TEMPTATIONS

TEMPTATIONS

OTIS WILLIAMS

WITH

PATRICIA ROMANOWSKI

G. P. PUTNAM'S SONS   NEW YORK

To Paul Williams, a true Temptation.

G. P. Putnam's Sons
Publishers Since 1838
200 Madison Avenue
New York, NY 10016

All chart positions referred to are from *Billboard* magazine and were
compiled from Joel Whitburn's Record Research, a series of books
available through Record Research, Post Office Box 200, Menomonee
Falls, Wisconsin 53051.

Photographs number 1–9, 14, 21, 22, 30–32, 35–39, 42, 43, 45–49, 51,
53, and 57 are from the personal collection of Otis Williams.

Author photograph by Aaron Rappaport.

Library of Congress Cataloging-in-Publication Data

Williams, Otis.
   Temptations.

   1. Temptations (Musical group)   2. Rock musicians—
United States—Biography.   I. Romanowski, Patricia.
II. Title.
ML421.T43W5   1988   784.5'4'00922 [B]   87-25778
ISBN 0-399-13313-5

Printed in the United States of America
1   2   3   4   5   6   7   8   9   10

Acknowledgments

I'd like to thank Shelly Berger, Billie Jean Bullock, Cherie Ann Dobbins of Star Direction; Marilyn Ducksworth, Stacy Creamer, Suzee Ikeda, Steve Martin, Robb Hogan, Howard Flash Jackson, my Aunt Lucille Woods, and Uncle Wade Woods; Brandy F. Davis for watching over my father, Edgar Little; my brother, Allan Little, and his family; Abe Somer and Jill Berliner, my attorneys; Cholly and Mae Atkins; Maurice King, Fred Moultrie, Edwin Lombard, Joe G. D'Oliveira, my business managers; D'Anza Bringier, Linda Penn, Bruceaud Terry Taylor, Ann and Willie Mitchell, Bill Tannen, Annie B. Cain, and Patty Romanowski and Phil Bashe—you're both wonderful. And my loving wife, Goldie, and daughter, Elanda, The Temptations, and my loving son, Otis Lamont, may you rest in peace.

—OTIS WILLIAMS

I'd like to thank Miller London at Motown Records, Bill Hathaway at Record Research, and the guys at Strider Records in New York and Memory Lane Records on Long Island for helping me compile the discography. Among the friends whose support was invaluable, I'd like to single out Elisa Petrini, Nelson George, Mitchell and Rana Schneider, Larry Geller and Joel Spector, Gypsy da Silva, and Sarah Lazin. My husband, Philip Bashe, as always, has a special place here.

Shelly Berger, Billie Bullock, and Karen Fisk at Star Direction smoothed the way. And Shelly and Stacy Creamer offered countless valuable suggestions and the kind of encouragement every writer should have.

Finally, very special thanks to the Temptations, for being. And to Otis, for his friendship, honesty, and trust, all of which made this assignment a dream come true.

—PATRICIA ROMANOWSKI

TEMPTATIONS

1

In 1986 I stood on the empty stage of Detroit's Fox Theater, the last of the city's grand old movie palaces and the only one to have been renovated. With its over five thousand seats stretching back between ornate plaster walls and glowing under the refurbished chandeliers, it struck me as a place, maybe the only place, that time forgot. Of course, I knew that these seats were not really the ones I sat in, surrounded by friends, all up and screaming for Frankie Lymon or Jackie Wilson. They'd been cleaned up, probably reupholstered, but they could have been the same. Coming in through the old stage door, I recalled all the hours I'd spent outside it, hoping to catch a glimpse of one of my idols, maybe one of the Cadillacs, or a beautiful woman, like Faye Adams.

They might have changed the stage, but not enough that I couldn't close my eyes for a moment and feel the rhythmic vibrations of our dance steps as we strut and glide through our first Motortown Revue or Christmas Show in the early sixties. Out beyond the edge of the stage I can see only a hundred or so illuminated faces, all smiling, all laughing, all bobbing in time to the music. Our music. Sometimes it feels like they might be the only people there, but then a thunderous roar reminds me that there must be hundreds, probably thousands just like them in the darkness. Beside me three of us swoop and spin behind a shining four-headed chrome microphone stand, while a fifth stands off somewhere to our left. If it's Eddie Kendricks, maybe he's singing "Just My Imagination," making the girls down front swoon. If it's David Ruffin, in a lightning flash he's sent his microphone flying skyward, turned, done his split, come up, caught the mike, and is heading down into the crowd. Every beat of every song prompts a move, a look, a note that comes so naturally, I might have been doing it all my life.

In those moments when this is all I think, when the adrenaline runs so high that it feels like a drug, time's stood still. This is the Apollo in 1966, or the Copacabana in 1967, maybe an English television studio in 1965, a little makeshift stage in a school gymnasium in 1963. And these are four of my very best friends, my brothers, all parties to a pact that says we will never part, that we—David Ruffin, Eddie Kendricks, Melvin Franklin, Paul Williams, and I—always will be the Temptations. After a couple more numbers on any given night, no one but me knows that mixed in with the sheets of sweat that pour down my face there are tears.

Then something always happens to remind me that time— about fifteen years' worth—has flown by. I notice that the women in the front aren't dressed the same, or I catch a hint of gray on one of our heads, or a move I've executed a million times calls for an extra hustle. It's not 1963 or 1967, it's 1982. The Temptations have been together for over two decades. Yet after a few more shows, only two of us—Melvin and I—will step onstage after an emcee winds up his introduction with ". . . the temptin' Temptations!" David and Eddie will have returned to their own careers. Paul Williams, though taken from us in his prime, we hope, is watching. And with us, as always, will be three other Tempts, guys whose voices are as much a part of our history as our own.

As the group's founder and spokesman I've always felt a deep responsibility to the Temptations, and not just because I'm part of it. Over the years I've been very proud to learn what our music has meant to our fans. Guys have played it to cheer themselves up in Vietnam, a young woman in South Africa asked to be buried with one of our albums in her coffin, and for countless babies some special Tempts song provided the soundtrack for their conception. As I keep edging closer to my thirtieth year as a Temptation, the group's role as part of one of the greatest phenomena in American popular music— Motown—becomes clearer. The only part I don't understand is how I could live through all this and still be just twenty-nine.

In everyone's life, there are certain key people and events— linchpin friends and incidents without which there'd be an entirely different story to tell. My life has been blessed with many such people and events, and not a small amount of good fortune. But at the heart of my story, of the Temptations' story, is the place where it all started, the place I will always go back to: Detroit.

I couldn't have been more than ten or eleven when my mother brought me up to Detroit from Texarkana to live with her and my stepfather, Edgar Little. She'd moved up north right after I was born, and though I'd visited her in Detroit since, living there was something else. Unlike small-town Texarkana, Detroit was a lively, thriving city, with tall buildings, seemingly endless blocks, and smooth, paved streets. I couldn't imagine a city bigger or more exciting, but even then I was too little to understand how extraordinary and special Detroit really was.

For decades Detroit had been the city of opportunity. Generations of Southern blacks emigrated to this integrated haven to man the city's auto plants or take other work, almost all of it better-paying than what they'd left behind. But I was too young to be concerned with such matters back then. All I saw were the nicely painted one- and two-family homes, the gleaming new cars, the big department stores crammed full of toys. Everything about Detroit was wonderful, newer, better. And I was fascinated.

Even though Texarkana wasn't more than eight hundred fifty miles from Detroit, the two places might as well have been on different planets. My birthplace was a plain, rural town that straddled the Texas-Arkansas border where my grandparents earned their living farming. My three surviving grandparents—Lucinda Eliga, Frank Fisher, and Della Gooden—each lived in what they call shotgun houses. You could stand at the front door and look right through like you were looking down a shotgun's barrel. There were three rooms, one right after the other; that was it. You can still see those little wooden houses in the rural South; back in those days, they were "fashionable" in those parts. To some, we may have seemed poor, but I never wanted for anything as a kid. Being the first grandchild on either side of the family ensured that I was loved to death and as spoiled as any kid brought up by two strict, God-fearing grandmothers could be.

Most of my early raising fell to Della Gooden, my father's mother. Her son, my father, was Otis Miles, but everybody in town called him either Sonny One or Bird Head, because he whistled so well. Walking home late at night on one of the dark gravel roads, he'd always be whistling. I'd hear him, and then my grandmother would say, "There goes Sonny One." It's probably an inherited thing, because I've always been one to break out whistling.

Despite my old man's peculiar-sounding nicknames, he was a lady-killer. The local women loved him. He was somewhere in his late thirties and single when he met my mother, Hazel Louise Williams. Hazel grew up in Texarkana, and her own mother, Lucinda Eliga, never wed Hazel's father, so what fate held in store for Hazel Louise wasn't viewed so much as a moral lapse but as the usual thing. Hazel, or Haze as I always called her, loved Sonny One, though she was a very young girl when they met. The attraction must have been mutual, but I think it was one of those hot, passionate things; my parents never did get married — at least not to each other. I was born on October 30, 1941, in my grandmother Lucinda's house, helped into this world by a midwife and handed over to my mother, a sixteen-year-old girl.

Though my birth never put too big a crimp in Sonny One's style, it changed my mother's life. I was a baby when she moved to Detroit, leaving me behind with Grandmother Gooden. Extended-family ties ran deep, and this kind of arrangement was common there. Grandmother Gooden's son didn't have to be married to my mother for her to love me. Sonny One would come to visit us every so often, and I saw him in church because he was our deacon. But our relationship never developed into a day-to-day, father-and-son thing. I knew that he was my father, but he was not the type to say, "Come on, boy. Me and you are going to hang, and I'll tell you about this and that." Luckily, my grandmothers more than made up for any lack of parental guidance.

Grandmother Gooden was the elder of my grandmothers. She'd been born only a couple of decades after emancipation. Grandmother Gooden took her job of raising me to be respectful and polite very seriously. She had worked very hard and owned her own house. Like Grandmother Lucinda Eliga and my mother's father, Frank Fisher, Grandmother Gooden loved me more than anything in the world, but if I ever misbehaved or got out of pocket, she'd light up my butt, no questions asked.

Both grandmothers loved the church, and every Sunday we sat in the hard wooden pews of the white, wood-frame church, listening to the Baptist preacher's sermon and singing the hymns, all full of joy and hope and the love of God. Church was very important to us, and even the little ones would be called upon to take part in different church activities.

By the time I was five or so, Haze had been in Detroit for several years. She came down for visits and sometimes took me up north with her for a few weeks at a time. We always sat together at the back of a Greyhound bus, eating fried chicken from a greasy paper bag. I recall just staring at her. She was very, very pretty, with gorgeous dark eyes and freckles. Although the few times we shared back then come back to me very clearly today, added up, it wasn't a lot of time, and as I grew older I became more conscious of the fact that she wasn't always around.

At church they'd picked me to stand up and recite a little poem about Jesus for a special church meeting. Haze promised to be there for my recitation, and so Grandmother Gooden browbeat me for weeks before the recital. "Boy," she would say, "you get in there and learn that now so you can make a good showing when your mother comes." I practiced and practiced my poem. I wanted to make Haze proud.

Came the big day, and I sat in church looking all around, waiting for Haze. After what felt like an eternity, the pastor called my name. I walked up to the front of the church, and my little heart broke when I saw that Haze wasn't there. All the practice was for nothing if my mother wasn't there, but I stood up and rattled off my poem. Everyone applauded. I was heading back to my seat, feeling crushed, when Haze walked in. She'd missed it. Grandmother Gooden talked to the pastor, who announced to the congregation that I would recite my poem again. I was just beaming, so happy to see my mother and to know that she hadn't forgotten me.

I also spent some time with Haze's mother, Lucinda. She was born in 1899 in Hope, Arkansas, and was another God-fearing woman. She always used to cook me what we called hot water (pronounced "hot-ta-water") bread, which is corn pone cooked on top of the stove in a big skillet full of hot water. Talk about something that's good! Jesus! I couldn't get enough of it. I close my eyes, and I can see Grandmother Eliga standing at the stove, saying, "Otis, Granny's fixin' you some hot water bread," and then she breaks into one of those sanctified shuffle dances, a lively kind of time step. She has one hand on the skillet handle and the other up in the air, her finger pointing to God. Her dress is flapping around her, because she's really strutting it and carrying on, and singing one of those old spirituals: "I'm going to have a little talk with Jesus, tell him all about our troubles."

Although both grandmothers were strict Baptists, they also believed in some of the old ways, things like curing sicknesses with homemade remedies, different potions and salves concocted from herbs and roots. They also had knowledge of other methods of curing disease, such as Grandmother Lucinda's treatment for my asthma. When I was older, she took me out to Belle Isle, near Detroit, and stood me up against a young sapling. As she marked my height on the scrawny trunk, she said, "Now, every year you grow older, and this tree grows older, your asthma will pass out of you." And it did.

The uses of the old learning went beyond breaking fevers and curing blisters. My mother's father, Frank Fisher, who also cared for me, grew up in New Orleans and was full of tales about bizarre occurrences, superstitions, and maybe a little bit of voodoo. My grandmothers knew and spoke of the powers various herbs and mixtures had, and what really stuck in my mind was their talk about how a woman could put stuff in a man's food to make him love her, or mix up something else to get back at him. And if that wasn't bad enough, a really determined woman could fix a guy for good if she could just get a piece of his clothing or a few strands of his hair. My cousin Delores, I, and a few other cousins listened to this for hours, fascinated and scared out of our wits. My grandparents were very matter-of-fact about it and made it sound like all women knew this stuff. Just their way of talking about it made you believe every word. After a few hours of listening, I'd lie in my bed afraid to close my eyes.

Years later I learned that I wasn't the only man of my generation and background who'd heard those tales. During the sixties, one of the Tempts made it a point never to leave any of his hair behind in a hotel sink or tub for fear that a maid might get ahold of it and do something to him. Another time, during the late sixties, a young woman who was in love with one of our road managers told me that she would "work some shit" on him and assured me that if she couldn't do it herself, she knew people who could. For these and many other reasons, I've made it a point never to underestimate any woman.

Whether it's real or not, looking back I think of my childhood home as a place where the unusual was accepted. Strange things happened down there. Our church stood across some railroad tracks, and about two hundred yards down the road, right next to the track, was a big old dilapidated house that all of us kids knew was haunted. In the daytime we'd run around the house, but we dared get only so close before we'd worked ourselves into a frenzy thinking about what was inside. In fact, a lot of corpses turned up there. Who knows where they came from—probably bar fights or crimes of passion—but we all imagined the worst.

I was walking home from church one evening after dusk. It was quiet except for the sound of mothers calling their kids in for supper. I was in my everyday clothes, rolled-up denim coveralls with no shirt underneath and no shoes, strolling along in no hurry, pitching rocks and pulling leaves off bushes. Suddenly I heard someone coming up on me from behind. Every so often I'd turn around, but it was pitch black and there was nothing. Closer to the tracks and the old house, I stopped under a streetlight, and when I whipped around, right along the outer periphery of where the lamp cast its glow, there stood a tall, shadowy figure that looked exactly like a man but without a head. I got one quick, terrifying glimpse before the thing lit out across the tracks and toward that old house. I stood there, paralyzed, watching it run until it disappeared by the house. As soon as I could move I took off across the tracks, around a wooded area, through a large clearing and up a hill, where the lights of my grandmother's house shone.

I never ran so hard in my life. When I finally got home, I pounded on the door, screaming at the top of my lungs. My grandmother opened the door, looked down, and said, "Well, boy, what is wrong with you?" I tried to explain it, though I doubted anybody was going to believe me. Still, she never said that it was impossible or that I was just seeing things, either. They carried me in and put my cut and bleeding feet in the big steel tub we used to bathe in. I didn't feel anything. I was just relieved to be safe at home.

Shortly after that we crossed the same road and the track to attend a neighbor's funeral. It was raining that day, and I couldn't help thinking about the house and that night, especially when we heard that the dead man was killed not too far from the old house. A train hit his car. In my imagination all kinds of things had happened to him, and I wondered if he'd seen the headless figure, too.

Even though most of my early memories are sweeter than that, Texarkana was in the South, which meant there was racism. We lived in a segregated community and attended an all-black school and an all-black church. Though an only child, I had many cousins by marriage, and one I liked to hang with was Calvin, who was a little bit older than I, probably ten or eleven. One day we decided to walk the mile or so into town. Our favorite place was the train station, where we sat for hours watching the long freight trains pass. Along the way was a little store where they sold all kinds of puzzles and toys. I never wanted for much as a kid except when it came to toys. I loved toys, and whenever we'd pass this store, I'd fantasize that we had money and make a list in my head of all the things I would buy.

Calvin and I were walking along when a couple of white boys started bothering us, calling us names and saying things like, "Come here, we'll jump on you. We'll kick y'all's asses." Thinking about it now, I can't say for sure if they even knew what they were saying or why. They were just little bigots, made that way by their parents. Calvin, who was quick-tempered, got crazy. He happened to be holding a sharpened pencil. As he got madder, he tightened his grip and held the pencil the way you would a knife. He was getting ready to walk over to those boys, when I grabbed his arm. "No, Calvin, don't do it," I said. "You might end up getting hurt." We could either walk away as if we didn't hear what they said, and nothing would happen, or Calvin could try something, and there would be trouble. Even young kids there knew to weigh their options.

Sunset Elementary School was a one-story building with one classroom for each grade, one through six. I liked school a lot, mostly because it meant being around other kids and especially girls, who, I decided early on, were wonderful. The first object of my affections was Verna Lillian Wright. She lived up the road from my grandfather, and I'd have done anything to catch her eye. She knew I liked her, but she wasn't making it easy. To impress her, I'd get on a swing and, being so tall for my age, could buck it so hard, I'd go flying. Once I did fly—out of the swing and onto the ground, knocking the wind out of me. I thought I'd die of embarrassment as I brushed at my coveralls and gasped for breath. I wanted to burst out crying, but didn't. Verna couldn't have cared less. Another time I was sitting on my grandfather's porch, pigging out on a big piece of watermelon when she happened to walk by. She caught me throwing the melon over my shoulder, wiping my face, straightening out my clothes all at once. She just stood in the road laughing. Verna Lillian was just so pretty, I couldn't give up, but nothing worked.

Once in Detroit, I got to know Haze and my stepfather better. He was very good to Haze and me, and I loved and respected him for it. He was more of a father to me than my real father. Plus, I knew plenty of kids back in Texarkana who either didn't have any kind of father at all, or whose stepfathers never liked them. Not long after the move, Haze gave birth to my half-brother, Allan. Several years later, a half-sister, Denice, followed. My stepfather was a hard-working man. The pace of life back in Texarkana was so much slower, and while people back there worked hard, holding a job in an auto plant seemed to take a different kind of stamina. I remember lying in my bed and watching him get up at four-thirty in the morning. It would be freezing cold and black as midnight out, but he never complained. He took care of his family, something I love him for to this day.

It didn't take too long to adjust to Detroit, and I soon had lots of new friends. After we moved into an apartment on Brush and Alfred, in the southeastern part of town, I got tight with a kid in our building named Joe Ratliff, whom everybody called Lucky. I was still young enough to be toy-crazy, and Lucky had tons of toys, which he shared with me. I was also into collecting and trading comic books—G.I. Joe, The Phantom, Blackhawk, Captain Marvel, Superman, basically everything except the romances. I always loved to read.

School was okay; I got mostly Bs and Cs without putting in too much effort. I hated math but loved art. I was a compulsive sketcher, always doodling on whatever was in front of me, and my teachers often took me off my regular lessons to work on a special art project, say, for a holiday bulletin board. My other great outlet was sports. The minute that school bell rang, I ran home, did my chores, and then took off for the playground. By then, baby Allan was traveling in his stroller, and it was my job to take him with me wherever I went, which seriously compromised my cool image. Allan was cute and well-behaved; the only thing wrong with him was that he was there. Having Allan at the playground wasn't such a problem because I'd park him over to the side of the field and keep an eye on him from the outfield. All I cared about was: is he still there and is he still in one piece? If he was, I'd done my job.

As I got older, I scheduled after-school rendezvous with young ladies for activities Allan could not watch. More than once he found himself and his stroller parked in a strange hallway facing a locked door while my latest love and I did what lovers do. Then again, Allan could be a nice little pal to have around. I'd ride him on my bike—a beautiful red and white J. C. Higgins with tassels on the handle grips—around the neighborhood.

I was around thirteen when I met James Bowman, whom everybody called Red. Red was in his later teens, probably about seventeen or so, and I looked up to him like a big brother. He was a sharp guy, and nice-looking, with light skin and red hair. Not only was he known to be something of a ladies' man, he also had his own singing group. I didn't sing with them but hung around enough to see what it was all about.

Before that, I also enjoyed music (I played tuba briefly in junior high), but wasn't really singing so much as listening to everything. The early fifties were the days of "race records," the music business's term for any music recorded by blacks and usually played only on black radio stations. It wasn't that easy to find the black station on your radio. Most of them were small operations, so you had to dial real slow and listen real close, or you'd miss them. Stations in those days played all the early R&B greats: Ruth Brown, B. B. King, Lloyd Price, the "5" Royales, the Orioles, Clyde McPhatter, the El Dorados, the Spaniels, Little Willie John, Harvey and the Moonglows, LaVern Baker, and the Drifters, and even the more risqué tunes: Billy Ward and the Dominoes' "Sixty Minute Man," Hank Ballard and the Midnighters' "Work with Me Annie," "Annie Had a Baby," and "Sexy Ways." We were barely in our teens, but the meaning of "Work with Me Annie" didn't get by us. When we realized they were singing about "doin' it," we liked the song that much more. But we also liked listening to the really smooth singers like Nat "King" Cole, Billy Eckstine, Vaughn Monroe, Johnny Ace, and Roy Hamilton. I loved voices and the harmonies of gospel singing. I'll never forget this one record a friend of mine had, "The Lord's

Prayer" by the Swan Silvertones, one of the greatest gospel groups of the time. Their lead singer, Claude Jeter, was a first tenor/falsetto whose voice radiated an awesome purity. He sounded like an angel. I was sixteen or so then, and we didn't own a record player, so I'd run over to my friend's house and beg him to play me that Swan Silvertones record over and over again.

In those early days I did a lot of my singing in the halls of Hutchins Junior High School. Another kid there, Lamont Dozier, would come walking down the hall from one direction, singing at the top of his lungs, and I'd hear him and start singing along, harmonizing on whatever hit of the day Lamont was doing. We weren't real close buddies, but sharing this special interest, we had a bond. We'd see each other, give a look like, "Hey, you sing too," and then go to our classes. Lamont's voice was a little bit higher than mine, a second tenor, like Paul Williams. He also had his own group, the Romeos, who recorded for Fox Records. He was quite a character too, even then. Every once in a while, we'd be hanging around the school at night, and there'd be Lamont along with some girl. We were pretty wild back then.

In most ways Detroit in the early fifties was a terrific town, but it was also a very tough place, especially for kids. Thinking back to all the kids I knew growing up recalls too many who got reckless or didn't know when to stop. Street gangs were all over the place, but the worst were on the east side. You didn't need to be a hood to belong to a gang; you just had to not particularly enjoy getting your butt kicked for not being in one. Some of the toughest, scariest gangs were made up of older kids, like the Ulus, the Kingsmen, and the worst, the Shakers. There's no doubt they were the most notorious and feared.

Everyone knew the leader of the Shakers, a truly frightening guy named Maurice. To me, he epitomized the ultimate bad guy. He wore his long hair parted straight down the middle and tied up in a doo rag; he had a big ugly scar above his lip. You could see that he'd been in some tough scrapes.

Many of the gang members' girlfriends had their own gangs. Those girls would walk around in skintight jeans with a handkerchief down in their rolled-up cuffs. As a rule, most of the gangs stuck to their own turf, but the Shakers went all over Detroit.

While the Shakers were the worst, no gang was really what you'd call good. And you could do your best to avoid them, but inevitably, you'd come out of school one day and find them waiting for you. There were times I'd have to say, "Well, let me see how fast I can get down," because they'd be waiting. I'd hightail it out of the yard and hear them behind me, yelling, "Get that one!" But they never did catch me.

In the end, I joined one, mainly for protection. I didn't do too much, and the other guys seemed to respect the fact that I had other things in mind. They didn't mess with me too much. They'd say, "Ah, he wants to sing, so we don't expect him to be serious about this." I got into trouble only a couple of times. Once James Bowman and I and another guy were caught fooling around with a girl in an abandoned house. Somebody called the police, and we wound up having to stay in juvenile hall over the weekend.

Another time, I was heading home when something just got into me and I didn't feel like walking. I had no bus money, and it struck me that I could steal it. I honestly can't blame this on peer pressure or anyone except myself. At fourteen or fifteen, I was almost six feet tall, and in the kind of black leather jacket only a JD would wear then, I must have been a sight. I approached my victim, a kid about my size, and said, "Come here, boy," scaring the hell out of him. "You got any money?"

"No," he answered.

"You're lying!" I shouted as I jumped him and took his money. My big heist got me a handful of change. I walked all the way home with the stolen coins in my pocket, wondering what the hell I'd done. This wasn't what my grandparents and Haze had raised me for. But they must have done something right because the guilt was eating me alive.

The next day a policeman came into my classroom and asked the teacher, "Do you have Otis Williams here?" She looked up at me and replied, "Yes. Otis, would you come up here? This officer would like to talk to you." My desk was way at the back, and the minute the policeman said my name, all the other kids turned to look at me. For a second, dying seemed like a good idea. I rose out of my seat and walked up to the front. "Come with me, son," the cop said, leading me into the hallway and out to the police car. I was booked and put in juvenile hall for the weekend. Naturally, Haze was upset to hear about it and worried about me being locked up, but she was cool. "Maybe this will teach you a lesson," she said.

No surprise: most of the kids in the juvenile hall were in gangs, too. Some had done far worse things than I had, but I didn't have any problem while I was there. We just hung out, shot some pool, messed around. Few of the other guys seemed to mind the place, which struck me as odd. The very idea of being locked up and having my freedom taken away, of being told what time to go to bed, what time to eat, what time to wake up—it just got to me. Then I started thinking about the gang business. It was bad enough feeling guilty and ashamed of myself for what I'd done to somebody else, but I knew most other guys felt guilty about nothing. What happened when somebody jumped me, or I jumped the wrong person? Only a fool could look at that street-gang nonsense and not realize that his days in it were numbered. The question came down to how far I was going to go with this stuff. I had better things in mind. That's when I started really getting into singing. I was never going to lose my freedom again.

2

Music was consuming more time and becoming a bigger part of my life. Suddenly I was listening to the radio in a different way—picking out different harmony parts or the way somebody sang a particular note or riff. The real trip-hammer fell when I started going to the rock-'n'-roll shows at the Fox Theater. The Fox was one of the loveliest theaters anywhere. It had these deep plush seats, big, grand columns, and all kinds of paintings. For ninety-nine cents or a dollar, you saw an amazing lineup, with up to ten or so acts, each doing a few songs, four or five times a day. Best of all, you could stick around all day and catch your favorites over and over. There were times I got so caught up in listening to LaVern Baker, the Royal Jokers, Chuck Berry, the Nightcaps, Frankie Lymon and the Teenagers—you name them—

that Haze and my Uncle Frank would have to come into the theater
and go row by row, looking for me.

Most of my friends then loved Frankie Lymon and the Teenagers, not only because they made great records but because they
were around our age. My real favorites were the Cadillacs, a
quintet out of Harlem. They did the usual four-part harmonies and
teenage-type songs, but their look and their movements were
original. They were the first really polished rock-'n'-roll group to
use a lot of professional choreography. As it turned out, their
choreographer was the man who would later work with all the
Motown groups including the Temptations, Cholly Atkins, and he
had the Cadillacs stepping. They performed their hits, like
"Gloria" and "Speedo," and they'd be wearing these loose, light
suits, that once they got moving would billow and sway as if they
were dancing on their own. And at one point in their set, they'd all
take a jump back from the microphones and slap one another's
hands in unison. They were really it, and when I saw the whole Fox
Theater—some five thousand people—going wild, screaming and
carrying on for them, I resolved that was what I wanted to do. Not
just sing around the neighborhood like everybody else was doing,
but take it someplace.

My mind made up, I started thinking about how it would be to
have fans. One day I happened to be hanging around the back of
the Fox when the Cadillacs came out the stage door. One of them
was signing something for a young girl, and she innocently asked
him why he had a pimple on his face. He angrily snapped,
"Because I ain't getting enough pussy!" The poor girl looked
crushed, and my bubble burst. There was no reason for that. I
knew that if anybody ever asked me for an autograph, I'd never do
anything like that.

Detroit was a real music town. You heard it everywhere, from
radios and record players, outside the doors of the clubs that kids
like us were too young to enter legally, from guys and girls standing
out on the street singing. It sounds like a scene out of a musical,

but that's truly how it was. At the time we were living on Seward Avenue between Twelfth and Fourteenth streets. The Gold Coast was on the corner of Seward and Twelfth, so I often saw the various groups who played there walking to or from their shows. I was lying in bed one night with all the windows open (in those days we went to sleep without even thinking about locking the screen door) when suddenly this beautiful sound filled the room. I jumped out of bed, and from the window I saw the Fresandos, a popular local quintet, coming down my street, singing their latest local hit a cappella.

What with rock-'n'-roll mania sweeping my generation, singers were easy to find, no matter what your age. I soon met David Cryor, a tenor who could sing the high parts in "Night Owl," and that was good enough for me. From here and there, we picked up some other guys: Herbie Murphy, the lead singer, myself, a guy named Eddie who sang bass, and a fifth guy whose name escapes me. We thought we were just *it*, and the highlight of our repertoire was "Stranded in the Jungle," a hit for the Cadets, a black quartet, in 1956. We sang that sucker all over the place, and soon some of our neighbors had us convinced that we could sing it just as good as the Cadets themselves. When we heard that the Cadets were performing at the Arcadia roller rink, we decided to go down and challenge them. We walked from the North End down to the Arcadia, about six or seven miles, singing all the way. At the rink we informed whoever was at the door that they had to let us in because we could outsing the Cadets on their own songs. Of course, we didn't get in, and we were pissed. Didn't they know who they were dealing with? Apparently not, but we'd show them. In the meantime, we turned around and walked all the way back home, singing as we went, our tails between our legs.

The walk was no big deal; none of us had cars, so we walked everywhere. Walking also gave us opportunities to meet more young ladies. We'd be strolling along, chewing the fat, talking about nothing in particular until we'd see a fine-looking girl. Then, look out. Our approach was, to put it mildly, forward. We were young and gregarious and we sang, so how could any girl *not* want to go out with us? God, we were cocky. "Hey, baby," we'd scream across the street, "you're sure looking good!" Then, regardless of the reaction, we just turned it up a notch. You could call it flirting, but it was more like a verbal assault. We had no finesse. Basically anything that got us some attention would do. Then, if any of us got a girl he really liked, no matter where she lived in Detroit, he'd walk miles to go see her, usually with one of us tagging along.

It was accompanying my friend Eddie (not Kendricks) to see his girl Vernell that first brought me to Twelfth Street, a thriving, jumping, dangerous place. It has since been renamed Rosa Parks Boulevard, and runs from the northwest end of Detroit south to the Detroit River. Twelfth was known for its gangs, hustlers, and players. At the time, I was living over on Custer, on Detroit's north end, so Twelfth and Lee Place, where Vernell lived, was foreign territory. You never knew what could happen to you on Twelfth, though you could expect to be hassled by tough guys asking you who you were, what you were doing there, if you had any money. It wasn't a place you wanted to go to alone. Eddie and I walked up to Twelfth, peeked around a building corner, and when the coast was clear tore across Twelfth, dashing up the steps of Vernell's building and running inside, all in about two seconds.

The only place tougher was Black Bottom, an area on the lower east side that ran between Gratiot Avenue and Hastings Street, the latter of which has since been torn down to make way for the Chrysler Freeway. Hastings was controlled by a gang of Jewish mobsters called the Purple Gang, but it was also a central shopping area. I went down there with Haze every Saturday morning to buy fresh vegetables and meats. During my teens I worked down there unloading trucks, just one of several jobs I held after school and on weekends.

As I got more serious about my singing group, I became more interested in perfecting my image. I had to be cool, and back in the mid-fifties that required a process. At fourteen or fifteen I got my first one. Processes were popular because they looked sharp and were easy to manage; you just ran a comb through once, and the waves just fell into place. Having a process was great, but getting it was less than pleasant, since the barber had to relax your hair first with a smelly combination of chemicals, including grease and lye. In inexperienced hands, a process could be a disaster; not only would your hair look like hell, but your scalp could get irritated and blistered. From the beginning, I always went to the best barber, a guy on Twelfth Street named Whitmore, who was a master at processing hair. After the process had straightened out your hair, he could mold it into whatever style you wanted: the New Yorker, which had a wave that went across your head; the 3-D, which was sort of what Little Richard wore in the fifties, but with three big waves in it; or, my favorite, the Tony Curtis, which was swept back in front and on the sides, then rolled up on top into little curls, and finished off in back with a DA, or duck's ass. Between everything, a good Tony Curtis took all day and didn't last more than a month before you had to get it done all over again, but it was worth every minute of it. No matter what style I wore, my pompadour was always so big that you'd see it coming around the corner before you saw me.

I kept putting little groups together, and inevitably someone would drop out. Some guys just weren't as dedicated as others. There was no pressure from home not to sing, and my heart was set on it, so I took everything about singing very seriously. I listened to all the music that I could, and soon I was writing little songs in my head. I didn't play any instrument except the tuba, which was no help, and couldn't write music, but these songs just kept popping out. For a while we had been doing one I wrote called "Pecos Kid," a tune inspired by the Olympics' hit "Western Movies." At this point my group was called Otis Williams and the Siberians. We had made something of a name for ourselves, singing at little hops around town. The Siberians were Elbridge

Bryant, whom we called Al, James Crawford, or Pee Wee, Arthur Walton, and Vernard Plain, our lead singer.

One day in 1958 I was standing at the kitchen sink washing the dishes, my regular after-school chore, and listening to the radio. It was tuned to Detroit's biggest R&B station, WCHB, and Joltin' Joe Howard was on. Joltin' Joe was one of those snappy, jive-talking jockeys with a high-pitched voice who did these ear-catching raps between the records. Joltin' Joe Howard said, "If anybody knows Otis Williams of the Siberians, please have him contact WCHB, CR1–1440."

A soapy dish slipped out of my hand and hit the bottom of the sink. Was I was losing my mind? "No," I said to myself, "he ain't talkin' about me." A few minutes later, though, he announced it again. That time I dropped the dishes and ran to the phone, leaving a trail of white suds behind me. I dialed CR1–1440—a number I'll remember for the rest of my life—and said, "This is Otis Williams. I just heard my name, and I'm calling in response."

Whoever answered the phone put Bill Williams on the line. Williams was another big jock at WCHB, and he was known for producing local groups. He had a real hot show that he always opened with a song called "Big Bad Train." Williams said to me, "Man, can you get the guys together and get on out here? We want to record you guys tonight. We love this 'Pecos Kid.'" I couldn't believe it. Stardom was right around the corner. We were going to make a record, and that was *it*.

I called the other guys, and we arranged to meet at Senator Bristol Bryant's. Bryant was an air personality on WJLB, and like a number of people around Detroit then, he was looking to make a killing in the music business. In his house he had a primitive two-track makeshift studio in his basement. It was a tiny little place, and the sessions would have to stop whenever anyone flushed the john, because the sound would be picked up on the tape. I sang lead on "Pecos Kid" and the flip side, "All of My Life."

Around this time Bill Williams became our manager on a part-time basis. During the brief period we were with him, we also met and worked with Milton Jenkins, another manager. Milton was an interesting character. He must have been in his early thirties then. Milton was a nice-looking man, with a high, receding hairline. He was a very sharp dresser, and he drove around in a big Cadillac convertible. Women were always around him, very hot-looking women. There's not too much else that I recall about him except that he always had his arm in a cast. "Damn, Milton," I'd say, "isn't your arm ever coming out of that cast?" We couldn't picture what Milton did for a living. Nobody we knew did that well without holding down a regular job. Milton had rehearsal space, which we used a few times, and there we heard two other groups, the Primes and their sister group, the Primettes. The Primettes, of course, would become the Supremes. We didn't get to know the girls all that well back then, but we could see they were working very hard at getting their sound right.

The Primes, however, were another story. They were a trio — Paul Williams, Eddie Kendricks, and Kell Osborne — that Milton had discovered sometime earlier. Paul, Eddie and Kell were originally from Birmingham, Alabama, where they had been friends since childhood. Being proud and somewhat competitive, my group would go up against anyone in these little group shoot-outs, but once we heard the Primes, we had to admit that there was no contest. We thought we were so hot doing our little doo-wop tunes — those "do-do-do do-do wah-wah"s and "dip-dip-dip dooo"s — but it was kid stuff compared to what the Primes were doing. They were just a couple years older than we were, but their three-part harmonies were heavenly. On a tune like "When I Fall in Love" their voices just soared. We were good singers and all, but we knew that to do the kinds of harmonies the Primes did, you had to have great ears, too. The other thing the Primes had over us were these fantastic moves, very smooth and sexy but classy at the same time, all the work of Paul Williams. We got to be friendly with them for a while, but over time we lost touch.

It wasn't long before Bill Williams decided that he didn't have the time to devote to us. He recommended that we see a woman named Johnnie Mae Mathews, who was also trying to get something together in the music business. Sometime in either late 1958 or early 1959 we met Johnnie Mae. She was like Milton Jenkins and dozens of other would-be pop-music entrepreneurs. They all knew it wasn't easy to make it big, but there was ample evidence that if you ever did, the rewards would more than compensate you for whatever you did to make it. Not long before, a local guy named Jackie Wilson had a moderate national hit with "Reet Petite," which everybody around knew had been cowritten by Berry Gordy, Jr., also from Detroit. Berry was also behind the success of another local group, the Miracles. We knew Smokey Robinson and a couple of the Miracles, and everyone was talking about their "Got a Job," an answer record to the Silhouettes' smash, "Get a Job." About this same time, my buddy Ronnie Taylor was living on Gladstone, and when we'd hang together on his porch, we'd see people coming in and out of Berry Gordy's house right across the street. The local music people seemed to agree that something was probably going to happen for him.

Johnnie Mae may or may not have known Berry Gordy personally, but she knew what he was doing, and she was trying to do it herself. Johnnie Mae was in her late twenties or early thirties then. She was a very attractive woman, and very sexy, too. Once we got with her, we would hang around her house on Carter and Lawton, working on songs or routines. People walking by would hear the music and stop in; one of those passersby was a singer named David Ruffin. We spent a lot of time with Johnnie Mae. She taught us tunes, and she had formed a label, Northern Records, on which she recorded us and several other acts. One group she had was Popcorn and the Mohawks, featuring Popcorn Wylie, who was a piano player in the Fats Domino style, and a tambourine player and sometime pool hustler named Norman Whitfield. Johnnie Mae also sang with her own group, Johnnie Mae Mathews and the Five Daps. At that time we used the word "dap" to describe a cool attitude.

Johnnie Mae was making a name for herself, and we heard that at one time she almost got to manage the Impressions, who were very big with "For Your Precious Love," and Mary Wells, who later became Motown's first female star. Mary was a beautiful girl, and during our tenure with Johnnie Mae, Mary and I carried on a secret romance in one of the offices. For some reason, Johnnie Mae's big break never came, but she had a good eye for talent. On her recording sessions she used a stand-up bass player named James Jamerson. Years later at Motown, Jamerson would be credited as being part mastermind of the Motown sound.

In 1959 a group called the Voice Masters released a song on Anna Records, a label cofounded by Berry Gordy's sister Gwen, called "Need It." They had had an earlier record out called "Hope and Pray," but it just didn't have the same punch as "Need It," a great song recorded in two versions, or parts: one slow and the other fast. The most striking thing about the track was the bass singing, a growl so deep, it didn't seem human. As I learned from asking around, that great bass voice belonged to a kid named Melvin Franklin. He was not a regular member of the group but had sung on just this song. Some of the Voice Masters became Motown's all-purpose male background group, the Originals, but this was years later. I kept Melvin in mind and vowed to look him up if our current bass singer, Arthur Walton, ever left.

I was still writing songs. After listening to the Isley Brothers' hit "Shout" for the millionth time, I found myself walking around saying, "Come on," as in "enough." I kept working with it and turned it into a song entitled "Come On." We sang it for Johnnie Mae, who liked it enough to record us. The problem was that Arthur was falling out on us. He'd made up his mind to go back to school; the singing life was not for him. "Come On" opened with some strong bass riffs and just couldn't be recorded without the bass. All I could think to do was to find Melvin, wherever he was.

As it turned out, Melvin attended the same school as I did, Northwestern High. He knew of the Distants, which we were calling ourselves by then, but I don't think he knew me. I finally figured out who he was and set out one day to convince him to join my group. When I think back about this time, I always see myself as Yul Brynner in *The Magnificent Seven*—out rounding up the guys I'd need.

I was walking down Woodrow Wilson at Seward when I spotted him. "There he is!" I said to myself. "Let me talk to him and see what's happening." When I crossed the street and yelled, "Hey! Melvin!" he took one look at me with my process, leather jacket, tight blue jeans, and white bucks, and thought I was a gang member coming to kick his butt, so he crossed to the other side. I crossed, he crossed. I crossed again, he crossed again. It went like that all down the block. Finally, I said, "Hey, man! Hold it! I just want to talk to you about singing."

Melvin stopped and waited for me to catch up. I introduced myself and said, "We have an offer to record." Melvin later told me that he'd just moved to the neighborhood and was walking up Woodrow Wilson so he could avoid the next parallel street, Twelfth Street. When I asked if he'd join us in the Distants he replied, "Well, I don't know you. You have to ask my momma."

Melvin came from a sheltered background and was kind of innocent by Detroit standards. I had no problem with talking to his mother, so we walked over and stopped across the street from where he lived, at 1160 Clairmount. He said, "Well, I live over across the street, and I'm going to stay *here*." With that, he hid behind a tree. I crossed the street and knocked on the door. Melvin's mother, Momma Rose, answered.

"Mrs. Franklin, my name is Otis Williams and I have a group and we have an offer to sign a contract and I would like to know if your son could sing with my group?" At the time, Melvin was singing with his close friend Richard Street, a guy named Maceo

Williams, and a brother and sister, Theodore and Barbara Martin. (In a few years, Barbara would be a Primette and sign to Motown as the fourth Supreme before leaving to start a family.) Melvin had a good little group; I'd heard them around. But we were set to have a real recording contract, and we already had a record out. I truly felt that we were offering him a better opportunity.

After I'd explained all this to Momma Rose, she said it was fine, and she called Melvin to come out from behind the tree and sit and talk with us for a while. Melvin had stayed across the street the whole time, just peeping out every now and then to see what was going on. When he finally crossed the street, she said, "Well, you can go on and sing with them, Melvin, because it sounds like Otis has his head on straight," and that kind of thing. That's when Melvin and I started. We started hanging together every day, and it developed into a very tight relationship that continues to the present.

Our lead singer Vernard decided to quit, so Melvin brought in his close friend Richard Street. Vernard remained in Detroit and later became deeply involved in the church. Richard had been in that little group with Melvin, but their relationship went back much further. Melvin had come to Detroit from Mobile, Alabama, in 1952 at the age of nine. He was a minister's son, and even though he'd been singing in church since he was three years old, Melvin remained a somewhat shy performer. Richard was also a quiet type, but seemed to have more confidence, and that helped Melvin. In addition, Melvin never got along too well with his stepfather. It was Richard who turned Melvin on to secular pop music and encouraged him to sing. Richard was a very easygoing guy and quite the ladies' man. In fact, back then he had a thing with one of the Primettes, Diane (later Diana) Ross. At the same time Melvin had a crush on Diane's groupmate Mary Wilson. But Richard was always a loner. He kept pretty much to himself, and still does.

Just a few days after that, the five of us—Al Bryant, James

Crawford, Melvin, Richard Street, and I—were in a studio recording "Come On" and "Always." This was done at Specialty Records in downtown Detroit, and while we were waiting for our turn in the studio, we heard the Falcons recording.

Considering it was only our second time in the studio, we acquitted ourselves well, I thought. "Come On" was a quick-paced doo-wop extravaganza, with God only knows how many parts in the background. The song kicked off with a guy from one of Johnnie Mae's acts, Albert Williams (no relation) coming in with this high, keening wail that was a real attention grabber. The verses were classic churchlike call-and-response, with Richard singing, "You know you make me want to love you in the morning" (then us singing back "in the morning"), "in the evening" ("in the evening"), "in the nighttime" ("in the nighttime"), and so on. "Come On" bounced and swooped all over the place, kind of like Frankie Lymon and the Teenagers' "ABC's of Love," but with a lot more fire.

Toward the end of "Come On" was a part where Richard would sing "I'm gettin' tired," and the four of us would do this heavy panting thing that was pretty sexy. Live, it drove the girls in the audience out of their minds. The flip side was "Always," a ballad that was different from a lot of the other stuff out then. It had a lot of "I love you"s and "whoa-whoa-oo-aa"s in it, but the ending was a beautiful, moody a cappella fade like the one the Diablos used on "The Wind."

"Come On" and "Always" may not have been the greatest records of all time, but "Come On" did cause a considerable splash locally. Listening to it today, I can say that we knew what we were doing, or at least what we were trying to do.

I'll never forget the day Johnnie Mae handed us our copies of "Come On" and "Always." The Northern Records version was very plain: a black label with gray lettering. I took my copy home and played it about ten thousand times. For lots of guys in this business, the excitement of it is enough to keep them going. We were thrilled to find out that a New York–based record company, Warwick, had purchased the rights to release it nationally. Maybe we'd be as big as Jackie Wilson or the Falcons. A few weeks later "Come On" was out on Warwick with the flip "Always."

At this point, it seemed like it was only a matter of time before we'd see our name up on the Fox marquee, but "Come On" didn't take off as we'd hoped. There were a few small local markets outside Detroit that picked up on it, and that made it possible for us to do more out-of-town dates, but we were basically still a big local group. None of us knew much about how a record company worked, or how much money was involved in a deal like the one Johnnie Mae made with Warwick, but we quickly figured out that there had to be more coming to us than what we got, which was zero. To be fair, she had invested time in us, and paid for our studio costs and first stage uniforms: white jackets, black slacks, and white bucks. But when we saw the response that "Come On" got at the hops we played all over town, we began thinking that there had to be some royalties going somewhere. Johnnie Mae was driving a hot-looking sky-blue 1957 Buick convertible with our group name, Otis Williams and the Distants, painted on the side. As we'd ride around Detroit, people would come up to us and yell at us from the sidewalks. It was only a taste of fame, but it was good. Good enough to keep us trying.

It was a fantastic feeling to be riding in a car and hear your song come on the radio. I'd turn up the radio so loud it would bust my eardrums. You started to feel like it could never get any better; it was almost as good as sex. We'd ride around and pound along on the dashboard, "Bmmm, bmmm, bmm, bmm, wachajam, dmm, dmm, dmm, dmm."

In just a matter of weeks, Pee Wee was also out, so Albert Harrell—Mooch—stepped in. At this point we were still the Distants, though God only knows, we changed our name so often. Mooch was an interesting guy. Not only did he have a great voice, but he really knew how to do all the vocal riffs. He used to do this

Ted Taylor tune, "Be Ever Wonderful," and he could stretch those notes like you wouldn't believe. Before joining us, Mooch sang with a group called the Ricardos, who were managed by a crippled man named Jimmy Smith. Jimmy bought them uniforms, their own station wagon—the whole nine yards—but it just wasn't happening for them. They all sang well enough, but they never got too heavily into the dancing because Mooch was as stiff as a box of Argo starch. I remember seeing the Ricardos at the Gold Coast Theater and Mooch taking over the stage on "Danny Boy." He could stand a good distance back from the microphone and his voice would carry all over the theater. We soon nicknamed him Scare Mooch, but I don't recall why. He was hot, and we were all sure that his voice would be our ticket. We had him, Melvin's bass singing, Al Bryant's great tenor and his popularity with our female fans, Richard, and yours truly.

With Mooch and Richard, we recorded another single, "Alright" backed with "Open Your Heart." "Alright" was the uptempo A side, featuring Mooch's wild screaming intros, and Richard on the lead. The lyrics were right out of the era—"Love her with all my heart / We'll never part"—but the music had a little more drive than a lot of other doo-wop-style records, with a wild rock-'n'-roll guitar line and intense but erratic tambourine banging by Norman Whitfield. The track also featured the high-pitched background vocals of the Andantes, a female group who'd been on our "Come On," and who were also destined to wind up at Motown years from then. They did the background vocals for everybody, including the Four Tops and the later Supremes records that Mary Wilson, Flo Ballard, and Cindy Birdsong weren't on.

The flip was my song, "Open Your Heart," which I sang lead on. It was a slow, pleading ballad ("Open your heart and let me walk in," and in the background, "Please, please, please"). The identifying factor in all four of our Northern releases was Melvin's unmistakable bass singing—those "boom, boom, boom"s were so deep you couldn't imagine anyone else ever going any lower.

Needless to say, we were certain that "Alright" would pick up where "Come On" left off and do as well if not better. But it was not to be, although years later Eddie Kendricks told me that he had heard "Open Your Heart" all over around Birmingham.

Even though our big break seemed always just out of reach, even minor local stardom had other perks. One evening Melvin, Richard, and I were out at WCHB's studios talking to Bill Williams. He hadn't been managing us for some time by then, but we liked him and he played our records and had sort of given us our start, so we went by to see him now and again. As we were standing there, in walked the Chantels. They'd had some big hits, their lead singer Arlene Smith's "Maybe" among them, and they were five fine-looking girls. The Chantels got in their car and we got in ours, and practically the whole way back to Detroit, the three of us were yelling at them out of the car windows, so thrilled to have met the Chantels we just about peed ourselves. "God," we kept saying, "the Chantels!" Nothing else came of the acquaintance, but it wasn't for any lack of trying on our part. It was a big kick, like the time I'd seen Faye Adams at the Warwick Records office in New York.

It didn't occur to us then to make a big thing about the money. Johnnie Mae was still booking us in lots of places, and we were young guys having a great time. The five of us hung out together and capped on each other. "Capping" means talking about someone's mother or something else personal and embarrassing. "Your breath is so bad I can see it" is an example. It sounds silly now, but you had to know how to hang with it or you were finished. We'd also be at each other's houses. I remember showing up at Richard's house around eight, nine in the morning. Richard would wake up, let me in, then we'd both go back to bed and sleep until a more reasonable hour, like noon or so. Most of the time Melvin would be there, too. Melvin was going through some rough times with his stepfather, and he often showed up at rehearsals upset about one thing or another. It finally got to the point that we all seriously considered jumping into the situation somehow, but we couldn't settle on what to do. In the end, we dropped that plan.

Without a big national hit, the only way to get our name around was to do shows wherever they'd have us. We spent countless nights playing little juke joints all around Detroit. A juke joint was a very informal place. Most times you'd have to bring in your own bottle. Some of them had little tables where you could sit and eat food they prepared there, like fried chicken. Juke joints didn't attract the most refined clientele, so playing them could be hazardous to your health. God knows how many times we had to run out a back door or hit the ground because some guy had come in looking for his woman and started shooting. Fights were common, and everybody knew it. Haze worried a little bit, but she understood this was what I wanted to do. She wouldn't stand in the way.

One time we were playing a juke joint in Mount Clemens, Michigan. Johnnie Mae was there with the Five Daps and us. We did a couple of shows each night. This night the place was packed so tight that you could not move an inch. The stage was set up near the kitchen area, where they were frying chicken, and along this little ledge between the stage and the kitchen sat a row of big tin cans. Johnnie Mae had tried to get across the floor to the ladies' room, but it was impossible and she was set to go on. She couldn't wait, so she just grabbed an empty can and went someplace backstage and discreetly peed. As she was going back up to the stage, she absentmindedly replaced the can on the ledge with what looked like garbage. As Johnnie Mae and the Daps were singing, Richard, Melvin, and I watched in amazement as a hand grabbed that particular can and poured its contents into a skillet of frying chicken. We almost died laughing, and did *not* eat chicken that night.

Johnnie Mae may not have given us the best deal in the financial sense, but she deserves credit for teaching us about the business of show business. She was a real stickler for punctuality and professionalism. I had always been a conscientious kid. If someone said to be someplace at five o'clock, I'd be there at four-thirty. Johnnie Mae noticed this and encouraged me to take on more responsibility for the group. At the time, I honestly didn't understand what it was all about. I thought singing was just about singing, and getting girls, and having a good time. But Johnnie Mae showed us that succeeding in show business was as much about taking care of business as having talent. And years later, when I saw countless talented people just blow their careers to hell because they couldn't keep the business thing together, I realized the value of what Johnnie Mae said. The awkward part came when she appointed me group leader. I wasn't the leader in the sense that I told people what to do; after all, I thought the group had to work like a democracy. But I was and continue to be the group's spokesperson and the person called whenever something has to be dealt with.

By 1960, Berry Gordy had made quite a name for himself around Detroit. The town was brimming with talent. Jackie Wilson had had a couple more big hits with songs Berry cowrote, and the Miracles had recorded "Way Over There," one of the first releases on Berry's Tamla label. That summer we were playing lots of the local hops. Each featured several local groups, and you'd do just a couple of tunes, usually covers of current hits, or, if you were lucky, your own record. It wasn't unusual for us to travel from one hop to another and cover several in a single night. Eddie Holland was doing the hops and was quite a hit with the girls. Eddie sounded a lot like Jackie Wilson, which drove girls wild with desire. They'd try to tear off Eddie's clothes, but Brian Holland would try to protect his older brother. We'd see him running after Eddie's fans yelling, "You aren't going to hurt my brother! That's my brother!" But having your shirt ripped off by a girl didn't look so bad to us.

Detroit boasted many other fine acts, like the Voice Masters and the Five Peppermints, who I've always thought were good enough to have made it. But as our manager, Shelly Berger, is fond of saying, all things being equal, timing beats talent every time. And in our case, the timing couldn't have been better.

One autumn night in 1960 we were playing a hop at Saint Stephen's community center. We were doing the heavy-breathing bit at the end of "Come On" and had that crowd going apeshit. Right about then, Smokey Robinson walked in with the other four Miracles and Berry Gordy. The Miracles were local celebrities then, and Smokey knew Richard, Melvin, and me from Northwestern High. The Miracles were supposed to close the set, but after "Come On" the crowd kept screaming for more. When we finally came off, I had to use the rest room. I was standing there at the urinal paying the water bill, as they say, and next to me doing the same thing was Berry Gordy. He introduced himself, then said, "I like what you guys do onstage and I like your record. If you ever leave where you are, come see me, because I'm starting my own label."

After a couple minutes of chitchat, Berry handed me his business card. It was just a plain card that said TAMLA-MOTOWN, with the number and address on it. Even if nothing ever came of it, everyone knew by then that Berry was a good person to know. Though he'd had some national hits, most of his successes had been regional, but he was doing as well as anyone else around and better than most. I knew right there and then that I would take him up on his offer.

As I would learn, personnel crises are just part and parcel of having a group. Each guy has his own personality, and as people change, the chemistry changes. You always have to be conscientious about getting along with one another and tolerating the other guys' quirks and bad moods. That said, however, there is a limit to everything, no matter how talented you are. Not long after meeting Berry, we had to let Mooch go. We all liked hanging with Mooch, and he always sounded great, but he had a temper that drinking tended to make worse. Now, none of us was a saint when it came to alcohol. Back then we didn't know about drugs, but we were into what was called "sneaky pete," a "mixed drink" mixed out of whatever we had—cheap wine and beer. It didn't taste as bad as it sounds; we enjoyed it, and gulping it down in cup-size swallows probably kept us from really savoring the flavor anyway. Mooch, though, was into something else—corn liquor, which not only gets you drunk but eats up your insides. Liquor seemed to irritate Mooch's stomach as much as his mood. A lot of times he had to get something to eat just so his stomach wouldn't be killing him.

Round about this same time, we reached the conclusion that it was time to leave Johnnie Mae. We'd worked hard over the two years we were with her, and though she did her best, we had been toying with the idea of leaving for a while. We needed to move up to some of the better venues; we also wanted a hit. The odds looked better with Berry. There was also the matter of the money. I don't recall us ever signing any kind of official contract with Johnnie Mae, but because she had put up the money for the four Northern recording sessions, she owned those masters. We expected that. But the day it finally blew up, we were shocked to learn that she also owned our car and our uniforms. And she claimed ownership of a song I'd written and that we had in the can, "This Heart of Mine." She paid for that recording session, so we figured to hell with it. We probably could have fought it, but it wasn't worth it. We didn't have a lawyer, and couldn't have afforded one anyway. And one other thing she kept—the name. We were no longer Otis Williams and the Distants.

As bad as all that was, we didn't take it too seriously. We were optimists and cocky, too. Something better was bound to come along. We were kicking around, just the four of us, without a manager or any kind of deal. Suddenly, Richard started missing rehearsals and dropping out on us. Always being a very private person, he didn't say much about what was going on, but he was caught up in the all-too-common position of having to choose between his singing career and his woman. Now we were essentially down to a trio—Al Bryant, Melvin, and I—but we were too young to worry. Singers were plentiful in Detroit. There were lots of clubs—Lee's Club Sensation, Phelps Lounge, the Flame Show Bar, the Twenty Grand—where you could see other acts and maybe pick out the next Distant, or whatever we would be called.

Meanwhile, I had lots of time on my hands. Not too long before this, my counselor at Northwestern, Mr. Stoll, had called me in for a talk. I'd been spending so much time on the Distants that my schoolwork had been suffering for some time. He and all the other teachers knew about our group, because Richard, Melvin, Warren Harris (a guy who would join Richard's group the Monitors in the sixties), and I would sing in the auditorium at lunchtime. We'd do a cappella versions of the day's hits: "Can I Come Over Tonight" by the Velours, "Oh, What a Night" by the Dells, "I Promise to Remember" and "Why Do Fools Fall in Love" by Frankie Lymon and the Teenagers. In fact, the inspiration for most of these in-school performances was girls. Girls loved guys who sang, and there was one very popular girl whom I loved, Jeanette McDonald, and I did lots of singing in school just for her.

Mr. Stoll was very nice and fair about it all, but he gave me an ultimatum. He said, "I'm going to give you ten days to decide if you want to get your education or if you want to sing. I'm going to suspend you, and when you come back, you let me know what you want to do." I thought about it a little, because neither of my parents had finished high school, and I understood why it was important to them. But then I realized that nothing in life is guaranteed. There were people walking around Detroit even then who had good educations and several degrees and still couldn't get jobs. From my point of view, it made more sense to go with what you believe in, and I believed in our group.

We were doing shows around the time of my suspension, and the day that I was supposed to be telling Mr. Stoll my decision, I was somewhere down South in Brian Holland's silver Cadillac coming home from a date we had backing Eddie Holland. And that sealed it. Now we had to make it. I took little jobs here and there, but spent most of my time rehearsing and getting the group together. I spent whatever free time I did have hanging out. Al Bryant and I would sit around for hours and talk about the important things — girls, seeing girls, chasing girls, clothes, sports — and sketch things. I even sent in those little things you'd see on matchbook covers, my renditions of the pirate or the Gerber baby or the little deer, into the correspondence-course art school. The other thing Al and I would do quite a lot was practice our signatures, perfecting every stroke until it looked just right, like the autograph of a star.

Maybe it was easier to believe that you could make it because you knew, or at least knew of, other kids from Detroit who had. For a while I dated Carolyn Franklin, the youngest daughter of the Reverend C. L. Franklin, of the New Bethel Baptist Church. Haze listened to the Reverend Franklin's sermons on the radio, and often his eldest daughter Aretha would sing. She'd also made some records, and that was a big deal, no matter what kind of music you were singing. I loved Aretha's voice, and still do. Just hearing it could move you to tears. Carolyn was a very pretty girl, built like a walking hourglass, and I was trying hard to get next to her. We were sitting around at Carolyn's house when Aretha just rushed into the room for a moment to get something she'd left behind. When I saw her, I was absolutely dumbfounded and totally in awe. She was a real star.

After our experience with Johnnie Mae, we wanted to be careful about the next person we got involved with. That town was crawling with people who were hustling young singers, promising them stardom when in fact all you might ever get out of these guys was maybe one record, a new car, some women, and maybe some drugs. Berry seemed different. He didn't wear flashy clothes or make promises. He was very businesslike and direct. I'd been watching the goings-on at Berry's from my buddy Ronnie's porch, and there was lots of talk about the activity over at the converted house on 2648 West Grand Boulevard. When I called him, he told me to get an appointment to see Mickey Stevenson and audition. We made a date for a couple of weeks later, even though we were still missing two key singers. I've always said that God has his hand in guiding the Temptations' career, and it must be true, because out of the blue Eddie Kendricks called me at my girlfriend Josephine's house. We hadn't seen him, Paul, or Kell in months and didn't know what had happened to them. As it turned out, Eddie and Paul went back to Birmingham for a spell after things with their manager, Milton Jenkins, fell apart. Eddie was still living down there and was just in town to visit Paul Williams, who was living in Detroit with a lady.

I told Eddie that we had interest from this company and asked him if he'd like to come into the group. He said, "Fine, I've got nothing doing." So Mooch's spot was filled. Eddie then asked if we wouldn't like to take in Paul Williams, too. "As good as Paul is, hell yes," I said. Richard wasn't officially out of the group yet, but it was only a matter of time. Paul and Eddie had been friends since their school days in Birmingham, Alabama, and they would remain tight until Paul died. We were bringing in two singers but getting much more than that.

Next thing, Paul and Eddie came over to see us at Josephine's. Paul brought his guitar and we started rehearsing right away, starting with a song called "A Hundred Pounds of Clay," a Gene McDaniels hit. The Primes had had those gorgeous, sophisticated harmonies, which we weren't really up on, so we worked on those, and Paul put us to work right away learning steps. He had learned a lot about staging and choreography from Peg Leg Bates, an old hoofer with a wooden leg who could still outdance anyone. I didn't think I could dance worth a damn, and that made me self-conscious. But Paul really worked with me and encouraged me. Eddie, Paul, Al, Melvin, and I put in hours working up our act. Eddie and Paul brought a new dimension to our sound, and Paul, who had a strong romantic baritone, starting taking the majority of the leads. Not knowing that the name was taken, we christened ourselves the Elgins, after the watch. A few days later I phoned Berry to tell him the news: "I got my group."

3

itsville, as they called the renovated two-story house where Motown was headquartered, was teeming with energy and excitement. It was impossible not to notice that people were busy doing something, but none of it looked like work. Everyone there—from the secretaries to Berry—exuded confidence and optimism, and for good reason. As we later learned, no one who fell under the spell there ever stopped to think that they'd never worked in the record business or that other companies operated differently. There was no reason to. Over the last couple of years, Berry had accomplished a lot: founded his Tamla label; cowritten two more Jackie Wilson hits, "That's Why (I Love You So)" and "I'll Be Satisfied"; penned a gold record for Marv Johnson, "You Got What It Takes"; and produced Barrett Strong's hit "Money." In addition, he'd worked consistently with the Miracles, helping Smokey Robinson fine-tune his songs and teaching him about record production. In 1961 Berry was assembling not only the artists but the musicians and businesspeople who would help him lead Motown to the top of the charts.

That first day we met Mickey (William) Stevenson, a writer and producer who, like most Motown employees then, had several jobs. Mickey headed the artists-and-repertoire (or, A&R) department, which made him responsible for who came into Motown and what went out. Choosing the musicians, the songs, the acts, and keeping schedules were all up to Mickey.

He led Eddie, Paul, Al, Melvin, and me down into the basement for our audition. There was an old beat-up piano, and because they were still renovating to make offices, rehearsal space, and a studio, boxes, lumber, and tools were strewn all over. During our latrine-side meeting, Berry had expressed interest in hearing our original tunes, so we made sure that our audition numbers included some originals and current hit songs. In those days you couldn't just walk into a bookstore and pick up a book on the music industry and how it worked. Almost all we'd learned about the business came by bending our ears and eavesdropping on people who seemed to know what they were talking about. We didn't claim to know it all, but the need to own and record songs we wrote was well understood. The real money was in the royalties that writers—not performers—earned on their hits.

Mickey wasn't the greatest pianist, but we sang "Oh Mother of Mine," a reworking of "This Heart of Mine," the song Johnnie Mae kept, and he picked out the chords well enough to accompany us. After we sang that, with Paul on lead, Mickey told us he liked our sound, especially the earthiness of Paul's voice. He called Berry down, we sang some more, and Berry was sufficiently impressed to offer us our first contract on the spot.

It was only a few days before signing when we discovered that another group was calling itself the Elgins and we'd have to change names again. Switching monikers was the last thing on our minds, but it had to be done. We first figured out what kind of name we *didn't* want: anything too damned long, or hard to remember, or meaningless, or silly, like the El Domingos or the Siberians. That in mind, the five of us were standing on Hitsville's front lawn with a guy who worked for Motown, Bill Mitchell. We were throwing around names when off the top of my head I blurted out, "Temptations." Bill said he really liked it, but when he asked the other four their opinions, we all took one look at ourselves in our raggedy, long winter coats and cracked up. We knew we weren't likely to tempt anyone or anything, but, what the hell, it was as good a name as any. As was typical of Paul, he saw something else in it. "It's just a name," he said, "but maybe it will give us something to live up to."

Paul's mind was always clicking, thinking of ways to make the Temptations look better, sound better, move better—be better. Of all of us, he was and will always remain the true Temptation. He kept us a step ahead. You can see today that it was the perfect name; it was about style and elegance but also suggested romance and, frankly, sex, something Paul deliberately made part of our image. Even back then he'd remind us, "We're selling sex." In our songs and our moves, the way we dressed and presented ourselves, we were subtler and more romantic than some other guys, who were always grunting and sweating and carrying on. Not to put them down, because we enjoyed their music as much as anybody, but we were different.

In recent years, a lot of information about Motown's contracts and its dealings with its artists has come out. All I can comment on is how it was for the Temptations. For example, our money didn't come to us on a strict allowance but in the form of periodic large checks for royalties and performance fees. Later on, we had an account for the Temptations' funds that required only my signature, Melvin's, or Beans Bowles's to draw a check for ourselves or the other guys.

When it came time to sign our first contract, the people at

Motown told us we could not take our copies out of the office, but that a lawyer of our choice could come in to look at them. Entertainment law then was child's play compared to what it is now, but still alien territory to your average Detroit attorney. We found a guy over on Twelfth Street who seemed competent, and he probably was—at divorces and workmen's compensation cases. After reviewing our contract he said, "It's a good contract. Standard contract. You can sign it." What he didn't know, and we didn't know, would haunt us for years to come. But that comes later.

The important thing then was that we weren't just five guys standing under the streetlights; we were recording artists, or at least a group with a deal. I don't recall what any of the other guys' families thought about our signing to Motown, but Haze and my stepfather were happy for me. Though they didn't know much about the business, they realized that a contract symbolized an important step. Except for Al Bryant, who had a milk route, none of us had full-time day jobs. Motown didn't give us a steady salary then, but we were big enough locally to get plenty of gigs in and around Detroit. To Motown's credit, they didn't bother with that or demand any part of our pay for shows until the hits started coming. We'd play Chappy's, Phelps, all around, and even do little tours of areas like Saginaw and Muskegon that took us out of town for a few weeks at a time.

By mid-1961 the Motown artist roster included our friends the Primettes, now the Supremes, Mary Wells, Popcorn Wylie and the Mohawks, and Eddie Holland, plus Marvin Gaye, the Contours, a blues singer named Singin' Sammy Ward, Jimmy Ruffin, and, of course, Smokey and the Miracles. Whenever we were home, you'd find all of us over at Hitsville. It was a great place to hang out. Everyone there was young and driven by the same dreams. You didn't have to explain yourself; we all had that passion about music and success. You wouldn't think twice about pitching in to help with whatever had to be done, whether it was singing backgrounds or mopping the floor. Joining Motown was more like being adopted by a big loving family than being hired by a company. This isn't just nostalgia talking, either. It really was a magical time.

It's the camaraderie of those early days that stands out in my mind. Whatever rivalries and jealousies would develop when Motown hit its peak a few years down the line were far away. Berry inspired us then. He knew what he was about, had a lot of confidence, and was full of piss and vinegar. He knew he was going to make it and made you believe you would too. We couldn't know then that we'd just latched onto the tail of a comet, but that feeling was in the air. I guess the world's now a more cynical place because people who weren't there with us find it hard to imagine a multi-billion-dollar record company growing out of that. But it happened.

Music was my life, so any other career was out of the question. One day I came home, and Haze said, "There's been a man here concerning your drawings. It seems that he is interested in you. You should stick around; he said he'd be back later."

I racked my mind thinking of who it could be. A couple hours later a very nice older man came by. His name escapes me now, but he was a white man with silver hair. He introduced himself, then sat down on a couch and pulled out some of the sketchings I'd sent off to the art school. People there thought my work showed great potential, he said. All I needed was some training in the technical aspects of drawing. He told me about how a good commercial artist earned five hundred, six hundred dollars a week working for magazines such as *Life*. Five hundred dollars! My head spun. That was all the money in the world to a guy who had nothing. He'd come all the way from Minneapolis and offered to take me back with him that day. I was a high-school dropout, and this stranger was offering me what sounded like the opportunity of a lifetime, to make a very good living doing something I loved.

After thinking it through a while, I declined, saying, "Well, thank you very much, but I've got a singing group, and we recently recorded our first single for a new label. I think something's going to happen, so thank you for coming and all, but no thanks."

"Well," he said, rising to leave, "if things don't go right with your singing career, give me a call. We're still very interested in you." He handed me his card and left. I never saw him again.

My romance with Josephine was going along fine. She was a year or so younger than I, and we'd been together a couple of years. We loved each other but never talked about marriage. Although the Temptations were starting to get somewhere (we thought), money was tight, so I couldn't support a wife. I knew plenty of guys who'd gotten themselves trapped into marriage, and I was too young to be somebody's dad, so we were always careful about using birth control. One night, though, the unthinkable happened. My prophylactic burst. We feared Josephine might have gotten pregnant.

My parents didn't raise a jerk, so I never really considered not doing the right thing if it came to it: marrying Josephine. But even if I had, there were forces at work that would have ensured that I did my duty. One was Josephine's mother, who let it be known from the start in no uncertain terms that no grandchild of hers was going to be illegitimate. Josephine's mother is an outspoken type, so you always knew where you stood with her, whether you liked it or not.

A judge downtown married Josephine and me. There was no question that I would marry her, but the judge still gave us a little speech about how he'd send me away if I didn't, because Josephine was underage. In a burst of nervousness, I guess, I hollered, "Which way's the county building, Your Honor?" Everybody in the room knew the county building was where you went to get your license and be married, so they all laughed. That was the only funny thing about it.

In the end, Josephine and I did have a child in the first year of our marriage: my only son, Otis Lamont, was born in June 1961. He wasn't a junior—we always called him Lamont instead of Otis—but his grandmother nicknamed him June, and it stuck. Lamont was a beautiful baby, with hair so thick we'd braid it up; sometimes he almost looked like a little girl. He was a sweet child, and very playful. Despite the fact that things between Josephine and me could have been better, it didn't change my feelings toward my son. I loved Lamont dearly.

Josephine and I went through the motions, getting an apartment, setting up house, and so on, but early on I told her, "This just ain't gonna work, Jo." We tried, though. I could live at home on my gig money, but it wasn't near enough to support two people much less three, so I was working on the welfare, as they say. That welfare card's still with me today, another thing I'll never go back to.

Berry had released our first single that summer on his short-lived Miracle label. You could read the label's slogan—"If it's a hit it's a Miracle"—two ways; in our case, it was a Miracle but no hit. "Oh Mother of Mine" was the A side. Berry and Mickey gave us some ideas and helped us make it a more complete, well-rounded song. Mooch sang lead on the original version, but Paul led this, and Berry produced it. The flip was "Romance without Finance," another of our songs, which Mickey produced. Unlike several of our early attempts, neither of these made it onto our first album, so I barely recall the lyrics, just "romance without finance is a poor paradise."

Without a penny in royalties coming in, we had to play wherever we could. I was management liaison, so to speak, Melvin was our secretary/treasurer, Paul planned our shows, Al arranged transportation, and Eddie's job was wardrobe.

Eddie always dressed beautifully. He had a knack for picking out sharp colors and cuts that looked hip yet classy, so he began putting together our stage uniforms. The first one was an olive-green suit made of a sharkskin-type material, which we wore with white shirts and black continental boots. Today these outfits hang in a case at the Hitsville museum in Detroit, and you can tell we wore those suckers to death. Back in 1961, though, they were brand-new and gorgeous, with creases sharp as a razor and the boots shining like jet beads. We were young, lean, tall, and with our patent-leather hairdos, as I call them, we were something.

Women noticed. During a run at Phelps, we saw four young ladies coming in every night and taking the same table, right down in front of the stage. They were fine, sexy girls, so we weren't complaining, but we gradually became aware that all they ever looked at was our crotches. Our pants didn't looked sprayed on, but they hugged a bit, obviously enough for these girls. We honestly couldn't figure it out, so I decided to ask them what the hell was going on.

The other guys were hanging out backstage between shows when I approached their table. We'd all been eyeing them too, probably as much as they'd eyed us, and there wasn't a night that we left Phelps without discussing each girl's attributes and saying, "My God, if I could get that one, uhm, uhm," like guys do. I introduced myself, and we made small talk. Then I said, "We noticed you're always sitting here, and we're glad you're enjoying the show and all, but why are you all staring at our crotches?"

The four girls looked at me like I was crazy, then one of them said, very matter-of-factly, "Hey, don't you guys know what's happening? That's what women look at, especially when they see guys looking as nice as you onstage and carrying on." Next, she listed all the other parts women looked at: asses, thighs, and so on down the line. Embarrassed, I got ready to say good-night when one of them added, "And another thing we like—you guys are all hung."

My jaw dropped. "Oh?" I replied. I wasn't a prude, but this shocked the hell out of me. Sure, guys talked about a woman having a nice this or that, but we never guessed they talked about us like that, too. Well, I learned you can't be fooled by those coy looks. I pulled myself together, and one thing led to another. They met the other guys, and each got her wish, so to speak. And we got ours.

Now that we knew we'd be recording on a regular basis, writing songs became a top priority. Walking home from the store one night I started singing, "By and by you knew that you'd make me cry, my love for you will never die . . . ," and before long I'd written "Check Yourself." During one of our many rehearsals at Hitsville, I sang it for Mickey, and he helped us get it together. Our rough version was recorded on a reel-to-reel and played for Berry, who also liked it. But when Brian Holland, who was there as a writer-producer, heard it, he said, "Yeah, Berry, that's great, but I hear something on that bridge where Paul is singing." Brian came up with some new parts that really improved the tune, and we used them. Hitsville was like a hit-record think tank. Anyone's two cents were welcome.

When it came time to record "Check Yourself," not all of the Tempts were around, so Brian is on that track singing some high tenor parts (like the backing vocal lines "the good times, the bad times"). He rearranged everything, so we could cover for whoever was missing. Melvin and I split that writing credit with Berry and Brian, and Berry produced it. The B side, "Your Wonderful Love," was one of Berry's songs, and he produced that, too. It's a ballad that reminds me a bit of the Impressions' "For Your Precious Love." As usual then, Paul sang lead. Our harmonies and singing in general had improved since Paul and Eddie joined, and working with good producers and crack musicians—James Jamerson, drummer Benny Benjamin, guitarist Eddie Willis, pianist Joe Hunter, and others—was the icing on the cake. But despite our strides and supporting talent, it was no deal on this one, either. "Check Yourself" was the last release on the Miracle label, which was discontinued. Most of our subsequent records were on Gordy.

The five of us had all gotten to know one another—living together on the road and spending so much time together didn't give you any choice. At first, Melvin and Eddie didn't get along at all. For no particular reason, Eddie made up his mind that Melvin shouldn't be in the Tempts. It made no sense, since Melvin's bass singing was crucial to our sound, and Melvin is generally well liked by everyone. There wasn't any real reason for Eddie to feel that way, but looking at it now, I suspect that he might have been bothered by the alliance Melvin and I had. We'd been there together longer, were about the same age, and were good friends. Basically, Melvin remained a sweet, quiet guy, so when Eddie, who was three years older, came on strong, Melvin felt picked on. Now and then they came close to blows and Paul, Al, and I would pull them apart. We'd just gotten in from doing a record hop, something was said, and one thing led to another. Once when they squared off, Melvin had a rock and Eddie had a can opener. Eddie was a great guy, but he could be mean, and he and Melvin were both hotheads.

Paul could also be quick-tempered if something got to him. Because he was in charge of how the show ran, if you slipped up onstage—missed a note, blew a step, whatever—he'd come down hard. One time Eddie didn't do something just so, and they got into one of those discussions that go:

"Fuck you!"

"Well, fuck you, too!"

The next thing I saw was Eddie holding a sharp object. He'd been stabbed during his teens, at a football game, and had a scar running up his stomach to show for it. Whenever he felt threatened, he'd try to grab something. This time he said, "I'm not going to be stabbed anymore. I'll be the one doing the stabbing."

"Oh, God," I said. "Come on, Eddie. You and Paul are friends from way back. Just stop it."

Over the years, there'd be quite a few silly fights. The thing is, no one remembers what the hell most of them were about. Maybe we'd just get tired of being around one another all the time, or somebody did something onstage someone else didn't like. There seemed to be a pattern, though. Something someone said would rub one guy wrong, then they'd be rolling around on the floor. I tried never to take sides, though more often than not I ended up going to Melvin's defense. By the same token, Eddie and Paul stuck together on most things. And Al and I were tight. You'd never get any five guys always to agree, so somebody had to end up against somebody else, no matter how you cut it. Back then, none of these scraps ever got serious enough to threaten our unity as a group. We fussed among ourselves, but to the outside world we kept up a united front.

We were in it together on everything, with a few exceptions. We'd finished a hop and were all changing into our street clothes at Lester Millard's house. He was a handyman at Motown, and Eddie and Melvin were staying with him. Melvin had gone around the corner to tell a girl I was seeing that I'd be around to see her soon. Lester was blasting the record player, and before long, the cops had arrived. One officer came straight upstairs, where he caught me getting into my street pants, and said, "That's right, keep on changing and move right on downstairs and get in the paddy wagon."

"Paddy wagon?" I yelled. "What the hell's going on?"

"We have a complaint of disturbing the peace, and we're taking you all in."

They had the six of us — Lester, his friend John, Eddie, Paul, Al Bryant, and me — single-filing it down the steps and into the paddy wagon when we suddenly heard this familiar whistling. There was Melvin coming around the corner, strolling along casually and acting like he didn't know us. It was funny as hell. Melvin got to somebody so they knew we'd been taken in, but we spent the night in jail, and the next morning the judge let us off with the warning that if we ever disturbed the peace again, we'd be in for a lot longer. It was a minor thing, but being in jail bothered me more than ever. I've never been back.

Besides doing our regular shows, the Temptations did a lot of background singing, both on records and on tours. After Eddie Holland had his hit "Jamie," we toured with him, singing background while Melvin played piano. In the very beginning, we also sang behind Mary Wells, who in those early days was Motown's leading star. It was as her backup group that we made our debut at the Apollo Theatre in Harlem. We did our two or three numbers, then backed Mary during her set, so we felt reasonably safe from the legendary wrath of a displeased Apollo audience. Plus, we were good, but at the Apollo what you thought about yourself counted for nothing. From the wings you could hear the crowd booing and hissing an act they didn't like. On amateur nights the audience would let you know in big, grand form that you weren't cutting it. They threw garbage, beer cans—about anything not nailed down—onto the stage, and a really bad act got the famous hook. The Apollo also had a microphone that came up from under the stage through a trap door. If the crowd had had enough, that microphone would start sinking. We saw some acts follow it all the way down to the floor until they were practically lying sideways on the stage. It could be a cold place, but if you ever got there, you knew you were doing something right.

Almost a year after we signed with Motown, one of Berry's dreams—to place a big hit on the mainly white pop chart—came true when the Marvelettes hit number one with "Please Mr. Postman" in December 1961. Berry used to throw a big Christmas party for everyone, and the early ones took place in the basement studio. I'll always remember our first one, because the Marvelettes walked in wearing big, fancy hats and with an attitude that let you know they were in the money now. I envied them—I'm sure everyone else did, too—but it wasn't a bitter thing. You just wanted the chance to prove you were as good, and that competitive atmosphere Berry encouraged was like a spur, driving you.

Another thing about those parties I'll never forget was how much fun they were. There was never any question that Berry was *the* boss, but he also has a very funny side that the business thing sometimes obscures. Whenever Berry got into one of his clowning moods, he'd have us laughing ourselves to tears. If Berry told a story, he didn't just tell it, he acted it out, playing all the parts, making faces, and using different voices. We'd be down there laughing and thinking that nothing could ever be better than this.

Even though our first two singles had stiffed, the Temptations remained a group to be reckoned with around Detroit. Paul gave us some original moves that set us apart from the pack. Our harmonies were tight and complex, and women loved us, and where the women go, the guys follow. We thought we had it, and maybe our high opinion of ourselves was obvious. One day Berry said, "You're all so hot around here, I'm gonna see how you are elsewhere," and sent us packing to the Keith 105 Theater in Cleveland to play a disc-jockey show.

The bill included the Halos, whose sole hit was "Nag," Shep and the Limelites, who had "Daddy's Home," some girl group, and Gladys Knight and the Pips. Gladys and the Pips headlined, riding high on their hit "Letter Full of Tears." Then there were four Pips— Gladys's brother Merald Bubba Knight, their cousins William Guest and Edward Patten, and Langston George (who left them not long after this). Gladys had been singing since she was a little girl and had been with the Pips since the late fifties. They'd toured with Jackie Wilson and Sam Cooke. They were pros and hot stuff.

We were the low guys on the bill, so we opened the show and, inexplicably, bombed. Maybe we were shell-shocked or didn't have enough experience working a big crowd like that, but the audience let us know they thought we stunk. We dragged ourselves offstage, mortified. Talk about performance anxiety. This had never happened before. We stood in the wings, watching the other acts get the applause and encores, and feeling worse. The capper, though, was Gladys and those Pips. The man who'd made the Cadillacs such showmen, Cholly Atkins, choreographed their act, and they were unstoppable. To be honest, they chewed up our butts but good.

Eddie, Paul, Melvin, Al, and I slunk back to our dressing room and sat around groaning. We didn't make any excuses and knew what we had to do: get back to Detroit and woodshed until everything flowed smooth as silk. To give you an idea how thoroughly Gladys and the Pips whomped us, even our friends at home were talking about how bad we got beat. Wasn't anybody going to humiliate us like that again. Our revenge didn't come for another year or so, but when it did it was sweet.

None of our 1962 singles did much. Our third and fourth releases, "Dream Come True" backed with "Isn't She Pretty" and "Paradise" backed with "Slow Down Heart," didn't even make the pop chart. All were good sides, but "Dream Come True" was especially interesting. It had a unique, dreamy feel that made it sound unlike anything else around, thanks to Berry's wife Raynoma's harpsichord playing. "Dream" made a minor splash on the R&B chart, at number twenty-two. Berry wrote "Paradise" in the style of the Four Seasons' hit "Sherry," and Eddie sang the lead falsetto. We later heard that it was a regional success in parts of California, but that was all. "Slow Down Heart" was, in my opinion, one of Smokey Robinson's best tunes. Paul sang lead, and it was beautiful, but no go.

We tried hard, and Berry, who had great ears for hits, produced most of our sessions, but something wasn't clicking. That's when Berry decided to revamp our act, starting with our name. That September, about the same time that "Paradise"/"Slow Down Heart" came out, Gordy Records released "Mind over Matter" and "I'll Love You Till I Die" by the Pirates, a.k.a. us. The Pirates? We'd have died for a hit, but if it meant going through life in pirate uniforms, no thanks. Our displeasure probably wasn't a big secret, and soon Berry was teasing us, saying, "Yeah, if that's a hit, you guys will have to change. Forget the Temptations. You'll be wearing pirate outfits." This was the only time we prayed for a flop, and God must have heard us, because that thing sunk without a trace. Ironically, Motown collectors today consider this among the label's rarest and most valuable singles. Not that these were bad songs. "Mind over Matter" was written by Nolan Strong, who was Barrett Strong's cousin and the Diablos' lead singer. Nolan had recorded "Mind" himself, but it didn't go anywhere, and Berry thought it would work for us. "I'll Love You Till I Die" was a nice bluesy tune that Clarence Paul—whose cousin was guitarist Lowman Pauling of the "5" Royales—wrote.

Even though most leads on these early releases were split between Eddie and Paul, there was no rivalry between them. Producers usually picked tunes that fit either Eddie's sweeter first tenor and falsetto or Paul's deeper baritone, but never both. The Cleveland debacle still fresh in our minds, we were practicing constantly. As I've said, Paul had a knack for choreography but we weren't going to let anything get by us, so when we were out scouting other groups, we'd watch for things to "appropriate" for our act. For example, early on we adopted that Cadillacs' bit of jumping back from the mike. Another group we kept a close eye on was the Vibrations, a quintet out of Los Angeles that was known for "The Watusi." They also recorded "Peanut Butter" as the Marathons, and their Ricky Owens would be a Tempt for a few weeks in 1971. Those guys tore up a stage. Not only did they sing and dance, but they jumped all around, doing cartwheels and splits. To our minds, the Temptations had something else, but we had to admit the Vibrations were stiff competition. If you ever found yourself on a bill with those guys you knew you'd be working doubly hard. The Contours were another raucous bunch who had us sweating a few times.

People at Motown gave us lots of input about how to improve our singing and our staging. We weren't in the so-called charm school learning about etiquette, dress, and makeup the way many of the young women there did, but some of the older guys, like Harvey Fuqua, Thomas "Beans" Bowles, Maurice King, and later, Shelly Berger, to name a few, taught us about wardrobe, staging, how to carry yourself and speak in public as situations arose.

Beans Bowles and Maurice King were two older, classy men

who came up as jazz musicians. Beans handled business for some groups, including us, and managed things on the road. Maurice was the Flame Show Bar's bandleader before he came to Motown as musical director. Harvey Fuqua, of course, sang lead in the Moonglows (of "Ten Commandments of Love" fame) and in 1960 married Berry's sister Gwen, with whom he started the Harvey and Tri-Phi labels. Harvey also discovered and brought to Detroit one of the latter-day Moonglows, Marvin Gaye, who would become Harvey's and Berry's brother-in-law when he married Anna Gordy in 1963. Harvey did some writing and producing, though his main job was to put together the Artist Development department.

One day when we were working with Mickey, we started talking about new songs for our repertoire. We didn't have enough of our own records to make a full set, so we had to perform other groups' hits. Mickey said, "You know that song 'Gypsy Woman' the Impressions do? I love that tune. I could see you guys doing that. All of you could break into this kind of move on the words 'gypsy woman.'" Then he showed us what he had in mind, a dramatic flamenco-style arm gesture accompanied by some smooth steps done on tiptoe that we worked into a routine. People loved it, so not long after, when we heard we'd be in a battle of the groups at the Uptown in Philly with Curtis Mayfield and the Impressions, we knew what to do.

Singing another act's tune on the same show was always done in good fun, but that didn't mean you wouldn't try to top them. When they saw us before the show, the Impressions said, "Man, that's all we've been hearing about. People are saying, 'Yeah, you guys sing it, but you've got to see the Temptations do it.'" That night they got their chance. Several things made that song work for us: Eddie's falsetto was similar to Curtis Mayfield's on the record, and we really were on that night. That one little move had the crowd eating out of our hands. Now, when Curtis and those guys sang it, they just stood there, so even though it was their song, it was no contest. Nobody was going to outsing us.

One thing Paul, Eddie, Melvin, Al, and I liked to do together was catch the gospel acts that came to Detroit. Although most gospel performers toured the South, few came to Texarkana, so I wasn't exposed to the live-performance aspect of gospel until I moved to Detroit. There, at King Solomon's Church, I saw Clara Ward, Mahalia Jackson, the Vocalaires, the Violinaires, and others. I loved them all, but I particularly liked the male gospel quartets, whose multipart harmonies left me breathless. Most of these men dressed conservatively, but there were those whose love of the Lord inspired a more extravagant, less inhibited, some might even say almost wild, singing style.

Paul's father, like Melvin's, was a preacher, and all four of us were steeped in the Baptist church, though I don't think any of us went to church regularly then. At the time, Motown had the one studio, and if a producer was set to record a song and couldn't find you, they cut it with whoever was hanging around. We recorded live, so all the musicians and technical people would be waiting, and Berry was not one to waste a minute. Unbeknownst to us, Berry had written a song with us in mind. He looked all over, calling our houses, asking people where we were, but nobody knew, so he gave up. As it turned out, we were watching the Harmonizing Four, the Highway QCs, and the Dixie Humming-birds at King Solomon's Church, but nobody thought to look there.

When we dropped in at Hitsville on the way home, everyone was saying, "Man, Mr. Gordy was looking for you guys. He had a song for you, but when he couldn't find you, he cut it on the Contours." Of course, it became a big hit, one of the few pop Top Tens for Motown that year: "Do You Love Me." Until the Contours hit number three with that, Motown's hottest act in 1962 was Mary Wells, whose "The One Who Really Loves You" and "You Beat Me to the Punch" had been Top Tens, too.

.   .   .

In early 1963 we cut our sixth single, "I Want a Love I Can See" backed with "The Further You Look, the Less You See." This single marked the first time we worked with the two writer-producers who would create the bulk of our greatest hits through the sixties and seventies: Smokey Robinson and Norman Whitfield. Both incredibly talented guys, they each gave us some of their best songs, but their styles—in their music and their work habits—couldn't have been more different.

"I Want a Love I Can See" was a Smokey Robinson song and production. By then, he'd been with Berry for quite some time. Berry discovered Smokey and the Miracles—then Claudette Rogers (soon to be Mrs. Robinson), Pete Moore, Bobby Rogers, and Ronnie White—sometime around 1958. By early 1963 they'd had a slew of records out: "Got a Job," "Bad Girl," "You Can Depend on Me," "Ain't It, Baby," "Mighty Good Lovin'," "Everybody's Gotta Pay Some Dues," "What's So Good About Good-Bye," "I'll Try Something New," "Way Over There," and the group's first two Top Ten records, "Shop Around" and "You've Really Got a Hold on Me." Berry and Smokey were always very close friends, and Smokey has credited Berry with helping him refine his songs. As good a group as Smokey and the Miracles was, though, Smokey's major contribution to Motown—to American music in general, I'd say—is his songwriting. The man is truly a genius.

Smokey is also the perfect gentlemen and has been a good friend to us from the start. Working in the studio with him was a dream. He was always at the sessions on time, with all of the instrumental and vocal parts worked out on paper down to the last detail. Being a singer himself, Smokey not only knew how to write for singers but how to create a comfortable, productive atmosphere for them. If you came up with a suggestion about how to sing a part, Smokey listened. He made everything so easy that you didn't feel right unless you gave him your best.

The flip, "The Further You Look, the Less You See," was

written by Whitfield, and although he didn't produce this particular track (Smokey did), it probably wasn't because he didn't want to. A very intense, competitive guy, Norman was born in Harlem and came to Detroit in his teens. Though he lacked formal musical training, he had worked with little groups around Detroit (such as Popcorn and the Mohawks when we were with Johnnie Mae), had done writing and production for Thelma Records, a label run by Berry's first wife Thelma Gordy, and joined Motown as a songwriter in late 1959. Over the many years we've known Norman, he was always a fun-loving guy but cocky as hell, even before he had a whole lot to be cocky about. In 1963 Norman wasn't much over twenty, and a few months later Marvin Gaye would have a big hit with Norman's "Pride and Joy." For us, though, no such luck. Neither of these sides did a whole lot, though "A Love I Can See" got played here and there, and our next release, which was Norman's first combined writing and producing credit with us, "May I Have This Dance," backed with Berry's "Farewell, My Love," died.

Despite that, "Farewell, My Love" is worth hearing today, because it features Paul and Eddie Kendricks on the lead. Paul did most leads then, and Al left us before our big hits, so his singing is not as familiar to the public as it deserves to be. He was a floating tenor, which meant his voice could roam all around up there, then blend back in on the harmony. It was something to hear him. When he'd come in with one of those parts onstage, it drove people nuts.

As always, it was back to the road. We'd been booked for some dates in Atlanta, so we drove down in our station wagon. Diane Ross was in Birmingham visiting relatives, and we were going there for Eddie and Paul to see their families, so we arranged to pick her up and take her back to Detroit. We were sitting in the car just talking about making records and wondering when we'd finally get our hits. The five of us were disappointed about not having cut a hit yet, but Diane was despondent. She was talking to me, and I was holding her hand, saying to myself, "Oh, Diane," but nothing ever happened between us.

"Diane, it's going to be all right," I said, rubbing her hand softly. "Just hang on. You can't give up; this is what you want to do."

She looked up at me and said, "Yeah, I guess so," but you could see that the idea of more failure was tough on her. It was tough on everybody to think you were good enough to have a contract but would never get a hit.

We needed a good kick, so we were thrilled to find that we'd be playing a weeklong string of dates with several other acts, including Gladys Knight and the Pips. The first date was at the Royal Theater in Baltimore. We closed with our biggest hit, relatively speaking, "I Want a Love I Can See," and with Paul singing lead, we looked, moved, and sounded fantastic. Some nights, you don't know why, but the magic just clicks, and everything works. And we were never afraid to improvise. This night Paul jumped down into a squat and scooted across the stage, so we all started doing it. We had that place jumping, and nobody could touch us after that. Each time we came into a new venue, everyone would be talking "Tempts this" and "Tempts that."

One time a stagehand said, "Yeah, we heard you boys tore the show up in Baltimore, and Gladys and them caught hell."

"Well," Paul replied, "damn right. Teach them to fuck with us." Paul was a gentleman but never shy about letting you know what he thought. He believed in us. Another thing, which few people today would know unless they saw us in the sixties or heard our live albums, is that Paul Williams was a fantastic showman. Still, he never hogged the spotlight. He might get the biggest applause for a number, but then he fell right back in with the rest of us.

Unfortunately, not everyone felt the same way about teamwork, and during 1963 Al became a problem. Lots of people assume that drinking and drugging is a natural part of being in show business, which is a shame. All of us drank now and again, except Paul, who never sipped anything but milk. Whenever he'd catch us guzzling our sneaky petes, he'd warn us about ruining our health with that crap, but we never listened. We all had it under control, except Elbridge Bryant. I don't know if it's true that people of American Indian extraction are more prone to overdrinking, but if it is, Al was living proof. At first, it seemed he was a little wilder than the rest of us, and we'd let it pass. We've kept to a long-standing rule that what a guy does on his own time is his own business until it affects the group. Then it's Tempts business. But Al hadn't yet crossed that line.

Every guy brings something to a group, and besides Al's voice, he, like Eddie, had this power to attract women. He was nice-looking and all, but his nose was quite large, so he was not a classic, out-and-out pretty boy. I don't know exactly what females saw in him, but he worked some kind of charm. Trouble was that on top of the drinking, Al developed a bad attitude. As happens to many stars, even little ones, that attention went to his head, and he ceased being a team player.

The four of us had started doing some preliminary scouting for Al's replacement in case it came to that. Now, that probably sounds cold, but we weren't all going to sink on account of one guy—never would, never will. At the time, I was living over on Philadelphia, and one block behind me on Euclid lived David Ruffin. We'd made an acquaintance during our Johnnie Mae days but lost touch. His older brother, Jimmy, had one Miracle release in 1961, "Don't Feel Sorry for Me" backed with "Heart," before he joined the service. Once he got back, he and David would hang out at my house. David had done pretty well on his own with "I'm in Love," "Mr. Bus Driver Hurry," and "Action Speaks Louder Than Words," the last two on Anna.

In the Temptations we always kept things to ourselves, so our problem with Al wasn't common knowledge, though in hanging with David and Jimmy I'd probably mentioned it. We'd sit in my kitchen, and the two of them would sing together, or try to outsing each other, which was something to hear. They were both fantastic singers.

One night when we were winding up a show at Chappy's Lounge, David Ruffin came up out of the audience and leapt onstage. We were singing "Shout" or "I Got to Know," some tune that got the audience worked up, and we had them going for it. But the minute Ruffin got up and did his thing with throwing the microphone up in the air, catching it, and doing full splits, plus singing like a man possessed, that was it. The crowd kept calling us back for encores. We had only so many songs in our repertoire, and we were tired, so after the third encore, Paul said, "Let's go. We've given them all we can give," and started walking back to the dressing room. Al, who thrived on adulation and could have gone back twenty times, didn't like Paul's attitude.

"Man, the people still want us onstage," Al said. But Paul walked past him. Al flew into a rage: "I'm going to kick that motherfucker's ass!"

"Hey, Al," I said, trying to calm him, but he jerked away and started after Paul. I called out to the others because Al was acting crazier than ever.

Back in the dressing room, Paul sat in a corner while Al stood over him, yelling, "Hey, man, the people want more. You know we got to go back and give the people more!"

Paul tried to reason with Al. "Look, Al, we've gone back three times. What are we going to do, just keep doing the same thing?" he asked.

Al kept screaming, "We've got to go back!" Then he suddenly grabbed a beer bottle. Paul looked up but didn't seem very scared, so Al said, "You don't believe I'll hit you with this bottle, do you?"

"Al, please," Paul said wearily, "I'm tired, and we are not going back." Paul had risen, but he must have thought the discussion was closed because he started to sit back down. No sooner was Paul in his chair than Al raised his arm and, as I stepped forward to grab the bottle, brought it crashing down across Paul's face. I called out for Melvin and Eddie, and closed the dressing room door. Paul was slouched in his chair with both hands covering his forehead, eyes, and nose. Blood gushed from between his fingers, so you couldn't tell if Al had cut open one of his eyes or what. We rushed Paul to the hospital, where they stitched him up and kept him overnight. Luckily, Al had missed Paul's eyes, but by less than an inch. The scar ran straight down the bridge of Paul's nose. It seemed obvious to us that Al was out. The next day at the hospital I said, "Well, we've got to let Al go."

"No," Paul replied, "let's leave him in. We've been friends for a long time. Let's just hang on."

"I hear what you're saying, Paul, but where is this going to lead? You got off kinda light this time, but you could have been blinded. Besides, it's one thing to have disagreements, but we can't have fighting and violence like this."

Paul's insistence that we keep Al surprised me. We were a good lineup, things were looking good, and a new guy is never easy to break in, so those were all considerations. But the overriding thing with Paul was that Al was still his friend, and Paul was nothing if not loyal. So Al stayed. For then.

We kept at it, but things were strained. After David Ruffin had caused such a sensation at Chappy's, you'd think Al would read the writing on the wall. Al's attitude didn't improve any, either, and it all blew up at the Fox Theater's annual Christmas show a few months later. I don't recall what song we were doing, but it was something uptempo because Eddie sang lead. Paul started doing another of his unrehearsed, impromptu moves, and Melvin followed him. Al and I were standing further back, and when I stepped forward to join the other two, Al nudged me and whispered, "No, no. We're the pretty boys. Let them do the work. We'll stay back here and be pretty for the bitches."

That was Al's last performance with the Temptations. When I told him he was out, he took it hard. He was devastated. I don't think he ever got over it, but you couldn't say he hadn't been warned. In his heart, I think he knew he'd brought it on himself.

Either David or Jimmy Ruffin could have taken Al's place, but after seeing how dynamic David was, we knew making him a Tempt would add an exciting element to our act. As with all of our personnel changes, we only had to notify management at Motown so they could take care of the legal details, and we were set. Not more than a week later, Smokey told us he'd booked the studio for us. He had this great song in mind for us called "The Way You Do the Things You Do."

That night the five of us met at Eddie's house on Hanover, then set out on the now-familiar walk to Hitsville. It was a cold, crisp January night, and each of us was bundled up in his long winter coat. As we strolled along, I dropped back behind the others and stood for what felt like a long time, looking ahead at my four closest friends. The whole city seemed to fall as silent as the stars that illuminated the silvery sidewalk. I didn't even hear their footsteps as they walked away. Suddenly, I felt overcome by a sense of purpose and the realization that this wasn't going to be just any group, or just a career for me, but a life. After all the turmoil and disappointment, we were going to make the Temptations into something bigger than all of us. It was in God's hands.

4

We finally broke out in early 1964 with "The Way You Do the Things You Do," a tune Smokey wrote with Bobby Rogers while they were driving on the Pennsylvania Turnpike. The first time we heard the song, we loved it. The melody swung, and the lyrics had lots of charm. They were silly in a way, talking about a girl you loved as a candle, a handle, a schoolbook, a cool crook, a broom, a perfume, but, typical of Smokey, he made it work. Paul sang lead on the flip, "Just Let Me Know." "The Way" got a good response whenever we did it live, so our hopes were up. We knew from past experience that even the best tracks don't always click.

Bringing in David was probably the best decision we made, but it wasn't all that smooth. In the beginning it was David and I who hung together. We had many wonderful times because David was a lively, funny guy. We walked all over the place, and David, who was known around then for always carrying a knife, would throw his knife into trees along the sidewalk or break into doing flips and cartwheels.

As long as I'd known David, he was always a very complex guy, very intense about things. I suppose a lot of it might be related to how he was raised. When we first met in 1959, he was with Eddie Bush, who I believe was his foster father, and David was known back then as Little David Bush. He was recording then. We didn't talk about it much, but from the little I did learn, it sounded like the Ruffins had come up from a rough beginning. He was originally from a little town called Wyanot, Mississippi, but up until the 1982 reunion tour, he'd always told us that he was from Meridian.

As badly as we wanted David in the group, the idea that he had been a solo artist played on our minds a little. When I finally asked David to join, I said, "Listen, David, we're not playing around. I'm serious. We need somebody who's going to stick with it." He assured me that he would, and I was satisfied. Although David was replacing Al Bryant, the structure of the Temptations was going to remain: five guys, any one of which could take a lead, with most leads split among Paul, Eddie, and David.

It would be a few years yet before any kind of competitiveness among those three came out. But it must be said that at first Eddie was not crazy about David coming in. Eddie couldn't have been threatened by David taking his spot because he was already splitting leads with Paul and, now and then, me. Besides, his voice and David's were so different. Still, David was an intense, dynamic singer and a natural-born showman. I guess it was just a matter of chemistry. Added to that was Eddie's suspicion that David planned to use the Temptations as a stepping-stone. We're aware that some books have presented the story so that it seems that we all suspected David's motives, but it's not so. Eddie's doubts about David cleared away as he saw that David was working as hard as the rest of us. And the other three of us never saw David in that light back then.

In actual fact, we were all tight with each other. Eddie and I were hanging pretty close. To give you an idea of the kind of friends we were, back in 1962, when we discovered—much to our surprise—that we were both seeing the same young lady, instead of one getting mad at the other, we laughed about it. It turned out she'd been playing us both, but we wouldn't let a thing like that come between us. Eddie had a real soft side. I recall him warning me about a woman who he thought was going to hurt me. Eddie was that kind of guy.

After we recorded "The Way You Do the Things You Do," we went out for a three-week gig in Saginaw, Michigan, hoping that our eighth single would be the one. Just about everyone who'd come to Motown around when we did was racking them up by then. Nineteen-sixty-three was a good year for Motown, what with Marvin Gaye's "Pride and Joy," "Hitch Hike," and "Can I Get a Witness," Martha and the Vandellas' "Heat Wave," "Quicksand," and "Come and Get These Memories," and the Miracles' "You've Really Got a Hold on Me" (from late 1962) and "Mickey's Monkey" (which we and Martha and the Vandellas sang backup on). Even Little Stevie Wonder had done it, with "Fingertips (Part 2)." Of all Motown's big acts, we were the next-to-the-last ones out of the gate. The only ones slower than us finally to bust into the Top Twenty were the Supremes.

The minute we got back in from Saginaw we stopped in at Hitsville, something we'd do even before we would go home. Everyone we ran into was saying, "Hey, haven't you all heard?"

"Heard what?" we asked.

"You're all in the charts."

We kept repeating, "Are you kidding me?" It was like a dream. Someone opened up the current issues of *Billboard* and *Cash Box*, and there it was: "The Way You Do the Things You Do" running up both charts with a bullet. By the time it was all over, "The Way" peaked at number eleven on the pop chart. When David saw those charts, he sat down on a long chaise lounge in the Motown lobby, took off his glasses, and cried like a baby.

"At last," he said, tears running down his face, "at last. I have been trying to get in the charts, and at last I'm in the charts."

I sat down beside him, kind of teary-eyed myself. All I could say was, "Yeah," and "Oh, man." There was no way to articulate that feeling. There'd be bigger hits, but nothing ever beat that first time. Everywhere we went, people were talking about us, or they'd see us in the street, point, and say, "Oh, that's them." We'd gotten a little of that with the Distants, but it was nothing like this.

I remember being at the Graystone Ballroom, a place where a lot of us went to dance and hang out. Promotion guys and jocks were coming up to us and saying, "Man, you all are number one in Chicago," and "You all's record is number one in Philly."

Back then disc jockeys ruled the airwaves, and could make or break just about anybody. Some of our earlier records, like "Dream Come True" and "I Want a Love I Can See," had been picked up here and there, but not on any consistent basis. Once those jocks got "The Way You Do the Things You Do" they must have known they had a live one. After that, we could do no wrong.

And the money was better. Ever since Josephine and I married, her mother had criticized me for not being in a more stable line of work. Sometimes Josephine would take up the cause, too. But I wasn't giving up. I'd felt in my heart that this day was going to come. Now it was here.

Between the release of "The Way You Do the Things You Do" and April 1964 when it peaked, Motown kept us busy. We sang backup for Liz Land, one of Motown's earliest artists. I believe she was a trained singer, and her range spanned two or three octaves. She'd get so high, the hair on the nape of your neck would stand up. She was a beautiful woman and an excellent vocal stylist. Her material was quite sophisticated and unique, mostly ballads. We had the pleasure of backing her on two songs, "Keep Me," which got a lot of play, and the flip side, "Midnight Johnny." But she never went as far as she deserved. Of course, today, that's another rare and valuable record.

Meet the Temptations, our debut album, was out in March, and though it barely snuck into the Top 100 albums chart, we couldn't have been happier if it had gone to number one. We'd prayed for that album for so long, we cherished it. Each one of us had his own copy, and when we were on the road and staying someplace, walking down the hall, we'd hear it playing. In those days albums weren't the main source of record sales, like singles, so having an album out then really meant something—that you had a hit, and you were on the rise.

Record companies' philosophies about albums were much different, too. Basically, selling an album was like reselling one, two, or three hit singles plus some throwaway filler tracks that nobody really gave a damn about. With *Meet* you got "The Way You Do the Things You Do" and its B side, "Just Let Me Know," along with ten other tracks culled from our seven-single string of flops. The only songs left out of our recorded legacy to that point were "Oh Mother of Mine" and "Romance without Finance," the two obscure Pirates tunes, and the Northern songs.

One of our favorite things about the album was the cover. Early on, Motown often used pictures of white people or some silly cartoon on the covers, thinking, I guess, that record buyers would be turned off by seeing black faces. The photographer wanted to do something different, so he posed us against a dark background. By carefully lighting our faces, he achieved an almost silhouette effect, not unlike that used on the Beatles' first American album. It was very dramatic and different for Motown and most other black albums of the day. I'm not sure that Berry deliberately chose that type of photograph and cover, thinking he would present us as an upscale act, but it fit in very well with the sort of classy image we were cultivating.

· · ·

We continued to write songs, but with time and hits, Motown became considerably less receptive to our stuff. When it came to what artists could and should do, Berry was very clear: artists performed, writers wrote, and producers produced. It was that simple. Because Berry wrote and produced himself, he respected writers and producers, often more than the artists. In his paternal, sometimes condescending way, he let it be known that he wasn't interested in having artists who wrote and produced. In the face of this, we got less diligent about pushing it. Maybe it was a mistake to let that happen, but once the Temptations became consistent hitmakers, Motown gave us the best material, the best production, and the best support. Maybe if we'd felt neglected things would have been different.

One of the last sixties tunes any Tempt had a writing credit on was our ninth single, "The Girl's Alright with Me," which Eddie wrote with Norman Whitfield and Eddie Holland. Onstage we did a thing where four of us stood around one microphone and snapped our fingers on the intro, and then glided right into our steps. It was hot. The more successful number, though, was the flip side, Smokey's "I'll Be in Trouble." At number thirty-three, it wasn't the smash follow-up we'd hoped for, but we'd take it. You'd think that Eddie's voice was high enough, but several producers at Motown preferred to record songs a half step or step higher than what you were comfortable singing. In some instances, like David Ruffin singing "Ain't Too Proud to Beg," it worked great, because that extra strain gave the vocals a sharper edge. Using that approach with Eddie, though, left him sounding a little squeaky if it wasn't done right, and what with "I'll Be in Trouble" being in a minor key, it didn't quite work. Our next hit was "Girl (Why You Wanna Make Me Blue)," a song of Norman's that Eddie sang lead on. We still switched off leads in our shows, but until late 1964 all our hits featured Eddie.

In those days Motown booked the Tempts on any tour that would take us. Motown handled all the financial arrangements and made the deals. All we had to do was show up and sing. Promoters then paid us several hundred dollars a night, against which Motown deducted travel, food, lodging, and other expenses. I remember being told that all the money due us would be kept safely in an escrow account until the tour ended. Then Motown would settle each act's account and write a check for the balance. Or so they said. In fact, we never saw a single penny from any of those early tours, nor did we see any kind of written statement breaking down where the money went. Since we rarely stayed in a hotel and weren't eating in the finest restaurants, it's hard to imagine what Motown's "costs" were. Something about it didn't hang right. Did this happen to anyone there besides us? I honestly cannot say. As success came to each of us, even if only in a small way, we kept to our own groups. You wouldn't be sitting around with other people outside your group and talking about it, even if you suspected something. I can't say why we were all like that. Countless times acts who were signed to smaller, less organized R&B labels or bigger, less friendly major companies told us how lucky we were and how they wished Motown would sign them. Hearing that gave us the impression that things were worse everywhere. In our case it was a matter of appreciating what you'd worked so hard to get and being mindful not to rock the boat. The five of us learned to carry a lot inside and, as they say in karate, suck wind.

Motown hadn't yet given us the power to draw on the Temptations account on Melvin's or my signature, but there never was a problem getting money if you needed it. If I saw a television I wanted to buy, I'd call up and there'd be a check waiting when I got to Hitsville. Every now and then, somebody might tell you your account was running a little low, or something along those lines, but money was coming in, so we probably didn't think about it as much as we should have. Following Beans Bowles's advice, we put ourselves on a budget. Even without an accountant's advice, we knew to pay our estimated income taxes, so we made sure we had some socked away.

Things picked up considerably in 1964, and we were either out of town or at Hitsville working on our act or recording. We did the Motortown Revue tours, as well as tours sponsored by Irving Feld, Henry Wynn, and Dick Clark. I recall being on the Henry Wynn tours with people such as Maxine Brown, who was hot then, Chuck Jackson, Gladys Knight and the Pips, and lots of others. The acts traveled by bus, and some were nicer than others. Motown's buses were in notoriously bad shape. As Melvin once remarked, a vehicle with wheels was a major improvement over what Motown had.

There wasn't much to do on the bus, so if you weren't into playing cards, reading, or constantly sleeping, you did a lot of talking. Generally, a bus carried five or six acts plus the band and whatever sidemen, chaperones, and other people there might be. It was very cramped, and there was no such thing as personal space, so you developed another kind of camaraderie.

These tours averaged thirty days each, and they weren't as strategically planned as they might have been. You might close a show in one town and have to drive six or seven hundred miles to the next show the next day. There were days and days we'd go without our heads ever hitting a pillow. On the rare occasion when we did check into a hotel for a night's rest or a few days' relaxation, if we were down South we might drive for a while to find a hotel that would take blacks.

For many people in places we visited the "old ways" died hard. Generally speaking, blacks in Detroit were treated better than in most of the South, so we found some aspects of racism pretty shocking. Even though you could predict what you were going to find down there, it still made you angry. All I wanted to know was, why?

One tour took us through my home state of Texas. Several young ladies had to use the rest room but weren't allowed to because they were black. The civil rights movement was growing, but in some of those little pockets, Martin Luther King, Jr., could have been marching on Mars for all those people cared. We had no choice but to reboard the bus and drive down the road a piece to where we could stop and people could go in the bushes. Some, such as Inez and Charlie Foxx, Maxine Brown, Blinky Williams, and Kim Weston, didn't go along with this crap silently, and some situations came close to turning ugly. Sometimes it made you wonder if it would ever change. The thing about any act of racism is that no matter how much you tell yourself what to expect or how many times you see the same nonsense, it never loses its power to shake you up.

Our first full Motortown Revue, in 1964, took us to South Carolina. From the stage, you could look out across the auditorium and see a rope running smack down the middle of the aisle: blacks on one side, whites on the other. Same thing for the balcony. We couldn't believe it. Angry, we asked, "What the fuck is the rope for?" but we knew the answer. There were far too many scenes like that to recount. Let's just say they were dealt with.

Sometimes we did see progress. Take that town in South Carolina, for example. When we got back there about a year or so later, the rope was gone, and it was a different scene. Everyone— black and white—sat together. In only a matter of months, some of those barriers fell, at least among the young people. This is not to say that getting blacks and whites together for a show solves any major racial problem, but it is a step.

As we came up in the business, we shared the stage with many of our idols. One was the late Jackie Wilson, a tremendous singer and consummate performer; I'd followed his career since he was in Billy Ward and the Dominoes. In fact, Berry often compared the Temptations to the Dominoes because our lineup and sound were similar. We were working the Regal in Chicago, and every night we watched from the wings as Jackie did his show. His style was dynamic, very athletic, and women found him irresistible. But Jackie didn't take care of himself. Back then he not only drank scotch and smoked cigarettes, but he snorted cocaine, and you could see that it was wearing on him. I knew he wouldn't go on like that too much longer without burning himself out.

One thing about the touring I enjoyed was being around women and getting to learn more about them, not necessarily in the romantic sense but as friends. Maxine Brown, Yvonne Fair, Dionne Warwick, and others would sit around and tell us how they liked men to treat them, and what they looked for in a guy. I never will forget Yvonne Fair saying, "If I look down at a man's shoes and he has those funny clodhopper shoes with the triple stitches, I don't give a shit how fine he is from the ankles on up, I will not talk to him. He will get no time, nor will he get any *stuff*." And then Maxine Brown said, "Yeah, child, if his hands ain't right—his fingernails right—if his teeth is cruddy, I'd say 'uh, uh.'" I'd listen to them talk for hours, fascinated and making mental notes.

Another one I liked to hang with on tour was Chuck Jackson. Chuck was a great singer, slick onstage, and always something of a ladies' man. He was a few years older than we were, and had been in the Del-Vikings. Around this time he had two substantial hits: "I Don't Want to Cry" and "Any Day Now." Girls couldn't seem to get enough of him. We made it a point to stick around Chuck because you could count on catching his overflow, if you know what I mean.

The one guy everybody loved was Stevie Wonder. He was much younger than the rest of us, about fourteen or fifteen, but he had a great personality and so much talent, you couldn't help thinking of him as a peer. Stevie liked to make people laugh and had an impish charm. Usually he sat at the back of the bus with the musicians and played his harmonica for hours. Everyone understood that he was woodshedding, but only to a point. When it got to be about two or three in the morning, someone would yell, "Stevie, man, put that damn harmonica down and go to sleep." If that didn't work, we tried, "Steven, we're going to beat your ass if you don't take that damn harmonica . . ." and he'd laugh, because he knew we'd never do that. Not that the thought didn't cross our minds now and then.

On a later tour Edwin Starr brought along his pet chimpanzee, who was cute but full-grown and not very well trained. This chimp amused himself—and Edwin, too, I guess, since he didn't try to stop him—by running around and peeing on people. Finally we put it to Edwin: "You got to get that monkey off the bus, or you get off." I forget what happened to the chimp, but he was gone.

So not everything ran that smoothly. You had to make an effort to readjust. You really liked everybody or you'd find out who you didn't like on there. And there were some times when we were not one big happy family. Once the Tempts went at it with the Contours. They were nice guys but a little rough around the edges, and a couple were downright unsavory. Not to brag, but we got our share of women, which one of their guys didn't like. I think we argued with them over that and a bottle of wine.

The young ladies from Motown were truly ladies, but some of them found the tours a little stifling. Motown made sure they were heavily chaperoned. That was probably not a bad idea, considering the fact that we guys were pretty much left to our own devices, and even though we were just in our twenties, Motown management treated us like grown men. Beans Bowles or one of the older gentlemen might lecture us now and then about using protection and how discretion was the better part of valor—a good thing to remember down South when white girls were after us—but that was the extent of it. We also managed to sneak in a few little love affairs and made friendships that continue today.

Around this time Josephine and I called it quits. Work took me out of town so much that even under the best of circumstances a real family life was hard to manage. I got an apartment over on LaSalle Boulevard and began dating again. One thing Hitsville did not lack was fine-looking women, and I wasn't the only guy to notice. At different times I dated Jeana Jackson, Sandy Tilley, Martha Reeves, Kim Weston, and Billie Jean Brown. Those were good times, but work always came first.

In 1964 we made our first and last appearance in Bermuda. We played at a club called the Forty Thieves and stayed in a big house up on a hill. Bermuda was beautiful, the people were friendly, and every night a bunch of girls followed us home and camped out on our front lawn. We'd come in during the wee hours, and there they'd be—dozens of beautiful women. Being young and wild, we'd party until five or six in the morning. The neighbors complained to the police and yelled out their windows at us, but we didn't care. It was just too damned good.

Despite all that, something happened, and Eddie and David locked ass one night. Melvin and I shared one room, David and Eddie had another, and Paul slept by himself. Melvin was asleep, snoring that big, thunderous bass snore, when suddenly, from the other room, Paul and I heard shouting. David was sitting on the edge of his bed, saying something that Eddie didn't like, so Eddie came at David as if he was going to belt him in the face. I grabbed Eddie, and Paul held David, and after making a lot of racket, they cooled out. I went into my room, sure that Melvin would be wide awake, but he continued sleeping like a baby. As a result of the commotion, the government of Bermuda banned us from the country, and we've never been back.

During the fall we did a nine-day stint at the Brooklyn Fox with Dusty Springfield, the Shangri-Las, Jay and the Americans, the Contours, the Ronettes, Martha and the Vandellas, Little Anthony and the Imperials, Marvin Gaye, and others. It was a lineup you couldn't slack off on. And we weren't slacking off a bit. Paul kept at us, and we worked like dogs. It's funny, but sometimes having a little success makes you hungrier than you were when you had none. Suddenly, great success seemed not only possible but probable. All we had to do was keep at it.

Aside from our singing and strutting onstage, we were known for our stage uniforms, which over the years would run the gamut from black-tux elegance to the psychedelic stomach-churning combinations of the late sixties. It was around this time that our uniforms started getting wild. Eddie was definitely ahead of his time in picking our clothes. Whenever we played the Apollo a salesman from F & F Clothiers named Dave would stop by and visit all the acts to show them fabric swatches. You could order just about anything your heart desired.

One day he showed up with some purple material, and Eddie fell in love with it.

"Eddie!" I exclaimed. "I'm too black to wear that purple!" And this was purple, as in pimp-clothes purple.

"Don't worry, man," Eddie said, laughing. "We're going to be sharp. They're going to love that purple on us."

Eddie ordered five purple suits with a white button, which we wore with white shirts and white shoes. I'd always trusted Eddie, but I couldn't see how this was going to work. The accepted thing then was red, white, and black. Maybe another color, but never purple.

But I was wrong. The minute the crowd got an eyeful of us in those suits, they went berserk. That purple drove the audience out of their minds.

The year 1964 closed on a high note for not only us but everyone at Motown. The Supremes racked up three number-one records in a row, then became the first Motown act to appear on national television when they debuted on *The Ed Sullivan Show*. It was exciting to see our friends on a program we watched every Sunday. When the Supremes made that historic appearance, they represented not just themselves, but everyone at Motown. As they would in several other areas, the Supremes blazed a trail the rest of us would follow, and we were all very proud. There were plenty of great female singers around Hitsville, and some truly fine-looking ones, too. But, as the world discovered, Diane, Flo, and Mary were born to this; they had "it," or as we'd say, the Jim Johnson. They were stars. Meanwhile, Marvin Gaye, Mary Wells, Brenda Holloway, Stevie Wonder, Martha and the Vandellas, the Miracles, and the label's latest signing, the Four Tops, kept spinning out the hits. After "Girl (Why You Wanna Make Me Blue)" charted in the twenties, we were looking for the next tune.

Back home in Detroit, Smokey Robinson caught our act at the Twenty Grand one evening. One of our numbers featured each of us singing a part. The title of it escapes me, but I do remember that we brought the house down with it. After we came offstage that night, Smokey approached us and, pointing directly at David, said, "I've got a song for you."

It turned out to be a tune Smokey and Ronnie White had written and planned to cut with the Miracles. It was midtempo ballad with a pretty, sweet melody. From the first lines — "I've got sunshine on a cloudy day / When it's cold outside, I've got the month of May" — we knew we had something very special. That fall, during a run at the Apollo, Smokey came to New York to work with us in our dressing room between shows. He taught us to sing the parts as he heard them and perfect those intricate harmonies. On December 21 we recorded "My Girl" in Detroit. It was David's first lead on a single.

We recorded our vocals over a basic track, so what we heard was basically bass, drums, and guitar. Smokey worked up those lush string parts with Paul Riser, a classically trained musician who wrote most of the orchestral music on Motown records. We listened in the studio as Smokey added the "sweetening," and by the time he was finished with the mix, it was the most gorgeous, magical love song I'd ever heard. There was no question in our minds that we had the big one here.

Sometime around then, the five of us were talking one day about how it seemed that so many good groups broke up just when things got good. We were thinking specifically of Tony Williams's leaving the Platters, but we knew of dozens of groups who'd let their petty nonsense ruin a good thing. It seemed to be one of the hazards of the business. Paul said, "Well, we don't care how big we get, we're going to stay together." And so we took a vow, promising one another that we wouldn't fall into that trap. Paul, Eddie, David, Melvin, and I were the Temptations and always would be. We truly believed that.

Christmas Day we did a Motortown Revue at the Brooklyn Fox with the Supremes, the Marvelettes, Marvin Gaye, the Miracles, and Stevie Wonder. The next day Motown released "My Girl," and it charted at number seventy-six three weeks later. Talk about a merry Christmas.

"My Girl" continued to climb to and hit number one on March 6, 1965. By then it had sold at least a million copies. Berry sent us a congratulatory telegram, which we received while we were playing the Apollo, and setting more records. I remember feeling like I was going to burst from pride. Everywhere you walked in Detroit that spring all you heard was "My Girl." By then, Motown had come to own Detroit. Wherever you went, if they knew you were with Motown, out came the red carpet. There was no more standing in line, no more waiting for anything. Despite all the success, Motown remained more a family than a business. When we didn't have shows, rehearsals, or recording, all of us would stand out on the front lawn and crack jokes half the day. I remember Marvin Gaye, Norman Whitfield, Shorty Long, Smokey, Lamont Dozier, the Holland brothers, and us out there. People would ride by and honk their horns at us and wave. Some fans even made pilgrimages to Hitsville as part of their vacations, like going to Disneyland. Once when I saw Esther Edwards leading a pack of tourists through the studios, I stopped one of them and asked, "You mean to tell me you all left beautiful L.A. to come and spend your time here in Detroit?"

"Oh yeah," the star-struck man replied. "We just couldn't help it. We wanted to see you guys."

Living in the middle of it, we had no real grasp of what Motown was becoming. For one thing, we had nothing to compare it to. How other record companies functioned was a total mystery to us, though as we would learn, there are two ways to run a record company: the industry way and the Motown way. And at that time, the Motown way was doing just fine by us. I remember somebody from the office boarding a tour bus and handing each of us a check—the royalties off one hit. Mine was for $18,000.

We felt that we were on our way, but even before the first hit, Paul had his sights set on where we should be going. "Man," Paul would say, "we've got to play Vegas and Atlantic City. The white folks don't want to see no guys out there bumpin' and grindin' and carrying on." Plus, we didn't want to be guys out there bumpin' and grindin' and carrying on.

The company was starting to boom. In March 1965 Harvey Fuqua convinced Motown to bring Cholly Atkins into artist development. We'd long been admirers of Cholly's choreography for Gladys Knight and the Pips, the Cadillacs, the Cleftones, Frankie Lymon and the Teenagers, the Moonglows, Little Anthony and the Imperials, and others. We'd finally gotten some of that magic ourselves when he devised a routine for us to use on "The Way You Do the Things You Do" in 1964.

Cholly was in his early fifties when he came to Motown after a long and successful career as a professional dancer. During the 1930s, Cholly was one half of a song-and-dance team called the Rhythm Pals, which appeared in several Hollywood films. After that, he joined forces with Charles "Honi" Coles, a tap dancer who at one time also managed the Apollo. It was through working at the Apollo that Cholly met many of the young vocal groups he later choreographed.

There weren't a lot of guys doing what Cholly did. What set Cholly's work apart from other choreographers' was that he built everything around the singing. Anybody can cook up a series of eye-popping moves, but to create dance that takes into consideration such things as the stage layout, the placement of microphones and cords, and how the hell you are going to move, sing, and still breathe takes a scientific approach and attention to detail. His routines incorporated dozens of tiny, nearly imperceptible movements—hitch steps, subtle turns and shifts, a little sway here or there—that when you followed them to the letter landed you in the precise spot at the exact second. However, miss one of those suckers and you were totally out of it. Just about anyone else's choreography allowed you a few beats for "correction," but not Cholly's.

It was one thing for Cholly to dream up these things, but it was something else for us to learn them. Of course, Paul had started us, and he'd even made a dancer out of me, the kid whose dance-hall name was "Wallflower." But as good as we were with that, Cholly took us into a whole other dimension. On average, learning a new routine took about two or three weeks of dance rehearsals for five or six hours a day. And while Cholly was a gentleman in all respects, he could be tough. His goal was to turn out acts with routines so ingrained in their minds that once the opening chords of any song hit your ears, your body went on automatic pilot. I remember going home after a long rehearsal, sitting down to watch television, and in my head hearing a little voice saying, "Kick, step, two, three, turn, one, two, three." In the studio Cholly didn't allow for one iota of deviation, and if you messed up he let you know it. We'd be sweating and concentrating, then one guy would miss something, and Cholly would yell, "You greasy snotsucker! Can't you count?"

"Pops, why do you have to call me that?" I asked once.

"I don't know. Because you are! Now, come on," he'd reply as he marched over and grabbed one of us by the wrist and start walking him through the steps.

Pairing us up with Cholly was a match made in heaven and would be so for years to come. In 1983 he worked up a routine for our song "Sail Away," a pretty ballad that ends with an African beat. During that part, Cholly had us moving back off the mike, tightening our midsections and hunching our shoulders. It was quite dramatic, and one day a woman who saw us said, "You know, when you all do that move at the end of 'Sail Away,' my seat gets wet."

When I relayed the story to Cholly, now in his seventies, he replied, "That's right. You want to touch them women and make them start thinking sexual. I know what them women like." And he did.

Also that March, the Motown Revue went to England. "My Girl" was not that high on the British charts, but from the moment we landed in London, we were in love with the country and its people, who ever since, for the past two and a half decades, have always treated us with love and respect. We didn't stay for the whole tour but did appear with the Supremes, the Miracles, the Marvelettes, Martha and the Vandellas, Stevie Wonder, and Dusty Springfield on a BBC special called *The Sounds of Motown,* which is now available on videocassette under the title *Ready Steady Go! Special Edition: The Sounds of Motown.* We performed "My Girl," "The Way You Do the Things You Do," and our then-latest single, "It's Growing."

At the time, we each had a group responsibility. Eddie took care of uniforms, Paul fined you if he caught you messing up onstage, Melvin handled finances, and David oversaw transportation. My job as group spokesperson and de facto leader was to see that nobody got too far out of pocket. I levied fines for things like lateness, excessive drinking, and smoking dope. This one day we were all at the Cumberland Hotel, and I decided to go down to David and Eddie's room and see what was happening. I knocked on the door, then one of them yelled, "Who is it?"

"It's me. Otis."

"Oh, shit!" one of them whispered loud enough that I could hear. A second later, the other one called out, "Just a minute," using one of those "I'm freaked but I'm cool" tones you get from guilty kids.

One minute, two minutes, three minutes went by. What the hell was going on in there? If I'd caught them smoking dope, I'd have fined their asses a hundred dollars, which in those days wasn't chump change. But whatever they might have been up to, I never did find out.

During the summer we did one of Murray the K's shows at the Brooklyn Fox. Murray the K was a hot New York City disc jockey who was also known as the fifth Beatle and, for a while, the sixth Temptation. Murray was a nice guy, and his shows always had the top acts. I recall one bill with us, Little Anthony and the Imperials, Tom Jones, the Ronettes, and the Shangri-Las. All of the girls were real cute, but, of course, the Ronettes were the hottest. At the time, Tom Jones's career had just taken off with "It's Not Unusual." He later smoothed out his appearance a bit, but then he was pretty rugged and chasing Ronnie Bennett (later Spector) of the Ronettes.

What I remember most vividly about that run was walking out the stage door in the wee hours of the morning and seeing people lined up, bundled in sleeping bags, waiting for the next show. These were great shows, and you worked your ass off for pay that averaged out to about ten bucks per guy per show. Still there was no place else I wanted to be then.

"My Girl" opened the door for us, and slowly but surely things got bigger and better. The crowds were wilder, the halls were bigger—even the groupies were classier. Of course that didn't mean that next week they wouldn't all be with the O'Jays or whoever else came through, but that was how it was. All that female attention could compromise your judgment, so you had to watch yourself. But overall, these were good times.

More than once, each of us was the target of a jealous boyfriend's rage. One night we were playing the Twenty Grand to a packed house. From backstage we could hear women hollering, "The Tempts! The Tempts!" Once the show ended, I was walking toward my car when a young lady called out, "Oh, please, would you sign your autograph for me?"

I said, "Sure," and took the paper and pen she offered me, but the whole time I could see that she wanted me to say, "What's your name, darlin'? What's your number?" As I was signing my name, a guy came and grabbed her tightly by the arm and snapped, "Not this one, motherfucker, this is mine."

"Hey, man," I replied coolly, "I'm just signing the autograph. I wasn't saying nothin' else to your woman."

"I just want to make sure," the guy said, "because she's my wife, and all I've been hearing from her is 'Temptations this, Temptations that.' I got so tired of hearing about the damn Temptations that I decided to come down and see you guys." He paused for a minute. "And you know what? Yeah, you all are bad. I like you. But this is my woman."

"Fine," I said. He offered his hand, we shook, and I split.

One time the jealous boyfriend was Kenny Gamble, who thought that David was moving in on his girlfriend (later wife), singer Dee Dee Sharp of "Mashed Potato Time" fame. Kenny was in a group called Kenny Gamble and the Romeos, which included future producer Thom Bell. We were playing the Uptown in Philadelphia when we got wind that Kenny might be thinking of bringing down some guys to jump David Ruffin. Naturally the four of us went to David's defense, and I told Kenny, "You might be in your home-town, but it ain't like we can't pick up the phone." David was unharmed, and Kenny and I became close friends. By the mid-sixties he and Leon Huff had their own label, and through the years produced Wilson Pickett, the O'Jays, Harold Melvin and the Blue Notes, the Jacksons, and others. Kenny and I would shoot pool and talk about the business.

For the most successful Motown acts this was the dawn of a golden era. But for others, the so-called B acts, whose hits weren't as big or as consistent, it was the beginning of a slow and, for some, bitter decline. Smokey wrote and produced most of our hits then, and since he was one of Berry's closest friends and a vice president of the company, some other artists assumed that we had an "in." We'd come to Motown with a group organization, and I dealt with Berry directly, just as I'd dealt with Johnnie Mae. Not all acts had that kind of thing with him, but I don't know why. We pretty much kept to our own business. Each act was out on the road almost constantly, so Hitsville wasn't the same friendly hangout.

Being back in Detroit meant being back in the studio. We recorded live then, with all the musicians in the room playing as we sang. The Funk Brothers, Motown's studio band, must go down in history as one of the best groups of musicians anywhere. Each of them was a master in his own right, and sometimes I'd get so wrapped up listening to them, I'd miss my cue and forget to sing. They'd also get their little barbs in. James Jamerson was a funny guy, and so was Eddie "Bongo" Brown, a percussionist. If one of us goofed, it meant starting the song over from the top, and that was always the musicians' chance to make a nasty crack, like, "Those damn doo-wops." Then someone else would say, "Yeah, you know they can't even doo-wop right." Or, "You guys better be glad that you got the Funk Brothers behind you, or you wouldn't sound like nothin'." Generally, we could cut a track in three to four hours and wrap up a whole album inside a week. Even though today technology affords artists the chance to make perfect records, they still haven't come up with the machine that puts in that special electricity and energy of those live records.

Our following two singles, "It's Growing" and "Since I Lost My Baby," featured David. "Since I Lost My Baby" is one of my favorite songs. That fall we released one of the few singles to feature Paul, "Don't Look Back." Although Norman Whitfield was getting in a song here and there, we were still primarily Smokey Robinson's act, and Smokey wrote with David or Eddie in mind. Paul wasn't exactly bitter about this, but he did make it known that he'd like to do more singing. "Shit," he would say, "I can sing too!" No one could argue with that, but no one seemed to be writing for him either.

I remember doing "Don't Look Back" during a run at Leo's Casino in Cleveland a couple years later. Leo's was small but well known for bringing in great acts, such as Chuck Jackson and the O'Jays. Once again we were in a battle of the groups, this time against the O'Jays. Cleveland being their hometown put us at a disadvantage. In those days there were five O'Jays—Eddie Levert, Walter Williams, William Powell, Bobby Massey, and Bill Isles— and from the dressing room we heard the applause through the walls. They were killing that audience with a tune called "Stand in for Love." We'd been on the road for a week, doing four shows a day, and we were dead tired, but somehow we rose to the challenge. "Okay, guys," I said, "we're really going to have to go for it."

We got onstage, did a little this, a little that, went into "My Girl," and bingo! We had that crowd dying for us. But the real capper came when Paul did "Don't Look Back" because we had a part in the routine where we all fanned out across the stage slick as water, leaving Paul in the center. At that point he'd start breaking the song down and really milking it as only he could. By the time we wrapped the show up, it was "O'Jays who?" From then on we did "Don't Look Back" just about every place we played.

Late in 1965 Motown released our third LP, titled after our now-famous introduction, *Temptin' Temptations*. Starting with the second album, *The Temptations Sing Smokey*, more thought went into the filler tracks, and so these records still hold up today. But as much as I liked most of the tunes (including "Born to Love You," on which Jimmy Ruffin sings with us), I can't look at the cover— with us in white suits and *black* shoes—without wincing a little. For all of our style and class, we didn't have those damn white shoes when we needed them.

Everything seemed to happen in 1965, and things moved in a

flash, so it's hard to find any benchmark. It was that year, though, when it struck me and, I'm sure the rest of the guys, that we were bigger than we ever dared imagine. I remembered back to when I'd have been walking on air just to get into the Arcadia and challenge the Cadets. Everything seemed so unreal, and the extent of our success didn't finally sink in until we did *The Ed Sullivan Show*.

The fact that the show was broadcast live and we would be seen by tens of millions of people didn't escape us. We stood backstage in our sleek black-and-gray tuxes, praying to God, "Please, please, please let me hit my note and make my steps. Don't let me make a fool of myself." Our tuxes were wringing wet with perspiration, and our mouths were dry as cotton. Of course, Eddie always had that cool exterior, so he seemed fine, and David had a way of making things seem more manageable: "It ain't nothin' but another television show," he said, then proceeded to go out and kick ass. I couldn't stop having one of my many conversations with myself. "Otis, there are millions of people out there watching your black ass. Do not mess up!"

Came showtime, we went out and sang "My Girl" and another tune. While we were singing, one part of me was really trying to focus on what my feet and my mouth were doing, while another part of me kept saying, "Shit, I am on Ed Sullivan. I am on *Ed Sullivan*." Then, almost the moment we started, it was over. It still didn't seem quite real until we got home to Detroit. My friends, neighbors, relatives—everyone, especially Haze and my stepdad, were so proud. I knew then I wasn't dreaming anymore.

5

One great benefit of all the travel was getting to spend more time with women. The chaperones on the Motortown Revue tours tried to keep us out of trouble, but love still found a way. There were many, many fine women around Motown, and I had my share of little crushes and more passionate things. Of them all, though, the one I recall most fondly is Florence Ballard of the Supremes. On the bus, we would sit together talking quietly or holding hands under a jacket that covered our laps so no one could see. In my mind's eye, I picture Flo on the tour bus, smiling, the wind blowing through her hair. She was one of those women photographs don't do justice to. Her beauty was understated and elegant, and in her way, she was stunning.

Back then Flo struck most everyone as a happy, fun-loving girl.

Quick and sassy, she could be the life of the party. In fact, it was Flo who taught me the expression "shoot the habit to the rabbit," which means make love. The first time she said it, I replied, "Oh, Flo, I like that." And she quipped in her sexy way, "Yeah, you know me, Big Daddy."

She was always one to tell you what was on her mind, and everyone knew how badly she wanted to sing. Not enough people got to hear Flo, so I'll tell you that she was one of the best singers I ever heard. All three of the Supremes had it, but even in the earliest days, whenever Flo took her part in "(The Nighttime Is) The Right Time," a Ray Charles classic they'd been doing since their Primettes days, she brought down the house. Her voice had a real depth of feeling and a strong, churchy sound. When Flo opened her mouth to sing, you sat up in your chair.

Our affair lasted only a brief time, mostly because both of our groups were always out on the road. Berry took a close personal interest in the girls, and they traveled separately from everyone else. And with Motown sending everyone everywhere, we didn't hang together like we used to. Like any group, the Supremes had their internal problems, but they kept them to themselves. I can't say that Flo harbored any resentment toward Berry or Diana, because she never discussed it with me. When we were together, we concentrated on us. She masked her feelings very well, and knowing what I know now about her background and the fact that she was raped as a young woman, I'd have to say maybe too well. We shared some very beautiful, intimate moments, which I will always cherish.

Another of my favorite romances was with Patti LaBelle. She and her group, the Blue Belles—Sarah Dash, Nona Hendryx, and future Supreme Cindy Birdsong—were on many of the same package tours as we were since their 1962 hit "I Sold My Heart to the Junkman." Patti sang as well then as she does now, and I thought she was very attractive.

I was not alone in that opinion; lots of guys wanted to get next to

Patti, but it was tough. The Blue Belles were managed by a married couple named the Montagues, and they kept their charges under tight wraps. You couldn't penetrate that barrier for anything. Many young men tried and failed, but I didn't let that discourage me. In fact, I was up for the challenge.

Fate intervened, and we found ourselves headlining a bill at the Uptown with Patti and the girls. Here was my big chance. Getting to Patti required getting around her chaperones, so I turned on the old charm. During my first meeting with the Montagues, I was the perfect gentleman. No matter what they said, I answered politely with a soft-spoken "Yes, ma'am," or "No, sir." Their defenses melted, and they finally said, "Oh, let's let Otis come in. He's such a nice boy." I smiled graciously, all the time saying to myself, "I'm going to slow-walk you to death," an old expression that's another way of saying, "I've plotted and I've planned, and I'll take my time, but I'm gonna get there."

Patti and I soon fell in love. She was a very nice girl, but matter-of-fact and dedicated to her career, something I understood and supported. I was in deep. Whenever we had time off, the other guys would say, "Well, we all know where Otis is going to be. He's going to Philly." And they were right. I'd take off for Philadelphia and stay with Patti's family. They treated me very nicely. Of course, that didn't stop us from sneaking away whenever an opportunity came along. All in all, it was a wonderful time.

Not to say we didn't have our problems. One was being able to go out together without being recognized. One day we were visiting one of Patti's friends when word got out in the neighborhood that we were there. Pretty soon the house was surrounded by fans screaming, "One of the Tempts is in there! Patti LaBelle's in there! Let's get their autographs!" We cut our visit short and ducked out the back. The bigger problem, though, was the business. After going weeks without seeing each other, our relationship cooled. I learned from this that when you lead a crazy life, you need a lover

◀ David English, a.k.a. Melvin Franklin, long before we met on Twelfth Street in Detroit.

▼ Me with my Aunt Lucille, the first person in our family to own a record player.

◀ Portrait of a well-loved and somewhat spoiled grandbaby, Otis Williams.

▲ Here I am decked out with one of my first groups. For some reason that's probably best left forgotten, I called these guys the El Domingos. Suave, no?

▲ The "Classic Temptations" lineup, which lasted from December 1964 to June 1968: *(back, from left)* Paul Williams and me; *(center)* Melvin Franklin; *(front)* Eddie Kendricks and David Ruffin.

MAVIS LEAK

The Rev. Martin L. King

ROEBUCK, STAPLES

REV. JAMES CLEVELAND SINGERS

THE MIGHTY CLOUDS OF JOY

THE CARAVANS

JAMES BROWN

MARVIN GAY

SAM COOK

PERVIS STAPLES

The Staple Singers

JACKIE WILSON

THE FOUR TOPS

CLARA WARD & Her GOSPEL SINGERS

SOUL STIRRERS

▲ They used to sell collages like this one in the Apollo Theatre lobby. Note the mixture of vocal harmony and doo-wop groups with our stylistic forefathers, the gospel singers.

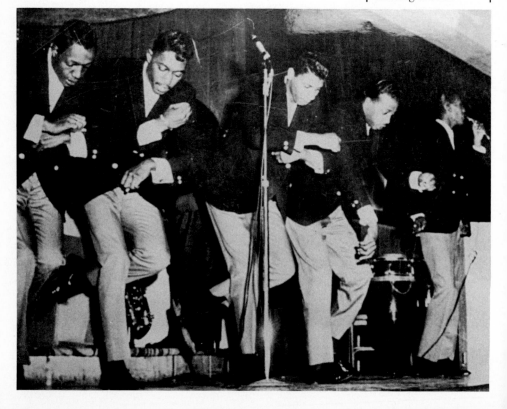

WESTERN UNION
TELEGRAM

◄ The Beatles sent us this telegram in 1964.

▼ It took a lot of fancy footwork—and coordination—to do moves like these and then all meet up around one microphone without missing a beat.

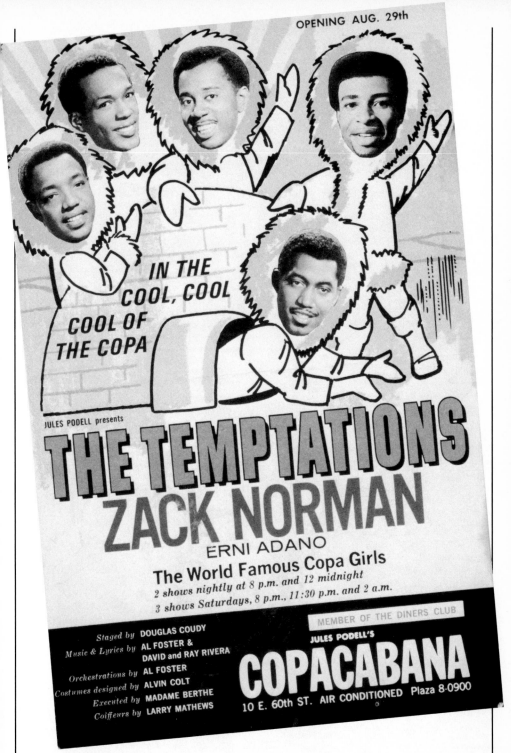

OPENING AUG. 29th

IN THE
COOL, COOL
COOL OF
THE COPA

JULES PODELL presents

THE TEMPTATIONS
ZACK NORMAN
ERNI ADANO
The World Famous Copa Girls
2 shows nightly at 8 p.m. and 12 midnight
3 shows Saturdays, 8 p.m., 11:30 p.m. and 2 a.m.

Staged by **DOUGLAS COUDY**
Music & Lyrics by **AL FOSTER &**
DAVID and RAY RIVERA
Orchestrations by **AL FOSTER**
Costumes designed by **ALVIN COLT**
Executed by **MADAME BERTHE**
Coiffeurs by **LARRY MATHEWS**

MEMBER OF THE DINERS CLUB

JULES PODELL'S
COPACABANA
10 E. 60th ST. AIR CONDITIONED Plaza 8-0900

▲ David Ruffin's replacement, Dennis Edwards *(upper right)*, joined us in time to perform at our second Copacabana engagement. No, the Eskimo costume was not one of our stage uniforms.

▲ Melvin, David, and Eddie backstage at the legendary Apollo, one of our favorite venues during the sixties. *Don Paulsen*

◄ More good times backstage. *Don Paulsen*

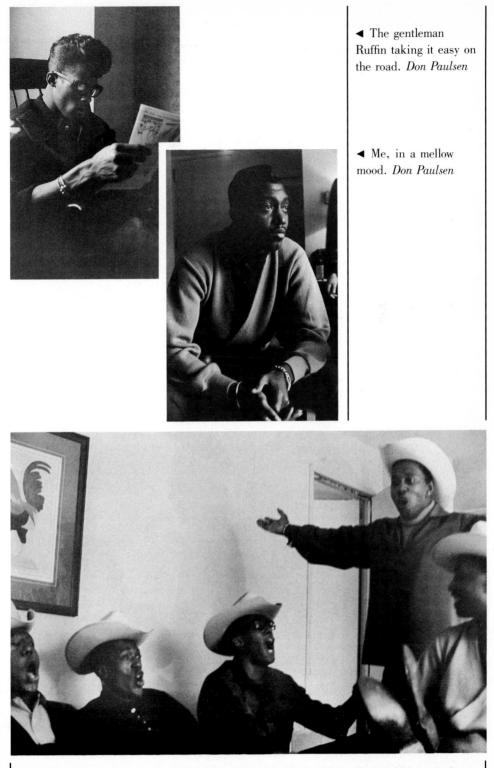

◄ The gentleman Ruffin taking it easy on the road. *Don Paulsen*

◄ Me, in a mellow mood. *Don Paulsen*

▲ We're the good guys in the white hats: *(from left)* Paul, Eddie, David, Melvin, and me.

▲ This is us in the early days. We weren't as flashy as we would be, but we were always cool: *(from left)* Eddie, David, me, Melvin, Paul. These were the best times. *Don Paulsen*

▲ As always, Melvin's the cheeriest of us all.

◄ Berry Gordy, Jr., founder and president of Motown Records, in a typical businesslike pose. *Courtesy Motown Record Corporation*

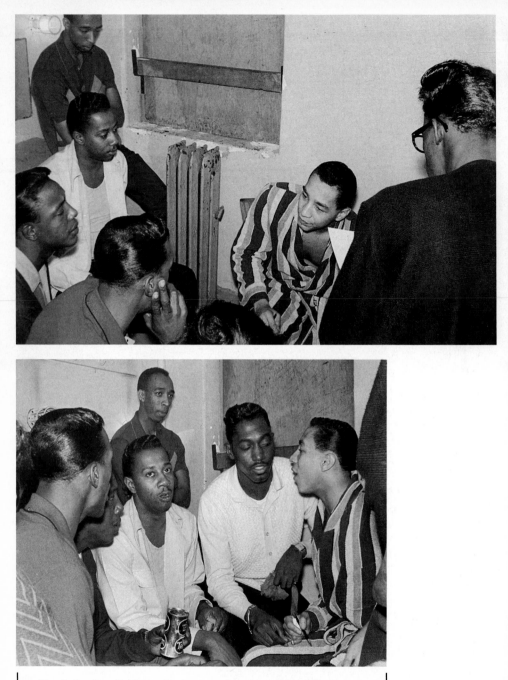

▲ Here's Smokey Robinson backstage with us at the Apollo, teaching us our parts for what would become our first number-one hit, "My Girl." *Don Paulsen*

▲ The product of David Ruffin's inspiration and our trademark: the famous four-headed microphone.

◄ The soul of the Temptations, Paul Williams, with a friend.

◀ Here I am backstage, getting ready again. *Don Paulsen*

▼ The second-next-best thing to singing. *Don Paulsen*

▲ Eddie Kendricks. *Don Paulsen*

▲ The Supremes and the Temptations performing "Rhythm of Life" on the historic *TCB* television special in late 1968. *(Left to right)* Cindy Birdsong, Diana Ross, Mary Wilson, Melvin Franklin, me, Dennis Edwards, Eddie Kendricks, Paul Williams. *Courtesy George Schlatter Productions*

▲ From the same program, obviously something lighter. *(Left to right)* Melvin, Cindy, Diana, Paul, Mary, and Eddie. *Courtesy George Schlatter Productions*

▲ Still one of the hottest acts around: Gladys Knight and the Pips at the Apollo. *Don Paulsen*

These photos are from a *Laugh-In* skit we taped at Los Angeles International Airport. Don Foster suggested that we use an outtake for the *Wish It Would Rain* album cover. *(Above, from left)* David, Paul; *(below, from left)* me and Eddie. *Courtesy George Schlatter Productions*

who's home when you are, not on the other side of the planet. Patti and I drifted apart.

For years I assumed that our affair was tucked away in our private memories. Then one day a year or so ago Cholly Atkins said, "What did you do to Patti LaBelle?"

"I don't know what you're talking about," I replied.

"You mean you haven't read *Ebony*?"

"No," I said.

"Well, you better go buy it," Cholly said.

I jumped in the car, drove over to the newsstand, picked up the issue, and started reading. In an interview Patti talked about me, saying that we broke up because I wanted her to quit singing and move with me to California. It didn't make sense. First, I was still living in Detroit then, and would never, ever ask another singer to stop. If anyone asked me to quit singing, I wouldn't do it. Still, it was flattering to be remembered.

Back in Detroit the competition among songwriters and producers was running hot. By early 1966 Norman Whitfield had scored a hit with the Marvelettes, "Too Many Fish in the Sea," a song he wrote with Eddie Holland, and was writing and producing for several other acts. Of course, Norman being Norman, he had his eyes on a bigger prize. Among the staff writers and producers it was pretty much accepted that no one was about to eclipse Smokey, at least not in Berry's view. And Smokey's streak showed no sign of cooling down, either. He had produced "My Girl," the Miracles' "Ooo Baby Baby" and "The Tracks of My Tears," Marvin Gaye's "Ain't That Peculiar," and the Marvelettes' "Don't Mess with Bill." The only producers topping him were Holland, Dozier, and Holland, whose string of successes is unequaled in the history of pop music, period. Through early 1966, HDH had eight releases on the Supremes, and six of those were number ones. Of course, every producer wanted a crack at the hottest groups, and every group wanted to be produced by a proven winner. But Motown took the position that each group should maintain a distinct sound. That's the reason a Martha and the Vandellas song doesn't sound like a Supremes tune, or a Four Tops record sounds nothing like one of ours. As far as producers went, most of the Motown's biggest acts were spoken for, so Norman set his sights on us.

Motown started hitting on all eight cylinders, and it never occurred to anyone to lay back a little. Instead, it was all turned up a notch. The recording studios ran almost twenty-four hours a day, seven days a week. With all the musicians on salary and under contract, they were "on call" whenever a producer wanted them. The hit single was still the business's coin of the realm, so if you got a hit, and people back at Hitsville thought you needed a quick follow-up, they pulled you off the road, flew you into Detroit, and had someone waiting at the airport for you, ready to whisk you straight back to the studio. In most cases, the producer had down a rhythm track, which the lyrics were written to, and some other instrumentation. Unless it was a song that was written with an act in mind, the track belonged to the producer. Then he or Berry decided who got to put on their vocals. All the charges for the musicians, the use of the studio, and so on were assigned to the producer until he recorded the vocals. At that point, those expenses were charged to the artists' account. It didn't matter that you didn't want to record a particular tune, or that it may never see the light of day and sit in the can forever. You still had to pay. Fortunately, we had very little unreleased material. Through its publishing division, Jobete, Motown got all the publishing royalties regardless of who recorded the song. The more often a Jobete song was recorded, the more it was worth. For this reason, virtually every act's hits were recorded by other acts, too.

Every Friday, the week's product was submitted to the Quality Control staff. Richard Street worked in this department, and the meeting was attended by a number of people, always including

Berry, Smokey, Billie Jean Brown, some of the promotion guys, and other department heads. No artist, with the exception of Smokey, was ever in on these. They evaluated each record for its hit potential, and releases were chosen based on the group's reaction. The rule for picking releases was simple: the strongest song got the release. This didn't make everyone happy all the time, but that didn't bother Berry. Quality Control was part of his scientific approach to making records. It kept Motown's percentage of hits well above the industry average, and that was all that mattered.

We were still Smokey's group, and in early 1966 we recorded his "Get Ready." It wasn't cute or sweet, and it wasn't a ballad. Smokey has called it the most direct song he ever wrote. It wasn't a bad song, but I thought it lacked an edge. Around that time Norman managed to cut his "Ain't Too Proud to Beg" with us, and the difference between the two was like night and day. Norman's melody had a touch of blues and sounded as anguished and desperate as Eddie Holland's words, which David Ruffin brought to life. David sang his ass off on that one, and by the time he was halfway through the session, he was drowning in sweat and his glasses were all over his face. I stood in the control booth with Norman, encouraging David. "Come on, man, you can do it!" I shouted at him between takes. Because it was recorded in a key higher than David was used to, it was strenuous, so Norman stopped a few times to let David catch his breath. Listening to that record some twenty-plus years later, you can hear that David was giving it his all. The first time we heard the finished track, we had a feeling in our bones that this one was going to do something big. It was a fantastic song, and even though it was a real departure from our previous hits, it suited us. Plus it showed off the earthier, soulful side of David's singing in a way most of our songs before it did not.

Feeling the way we did about "Ain't Too Proud," we were certain it would be released next. When the two songs came up at the same

Quality Control meeting, the nod went to "Get Ready." Apparently people thought it was the stronger tune. Berry told Norman, though, that if "Get Ready" failed to crack the Top Ten, they'd release "Ain't Too Proud." We were on the road while this went down, so we didn't even know the song was out. We'd stopped in Los Angeles to do Dick Clark's *American Bandstand* when Motown called to tell us that "Get Ready" was starting to break and that we should perform it. With the taping less than an hour away, Paul rounded us up in a hotel room, and in thirty-two minutes, we devised, learned, rehearsed, and mastered the routine.

Despite our superhuman efforts, though, "Get Ready" peaked at number twenty-nine. Berry kept his word and released "Ain't Too Proud to Beg," which got to number thirteen. More important, it marked the beginning of a shift in direction for us. Norman Whitfield could and did write and produce soft, smooth ballads with the best of them but, stylistically speaking, he was headed into another realm. His backing tracks crackled with more intricate percussion, wailing, almost rock-style electric guitars, and arrangements that presented us as five distinct singers instead of one lead singer fronting a homogenized doo-wop chorus. Norman's greatest accomplishment, I think, was that he did with us what a producer should do: took us in new directions without losing the heart of our sound. "Ain't Too Proud to Beg" was nothing like "My Girl," and years later "Papa Was a Rollin' Stone" would be nothing like anything else. Yet they all sound like the Temptations. Norman's productions seemed to illuminate every aspect of our sound—the highs were higher, the lows were lower. Norman Whitfield and Eddie Holland wrote our three biggest hits in 1966: "Ain't Too Proud to Beg," "Beauty Is Only Skin Deep," and "(I Know) I'm Losing You." Our guitarist, Cornelius Grant, cowrote the last song; that's his killer lead guitar hook that opens the track.

The funny thing about success is that the more you get, the harder you have to work, and that meant touring. When a Henry Wynn tour we were on with Jackie Wilson and Chuck Jackson stopped in Birmingham, Alabama, we stayed over so that Eddie and Paul could visit their families. For years Paul had been telling us that his father could sing a deeper bass than Melvin, which seemed humanly impossible. But we got down there, and sure enough, he could. It just goes to show that God never makes one of anything.

Our bus pulled up at the A. G. Gaston Motel, and we were getting off when a fan approached us. She said, "Oh, that's the one I want to meet," pointing at me. "I like him. Please hook it up with him."

"Otis, come here," Paul said, waving me over. "I think you should meet her."

"Oh, yeah?" I was interested.

"Yeah," she replied, smiling at me. "What are you doing after the show?"

"Well, I hadn't planned on anything. Just coming back, because we're leaving early, but if you want to stop by . . ." You get the picture.

After a couple minutes of chitchat, she added, "Well, I am married, you know, but I'll take care of that."

I should have known better, but being young, dumb, and full of come, it didn't occur to me that having a married woman in my motel room in a strange town might be a bad idea.

Back in the room, I got things ready for the big night. Ever prepared to create the ultimate romantic atmosphere wherever an opportunity might arise, several of us always brought along three important things for *l'amour:* a portable record player, a stack of make-out records (usually some of our own and Smokey's), and a red light bulb.

Tyrone Burstyn, who worked with us as a road manager, the fan, and I were listening to records and relaxing. Nothing was happening yet, and thank God for it, too, because suddenly the door was banging so hard we thought it was going to fall off the frame. A loud, angry voice screamed, "Open the door, you motherfucker!

I know she's in there!" *Bam, bam, bam!*

"Hey," I whispered to her, "I thought you told me this was taken care of."

She didn't offer any answer, and the room got as quiet as a rat pissin' on cotton. After a few more seconds of silence, *bam, bam-bam, bam-bam.*

"Open the door, motherfucker! I'm going to kick this damned door in! I know you got my wife in there!"

After a few agonizing, heart-pounding moments, we heard the sound of his footsteps fading in the distance. I eased up to the window, pulled back the curtain, and peeked out. He was gone. I walked over to my would-be date and said, "Get your ass out of here. Now." Tyrone and I switched rooms in case her husband came back. Luckily for me, he didn't.

The next morning we got on the bus to go, and I must say it was the most beautiful Sunday morning I ever saw. I noticed all those little things: the dew on the grass, the bright sunshine, the fresh air. I felt so thankful to God for being alive. Corny, huh? After careful consideration I decided to eliminate married women from my bachelor diet. It wasn't worth getting hurt or killed.

A couple years later Melvin found himself in a similar difficulty. We were playing the Carter Barron Amphitheater in Washington, D.C., when Melvin set his sights on a particular girl. Now, once Melvin gets himself into overdrive there's nothing that can stop him, so when an older man asked him to lay off the girl, Melvin didn't take it lightly.

"You old son of a bitch," Melvin snapped. "She's too young for you anyway."

"Well," the old gentleman replied sternly, "that is my daughter, and I am a judge here, so—"

About then Melvin got as weak-kneed as a chitlin, and we had to do some fancy footwork to keep this judge from nailing Melvin's butt to the wall.

We can laugh about that kind of thing today, but in fact violence was a fact of life on those tours. Angry boyfriends, fathers, and husbands are one thing: at least you can see them coming—sometimes. Racially motivated violence, however, was unpredictable and could erupt anywhere, at any time. We saw the worst of it in Kentucky. We and the Four Tops had finished our show, and their valet, Frazer, was standing outside the bus, taking down equipment. What happened then was unclear, but some white guys struck Frazer in the head. I don't know what they hit him with, but it must have been heavy, because it left a serious, ugly wound. It was the first time I had ever seen all the flesh torn away from a human skull. The skin was gashed open, and Frazer's skull was dented. Everyone insisted that he go to the hospital, but he refused, saying, "I'm okay, I'm okay." The men who attacked Frazer threatened to come back the next night and disrupt our show, so for the remainder of our run, we and the Tops took turns guarding the stage. When they were on, we stood in the wings, armed with guns and baseball bats; when we were on, they did the same for us.

After the show, we returned to the hotel. As we were loading up the bus, a bunch of young white boys drove by and shot at us. We dove to the ground and lay there, scared to death, listening to them yelling, "You niggers, you motherfuckers, don't you ever come back here again!" as they circled us in their car. As soon as they split, we got out some bats, just in case they came back. Thank God they didn't, because it's impossible to see how another confrontation like that could have ended peacefully.

As well as things were going, we never fell into believing that we couldn't be any better. We were always working new things into our act. One of the bigger brainstorms hit in Philadelphia, where they'd booked us to perform in another battle of the groups. This time we were up against Gladys Knight and the Pips, the Four Tops, the Contours, and the Vibrations (whose "sloop" dance step we adapted into our trademark Temptations Walk). We were sitting around talking during a break in rehearsals. "Man," somebody said, "we need something that will make us different."

"If we had a microphone stand with four mikes on it, that would be different," David offered. "Instead of four of us bunched up around one mike, and one of us on the other, we could really do our steps, and it would be something unique."

As it turned out, Lon Fontaine, a choreographer who worked with us, knew someone who could make such a stand. The first time we brought that out onstage, it was the talk of Detroit. It allowed each of us to stand a distance away from the others and execute our moves without stepping on each other. Benny Welburn was in charge of the stand, and before long fans everywhere knew that the stand meant only one thing: the Tempts were coming on. At the time, most groups simply walked onstage and took their places when they were announced. Once we got that stand, we made a different presentation. The curtains would be closed, and Benny would place the mike stand on the stage. The buzz in the crowd would start, then we'd get into position behind the curtain, the announcer would introduce us, the curtain would go up, and we'd be standing there, sometimes decked out all in white, like five soldiers standing at ease. We were in all our splendor in any of twenty or thirty flashy suits and our then-cool slicked-down hair. The applause seemed to build like thunder, and by the time the curtain rose, we'd almost get a standing ovation just for being there. It made you feel so damn good that you couldn't help smiling. It was a wonderful feeling.

Motown wouldn't stop growing, and in mid-1966 hired a new staff manager to oversee us and the Supremes, Shelly Berger. He had studied acting and, on the recommendation of an agent from William Morris, got this job. Berry hired Shelly sight unseen, and when they finally met face-to-face, Berry was surprised to find that Shelly was white. Not that Berry didn't like having white folks working for him. A sizable portion of Motown's upper-echelon management was white by then. Shelly just wasn't what Berry had expected.

Motown was still the only major record company in Detroit. As we later learned, industry people on either coast didn't quite know what to make of the label. There were rumors that all of us lived at Hitsville, or that we were a group of black nationalists. Hardly anyone from New York or Los Angeles ever came to Detroit, so there was nothing for them to base their information on but rumor. Despite all the success, how Motown functioned remained a mystery to outsiders.

Berry's instincts were nearly flawless, and hiring people because they showed energy and commitment was working well enough. One indication of Berry's positive attitude was a memo he circulated around this time. Apparently, Motown was in a "slump," which meant none of us was in the Top Ten. Berry's solution was to write: "We will not put out any records that are not Top Ten records. For the Supremes, they must be number-one records." It sounds funny now, but the funnier thing was that it worked. Before long Motown was moving beyond the pop-record business and into show business. Along with Berry, Shelly had a clear vision of where Motown acts should be going: more television, broader markets, clubs like the Copa. In other words, *crossover*.

Throughout the sixties and into the early seventies, we made countless appearances on variety television programs. Most people recall Ed Sullivan's show, but there were many others through the sixties and early seventies, such as *The Hollywood Palace*, *The Dean Martin Show*, *Shindig*, *Hullabaloo*, *The Tonight Show*, *Where the Action Is*, and *The Smothers Brothers Comedy Hour*. Several programs, particularly Sullivan's, cooperated with Motown in scheduling and presentation. We often debuted a new single on national television days, sometimes just hours, before its release. In addition, Motown made sure that we did at least two numbers: our current hit and a standard.

Through putting so many acts on national television, Motown was responsible for a number of innovations in presenting pop music on television. It's difficult to get a good mix on television even today, which is why so many people still lip-sync to their records instead of singing live. Generally, each show had its own band, but Berry wanted to achieve the perfect balance between the various instruments and vocals. What sounded great on a car radio, which is what Motown's records were produced to do, fell flat on television. To solve this, Berry recorded the show's band and the background vocals, then mixed it for television. The end result was that for most television shots, only the lead singer was singing live and the background vocals were synced. This approach is still used today.

Of all the television appearances we made then, the one that I'll never forget is *The Hollywood Palace* with host Bing Crosby. We all admired his singing, so it was quite an honor to be on the show with him. The highlight was when he sang "My Girl" with us, trading off lines with David Ruffin. The minute he started to sing, "I've got sunshine," I said, "Whoa!" It just blew me away. He approached the song with a whole different attitude, almost a reverence. It was all I could do to keep my mind on what I was doing and not stand there with my mouth hanging open.

During a break in the taping, Melvin and I went to the cafeteria. As we were eating, I noticed a guy sitting across the room.

"Blue," I said, using Melvin's nickname in the group, "that guy over there looks familiar. I've seen him somewhere." Melvin agreed but couldn't place him either. Then it hit me. "Melvin, do you know who that is? It's Lash LaRue."

Probably not many people today know who Lash LaRue was, but when we were kids we idolized him. In the forties and fifties he was a movie cowboy, like Whip Wilson, Durango Kid, and Allen "Rocky" Lane, from the serials. I remember being a little guy, meeting my buddies at the theater, getting a couple boxes of popcorn, then munching our faces as our heroes rode into town and beat the bad guys. Lash was the coolest. Dressed all in black, carrying two guns, and thwarting the villains with his namesake whip, he was it. We were thrilled when he recognized us. He walked over and told us he'd given up being a Hollywood cowboy for religion. It was funny; we were meeting so many big celebrities, such as the Beatles, Bill Cosby, Muhammad Ali, and others, but we got the biggest kick out of Lash LaRue.

One of the first things Shelly did was team us up with the Supremes for several concert and television appearances. It made sense because we had wider acceptance from blacks, and the Supremes had a larger white audience. It was thought that if we opened for the Supremes on tours and made television appearances with them, our audience would broaden, and it did. A second thing Shelly did was move us from the A.B.C. booking agency to William Morris, the largest all-service agency in the business. Despite all of our hits, the William Morris people wanted to see us audition. That August, Shelly booked us on a show with the Supremes and Stevie Wonder at the Forest Hills tennis stadium, outside New York. I will never forget that show. The whole world loved the Supremes, it seemed, so we felt pressured to work that much harder. When we came off, I said, "Well, Shell, what do you think? Do you think they like us?"

He replied, "Don't even worry about it. You got it." Ever since then, Shelly's been a good friend, and he still manages us today.

Probably our most important joint appearance was on Ed Sullivan's program. For one show that aired toward late 1966, we performed some Supremes hits, and they sang some of ours. It was a cute idea. During rehearsals we were all giving it our best, and David's best was always fantastic. David could wipe a stage with anybody, so it's not slighting Diane to say that he blew her away. Diane, however, took it hard and began whining that the key was too low for her. Maurice King, our musical director, was cool about it and tried to reassure us, saying, "Don't worry, fellas, she's just saying that because you all are giving her hell." But next thing we heard was that she had taken her complaints to Berry, and Berry had instructed Maurice to push up the key of the entire medley so that it was barely within David's range. In the meantime, Diane devoted hours of extra time to rehearsing her parts. By showtime she was in great form.

Another thing Shelly did for us was negotiate better terms for appearances. We'd done all right, but once Shelly arrived we began doing a whole hell of a lot better. Before Shelly, we were earning an annual group income in six figures, which Shelly instantly moved over the million-dollar mark. Now each guy's royalty check wasn't $10,000 or $15,000 but maybe $50,000, $60,000, and that was our take under Motown's tired-ass contract terms and royalty rates. The only thing wrong was that Motown continued dealing with its artists and their money the same way they had when we were kids making a couple thousand a year. There was never any discussion about forming a corporation, tax planning, investments for retirement; we didn't have basic health insurance. When I think about how even that money could have worked for us if we'd invested it correctly, my head spins. All I knew was that I was sending Uncle Sam five figures every quarter in estimated personal income tax and that once one bank account reached the FDIC-insured limit of $100,000, I'd have to open another. Not exactly what you'd call sophisticated financial planning.

Now, do I blame solely Motown for this? Frankly, I have mixed emotions. The tack Berry took with his artists when it came to money was an extension of his attitude toward them in general: he believed that he knew what was best for us. Motown provided our lawyers, accountants, and managers. Today we'd call this a clear conflict of interest, but Berry's term for it was "complement of interest." On the plus side, it saved us a lot of what we did get: rather than each artist paying a double-digit percentage of his earnings to each one of several professionals separately, Motown did it all for one considerably lower figure. Unfortunately, most people at Motown, while smart, hardworking, and well-meaning, were out of their depth. Motown's tax advice was hyperconservative, and we suffered for it. About the only good thing you can say about Motown's accounting was that as long as they handled the artists' tax returns, none of us ever had trouble with the I.R.S.

Up until this time and a little bit beyond it, the five of us still hung tight. You could always find us over at one another's houses, eating dinner together and enjoying ourselves. Melvin would cook up a batch of beans and cornbread, which Eddie loved, so we called Eddie Cornbread. I was a bachelor then, a noncooking bachelor, and they knew I was existing on Kentucky Fried Chicken and Frosted Flakes, so somebody's wife or girlfriend would whip up a big meal and invite me over. We loved one another, like brothers, and I'm not ashamed to say it.

As we'd seen with a number of other singers, and closer to home with Elbridge Bryant, some people just cannot handle the adulation that comes with fame. Added to that is the "problem" of money. When we started raking in the bucks, we ceased living in a dream and started living out the old cliché: money changes everything. James Brown said that money won't change you, but he was wrong. When your pockets are empty, it's impossible even to imagine that money could ever be a problem. It's what money does to you as a person. When I think about what happened to the five of us, it seems that everything started to unravel about this time. But these things—the pressures, the money, the success, the temptations of drinking and drugs—didn't destroy us. We weren't stupid, but we were young, and sometimes that's just as bad. In our own way, it seems we were bent on destroying ourselves.

Not having money or people falling all over you keeps you in check. When you need something, you buy one, maybe two. When you relate to people, there's a give-and-take. Take away those restraints—walk into a store to buy one thing and come out with ten, or suddenly have people letting you into places for nothing, or insisting that you get the better table, the better view—and it can be overwhelming. For years, your whole motivation is wishing and hoping for things. One day you wake up and there's nothing to want. You go to Hitsville, pick up a check, run to the bank, and walk out with a pocket full of hundreds. All five of us were lavish spenders, buying lots of clothes, cars (except for me, since I didn't get my license until 1968), our first homes, and giving money to our families. It wasn't all bad. It felt very good to help our loved ones, of course. But in the long run the effect on us was more negative than positive, and success in general became an ugly force among us.

At the start, the two guys most affected by it all were Paul and David. In Paul's case it's difficult to pinpoint what it was all about. His background was similar to ours, and he was a real pro, but something inside him began to crumble. I've turned it over in my mind a thousand times, but where the trouble started for Paul remains a mystery. While David and Eddie got most of the leads, Paul was acknowledged as the Temptations' creative force, and people at Motown listened to him. And to our fans, Paul was always a star. Audiences would get off on seeing Eddie or David do one of the hits, but the reaction Paul got with one of his show-stopping numbers was equal to none.

Around this time Paul fell in love with a woman named Winnie Brown. She was a relative of Flo Ballard's and toured with the Supremes as their hairstylist. Paul had married young and had five children. He was devoted to his family but torn between them and Winnie. Before too long Paul, who never took anything stronger than milk, started drinking.

David's problem was different. To put it bluntly, success went to his head. It started off with little things; for example, he refused to travel with the four of us in our two group limousines and got his own, complete with mink-lined floor and his name painted on the side. To some it seemed that Eddie's early fear—that David would put his solo career ahead of the group's—might be legitimate.

Exacerbating the problem was a group of hangers-on who stuck with us, and one guy in particular: Royce Moore. I don't think

Royce was a bad person. He was just one of those guys who likes being where the action is, and he figured out early on that David appreciated stroking the most. I can't count the times we'd come backstage after a show and there'd be David sitting in a chair and Royce rubbing David's shoulders and back and giving him a pep talk. "You know, Papa"—he always called David Papa—"they came to see you, you know. You're the one." None of us said anything about it, but we watched. The minute Royce started in with the rap, you could practically see it taking effect on David, like a little light bulb was going on inside his head. And David Ruffin wasn't exactly what you'd call humble to start with, so that kind of flattery, pitting us against him, was like pouring gasoline on a fire.

We got a little preview of where David's head was one day in Puerto Rico. He called a meeting of the group and our road manager, Don Foster, to inform us that he wanted the group to be known as David Ruffin and the Temptations. He calmly explained that he was the dominant lead, even though we still got hits on songs sung by Eddie and Paul, and he felt that it was time he got his due. Considering how almost every other group of the time had its one lead singer, and the trend toward calling a group "So-and-so and the Whatevers" was starting, you can understand David's thinking. But this wasn't just any group, this was the Temptations, and no lead singer, no matter how great, would ever be set apart from the group. As Berry said, no man is ever greater than the group. After he finished his speech, I said, "Oh, no. You can forget that. We are not changing to no David Ruffin and the Temptations. It's going to be the Temptations, and that's it." David backed off then, but I think the die was cast.

The one truly good influence on David around this time was his lover, Tammi Terrell. Tammi signed to Motown in 1966, after having recorded unsuccessfully for James Brown's Try Me label, and Checker and Wand. She was just twenty then, and a beautiful young woman. None of her solo releases did that well, but starting in 1967 she and Marvin Gaye recorded a series of Ashford and Simpson duets that are classics: "Ain't No Mountain High Enough," "Your Precious Love," "If I Could Build My Whole World Around You," "Ain't Nothin' like the Real Thing," and "You're All I Need to Get By."

Tammi was very good for David. Since she was a performer, too, she had a deep appreciation for what his priorities should be; she kept him straight. She always made sure that David was on time for whatever we had to do. She'd say, "You guys have got a rehearsal, so get up, David." This was a great thing for David, especially since so many women who gravitate to stars would more likely say, "Baby, just lay back here. You're the lead singer, you ain't got to go nowhere. Let them go and do it." But not Tammi.

In addition to being so beautiful to look at and a great, very soulful singer, Tammi was a hell of a person. She was sweet, fun-loving, and fun to be with. She'd had a rough couple of years before coming to Motown, and would have a rougher few after, but she never lost that vibrancy. When she and David moved in together, she kept a nice house and was a good cook. There was nothing she wouldn't do for David. She loved the hell out of him, and liked to be with us, so she'd come out on the road, too.

Contrary to a popular rumor at the time, David was not married when he hooked up with Tammi. He had been married when we first met him, to a woman named Sandra, but they were divorced by then. His thing with Tammi was intense and quite tumultuous. Later on, they began to fight a lot. Their relationship was definitely a rocky one. But none of us knew what to do to help. Still, no matter what problems they had, one thing was certain: she loved David, and I'm sure David loved her.

Despite all that and his ego-tripping, though, David was still basically a likable guy. Everybody knew how David was, that at times he could be arrogant, but people took him for what he was. Of course, there were others who didn't care for him at all, those who would say, "Well, he can sing, but I don't like his attitude," but then that's been said about each of us at one time or another. We figured that this was what we had to deal with. As long as David took care of business, there was nothing we could say.

Toward the end of 1966 we learned that we'd be making our debut at the Copacabana in New York the following summer. We began preparing for the show by taking our act to similar venues all over the country. One was the Cave in Vancouver, British Columbia. It was a supper club out of a forties movie, with girls walking around carrying a little tray and saying, "Cigars, cigarettes?"

It was during one of our shows there that I split my pants onstage. It was one of the hazards of our kind of act. Amazingly, out of all of us, the only one who never ripped his pants was David. Whomever it happened to would leave the stage, change, then fall right back in, usually to great applause and good-natured laughter.

Recently Richard Street had a slightly different problem when he unknowingly came onstage with his fly open.

After ten days at the Cave, we were to fly to Toronto, where we'd pick up a flight into Washington, D.C. After only a few years on the road, we'd heard almost every conceivable horror story about the dangers of constant travel. Everything might be as safe as can be, but so much of it depends on the human factor and the whims of nature that your number could come up at any time.

Except for the fact that former heavyweight champ Jack Dempsey was on board, the flight was uneventful, and we were finishing our snacks during the final approach when the plane dropped about two thousand feet like a piece of lead. The sudden force of the plunge threw a flight attendant up against the ceiling and sent everything not tied down flying through the cabin. The second we hit what felt like the bottom of our plunge, the wind swept under us and carried the plane up and sideways so that it was as if we were riding a swinging pendulum. First we'd arc up on one side until we were all sitting perpendicular to the ground, then—whoosh—we'd be plummeting down, across, and up again until we were 180 degrees from where we started. All I heard was this monstrous, loud *whoom* noise and the sound of every piece of metal vibrating like it was ready to bust.

Before this, whenever I read or heard about people dying in a plane crash, I wondered what it was like, what went through their minds knowing they were about to crash. Now I know. People were throwing up from the fear of death and crying, "Oh, God. Please, God. If you're going to take me, please don't play with me." Some prayed. It was total chaos. I glanced out the window and saw those steel wings fluttering like a piece of paper stuck to a fan. To top it all off, the captain came on the intercom to say, "Fasten your seat belts, and maybe we'll make it." You could hear the fear in his voice, and knowing how well pilots are trained to keep their cool, you knew that this really could be it. I grabbed the armrest, looked at the other guys, and said to God, "So this is the day, huh?"

After another five or ten minutes, we finally got out of it and landed. The minute the plane rolled to a stop all the passengers gave the crew a standing ovation, and then paramedics came aboard to take care of the injured. We found out that we had been caught up in clear-air turbulence—wind shear, as they now call it.

Tyrone came into the terminal and, in the middle of a crowd, fell to his knees and kissed the ground. Eddie, being a brave fellow, connected with the next plane to Detroit and flew out. I phoned Motown and said, "You all have to get another act because we cannot get on another plane. We almost crashed." Taylor Cox, who was in charge of Management, arranged for Little Anthony and the Imperials to substitute for us in D.C.

The other four of us and our crew chartered a bus to take us from Toronto to Detroit, which is a pretty short hop. The sun was setting that day, and it was fantastic, beautiful. As I sat on the bus, it struck me how close I'd come—we'd all come—to not seeing it. Melvin, David, and I were all pretty bent out of shape, and not saying much. Paul sat there crying.

We stayed off the road for a few weeks, but we were booked to appear on Ed Sullivan's show and couldn't get there on time without flying. We reluctantly boarded the plane, and as we were coming into LaGuardia Airport, a severe electrical storm broke. Our pilot kept circling the airport, waiting for instructions to land, but I guess he got impatient and landed without permission. I was holding on to my seat, thinking, "Oh, no, not again." But we made it, and once inside the terminal watched as a bunch of officials hustled our pilot off somewhere. Ultimately, though, I guess it's always all up to God.

We were traveling, living high, making money, and having a generally good time, most of us without having finished high school. So imagine our surprise when Northwestern High invited the Temptations to speak to students about the importance of staying in school. The funniest part of it was that back when Melvin, Richard Street, and I had been in the Distants, Northwestern had expelled Richard and Melvin for singing in the halls, and Mr. Stoll, my counselor, had all but invited me to split, too. Melvin and Richard were walking the halls and singing with future Monitor Warren Harris when they ran into a woman teacher they didn't like. Allegedly, Warren referred to her as an old bitch, but she thought Melvin did it. When Richard went to Melvin's defense, they both got thrown out. Melvin then transferred to Northern High.

So there we were, standing up in the same auditorium where we'd spent so many hours practicing our harmonies. Looking out across the audience, I couldn't help flashing back to the days when we sat in that same auditorium. We didn't sing this day, we just told the students to please stay in school, that education was important. That the kids really listened to us because we were the Temptations made us feel very proud. We also saw many of the teachers and counselors we knew. In fact, if I remember correctly, Mr. Stoll was there. He didn't say anything, but he didn't have to. Ah, poetic justice!

Our first single of 1967 was "All I Need," a tune I loved. Listening to it recently reminded me that our vocal parts had been all switched around, so that I was singing a high second tenor, with Paul under me. It was the kind of thing you can only do when you're young and your vocal cords are strong and supple. "All I Need" is a shining example of the one thing that Motown did well consistently: came up with great songs. This one was written by Eddie Holland, Frank Wilson, and R. Dean Taylor. The best part about it was Eddie's lyrics about a guy who'd cheated on his girl begging for forgiveness, a common theme, to be sure. It wasn't a coincidence that most of our songs were about that very subject. We knew that women love to hear guys pleading, begging, confessing, and basically admitting they'd made mistakes. After all, it works so well in real life. So most Motown lyricists—Norman Whitfield, Eddie Holland, and Smokey Robinson—wrote to appeal to that sensibility. What made this one different was Eddie's words. I'd never lost my interest in songwriting, even though Motown did nothing to encourage it, so I'd pay attention to how those great writers and producers put things together. I found the whole creative process fascinating. "Eddie," I said one day, "you have to tell me how you do it."

"Otis, the greatest thing you can do is sit and listen to women talk," he answered. "Every once in a while, one of them will say something, and I say to myself, 'I'll use that,' and I go home and write it down."

"Aha!" I thought. My lifelong fascination with women had a second, more practical, application.

A couple months later we released the only single on which David and Eddie switch off on the lead, "You're My Everything," something Norman and Cornelius Grant cowrote with Roger Penzabene. Within the year Roger cowrote two more hits for us, "I Wish It Would Rain," and my favorite, "I Could Never Love Another (After Loving You)." We also recorded his "The End of Our Road," a hit for Marvin Gaye in 1970, on our *Solid Rock* album. On the last two, David sang like he was ready to cry, especially "I Could Never Love Another," with its lover's plea.

We liked Roger a lot. He was young, nice-looking, but kind of quiet and reserved, and very humble. Ironically, the inspiration for these great songs was his unhappy personal life. He was madly in love with a woman who gave it up indiscriminately and was quite indiscreet. Everyone who knew Roger knew what was happening, but he couldn't stop loving her. It tore me apart to see how badly she hurt him. We were playing the Latin Casino in Cherry Hill, New Jersey, on New Year's Eve when we got word that Roger had shot himself in the head and died. Later, Norman told us that Roger reached the point where he couldn't take it anymore. His death was a great loss.

That July Motown released *With a Lot O' Soul*, one of our top-charting albums. Although we always strive to make an emotional impact with our recordings, it's always strange to witness the actual effects. I recall Sandra Tilley, a onetime Velvelette and future Vandella, sitting at my house and crying her eyes out over a beautiful song that Eddie sang called "Two Sides of Love." We'd sit on my beige-and-brown checkered fur bedroom rug, and Sandra would play that tune over and over again. The album also contained the only track we ever cut with Holland-Dozier-Holland, "Just One Last Look," which featured one of David's best performances. Brian had complained to me that with Norman doing so well with us, it was impossible for him, Eddie, and Lamont to get near us. Something must have happened, though, and when we found we'd be working with those three, we were ecstatic because they were so hot. For some reason, though, that song wasn't released as a single.

Though ninety percent of the leads went to David and Eddie, Paul had one nice tune on this album, "No More Water in the Well." You could hear that he still had the goods. "Don't Look

Back," a moderate hit in the fall of 1965, would be Paul's last lead on a single. The concept of the Tempts as a group with several lead singers basically ended, at least as far as the records went, and David dominated the singles until he left the group. This wasn't intentional, it's just how it happened. We all felt that more songs should have been cut on Paul, and he still complained. When it came to creative decisions, folks at Motown might hear you out, but that's as far as it went.

As summer approached, the group got more excited about the Copa date. Success there was crucial for us, since it symbolized acceptance by the entertainment business at large. Though the Supremes were a smash there in 1965, not all the Motown acts who followed them did as well. Marvin Gaye, for example, whose biggest ambition then was to be a slick balladeer in the Nat "King" Cole style, was received coolly, as were the Four Tops and Smokey and the Miracles. It was all chemistry.

We've always retained a healthy level of preshow jitters, no matter where we play. In my opinion, if you're not at least a little nervous about getting up in front of people who've paid good money to see you, you probably don't know what the hell you're doing. Even now, after umpteen thousand performances, I can feel that preshow butterflies-in-the-stomach tingle. It's not fun but, like it or not, it's probably a good thing.

None of us ever studied voice or used vocal exercises, but we'd warm up in the dressing room with a tune called "Cindy," from *Wish It Would Rain*. We also kept to a couple of old superstitions. We did not allow whistling in the dressing room, for example. We've heard that Frank Sinatra doesn't either, and if it's good enough for him, we'll stick with it. Last but never least, we held hands as Melvin led us in a prayer, as he usually does before every show.

Like everything else, the Copa today is not the same place it was then. In those days they still had the Copa Girls, a bunch of showgirls who did a little opening act. When they finished their numbers, guys came out and carefully swept the floor for any beads, feathers, or sequins that dropped off their costumes.

From the first downbeat, we knew this was going to be our night. We could do no wrong. Everything was proceeding along without a hitch. We'd reached a part in the middle of "Don't Look Back" where Paul always got deeply into it. Our routine called for us to do this little thing where we danced and sort of turned around, so that Melvin ended up behind me. I went to stretch out my arm when I heard this tremendous thud under my feet. I whispered, "What the—" and spun around to see Melvin flat on his back, spread-eagle all over the stage. Our shoes were made for dancing and didn't have a thread of traction to them, so when Melvin hit one of the Copa Girls' beads it threw him flat on his butt. Without missing a beat, he shot straight back up and came in right in time, like nothing happened. Everyone there about died laughing. Even with the slip, we were a smash. We played the room every year for the next four or five years.

One of the good things about playing rooms like the Copa was that we got to work more standards into our act, which we loved. Probably the most difficult of all the songs in our repertoire is "Ol' Man River," a tune we started doing in 1964 after seeing the Flamingos do it at the Uptown in Philadelphia. We changed it around a little, but Melvin sings lead, as the Flamingos' bass singer Jacob Carey did. Shortly before the Copa opening we recorded *In a Mellow Mood*, a collection of standards such as "Hello Young Lovers," "For Once in My Life," "That's Life," and "The Impossible Dream," complete with full orchestration. Produced by Jeffrey Bowen and Frank Wilson, the record featured Eddie, David, and Paul equally, but David's renditions of "The Impossible Dream" and "Somewhere," Paul singing "That's Life," and Eddie's "Try to Remember" are standouts. Even though we loved the record and enjoyed the challenge of singing the tunes, there was some apprehension about how our fans would take it. A few of us, Paul in particular, worried that it wouldn't go over, but when it went to number thirteen, we quit worrying. It was gratifying to know that our fans were willing to let us try anything. This isn't to say we didn't get some flak for it, but you get that no matter what you do, so we figured we might as well do what we wanted. I've heard that these days a copy of the *Mellow Mood* album in its original purple jacket goes for about fifty dollars and is considered a find. It gives me a feeling of satisfaction to think that something we are so proud of has stood the test of time.

Mid-1967 brought all kinds of changes to the group. Paul was drinking more, and he wasn't any closer to deciding between his family and his lover, and was more confused than ever. So many times he'd come to me and say, "Otis, I just don't know what to do." David was only beginning to get pumped up, ego-wise, with each new hit, so we were all definitely starting to feel some strain. God knows we didn't want to lose David, but the possibility was there. We began scouting around for a guy who might take David's place, if it had to come to that.

Eddie and I first noticed a singer named Dennis Edwards at the Howard Theater in Washington, D.C., when he was still with the Contours. We watched from the wings as he sang lead on Lou Rawls's hit "Love Is a Hurtin' Thing." Dennis not only had a stirring, soulful voice, but he was a showman with real command of the audience. His style was a little rougher and grittier than David's, but we could tell that Dennis would be able to handle David's songs and bring a new sound to the Tempts as well. Eddie looked at me and said, "That's who we should get. If David don't straighten up, that's who we should keep in mind."

"You're right, Corn. That brother can sing."

I wouldn't necessarily say we were plotting, but we were taking mental notes. The feeling that David was going to be leaving—one way or the other—was undeniable.

Eddie was my ally then when it came to David, but little by little I noticed that he was going through some changes himself. He'd gotten married, and maybe he felt he had to make more money or something. Whatever it was, the result was that he became less fun to be around and started talking about doing his own solo album in addition to recording with the Temptations. Today people do solo records all the time and still stay with their groups, but in the sixties a solo record meant that you were either leaving a group soon or thinking real hard about it. We flatly told him to forget it, and that's when he started pulling away. But it was a very slow, subtle thing, and we continued working together day to day with no big problems. Our focus was on David and Paul, and where that was all going to lead.

The Temptations weren't the only people at Motown having problems. We'd been hearing rumors that Flo Ballard was drinking too much and that she and Diane weren't getting along. Being Motown's flagship, the Supremes probably got more pressure than other acts, though it's hard to say, since we saw them only every so often. Every time I did see her, though, it was obvious that Flo was deteriorating. Still, when it got back to us that she was so drunk she couldn't make a show, I was shocked. She'd always been so dedicated. Even on a night out at the Twenty Grand I'd never seen Flo take more than one or two little mixed drinks. When we heard that Flo was missing shows and laying down ultimatums, we figured it was only a matter of time. Berry wasn't going to stand for too much more of that.

Around June, Flo finally left the Supremes. Melvin sent Mary Wilson a telegram, urging her to stick by Flo. I don't recall seeing her much after that, or if I did it was for so damn brief a time, it was like not seeing her at all. It was like she dropped out of sight, and people missed her. She was always that kind, fun-loving girl. Even after she'd achieved great success, she was never bitchy, like some people got to be.

There's no question that Flo had the voice to make it as a solo. The problem was that she didn't get the right material or the right direction. Like a lot of us, she was a group person, and regardless of what anyone might think, Diane and Mary were her friends. She came from a place that no one would go back to if they didn't have to, and she had the drive. Unfortunately, nothing came together the way it should have.

Also that summer, Tammi Terrell's health declined. She was on tour with Marvin Gaye, and they were playing a college date in Virginia, when in the middle of a song, she collapsed in Marvin's arms. Tammi had been complaining of excruciating headaches for as long as we'd known her but had never had it checked out. The doctors discovered a brain tumor, and over the next few years she underwent several operations. Eventually she went home to her family in Philadelphia. It's strange, but as close as we were, I never knew how David took it. I do know that he loved her very much. We last saw Tammi in 1969, I believe. She had lost some muscle control as a result of the tumor and operations, but made a valiant effort to be the old Tammi. There was some talk that she was on her way to recovering, but I could see that she never would be the same again. She died in March 1970.

One of the better things that happened to me that year was meeting Ann Cain, the woman who became my second wife. I was taking a stroll in a stadium we were going to play when I saw this beautiful woman walking Stevie Wonder around. She was all dressed up, and talk about pretty. She carried herself like a lady, but something in her attitude told you she had moxie. All I could think was, "Mercy." At the time she was dating Stevie's conductor, Clarence Paul, but something happened. Not long after that we were doing a big show in Los Angeles with Ike and Tina Turner, the Fifth Dimension, and Martha and the Vandellas. As Shelly and I pulled into a parking space, who should be in the next car but Ann. I did a double take. This was too good to be true, and I took it as an omen. My first impulse was to hang back a little, thinking this could be a little too heady, even for me. On second thought, though, I figured what the hell. I was feeling my Cheerios.

We talked for a while. She was working for Ike and Tina's booking agency, Sputnik. Our next date was in San Francisco, but Ann and I exchanged numbers and agreed to get together when I returned. The time didn't pass quickly enough, and the second I got in, I called her. The die was cast, and we stayed together for the next five years.

Ann and I became an item just in time for the Detroit riots that summer. The night all hell broke loose, I had been driving around town, visiting friends and checking up on my family. It was getting late, so I decided against dropping into the Chit Chat Lounge on Twelfth Street. For some reason, I got a creepy kind of feeling and decided to take myself home. I left Twelfth Street, and by the time I got home, settled down, and turned on the news, the riots had started, in fact, right near the Chit Chat. Watching the news was like seeing a nightmare. The violence, looting, and burning got worse by the hour. Finally the National Guard and the Army came into the city and started shooting near our building.

You couldn't go out, but the gunfire was so close you didn't want to stay in either. Luckily, our place was laid out in such a way that most of the rooms opened off a main hallway in the center of the apartment. They were firing rounds all over the place, and it didn't seem to stop. I was afraid we were going to get hit, or at least cut by flying glass, so we went into the hall, closed all the doors, and stayed down on the floor for hours. It was one of the most terrifying experiences of my life.

The next morning I went out for groceries. I was walking down Davidson, and on every corner stood soldiers with guns, looking at everybody who came by as if we'd all done something. They had orders to shoot looters, and the tension was so thick you could choke on it. It was the strangest thing. Here I was, a perfectly innocent, tax-paying citizen walking in my own neighborhood. I shouldn't have had a thing to fear, and yet I found myself consciously keeping a look on my face that said, "Hey, I'm not up to anything. I'm cool. Don't shoot." With every step, the possibility that someone could have lit up my ass at any moment became more real. It was spooky to feel that you had no freedom or that someone could kill you in the blink of an eye, no questions asked. By the time I got home I was shaking out of my skin.

Eventually the soldiers left, and then we realized the full impact of what had gone down. Many of the places we knew, stores we'd patronized over the years, places we'd hung out at were gone, destroyed beyond salvation or burned to the ground. Someone broke into our dry cleaners' and stole parts of our uniforms, so we ended up giving pieces of what was left to Richard Street and his group the Monitors. It was a little thing—they were just clothes— but there was something creepy about it. I'll never forget walking out that first day. I loved Detroit and still do. Afterward lots of people talked about bringing Detroit back, but no matter how much money they threw at it, that beautiful city wasn't ever going to be the same again.

6

Throughout the years, our relationship with Motown remained essentially good. I believe that Berry cared about the Temptations. Now and then he might offer his opinion about a matter, but I never felt that we were being browbeaten or dictated to. If a problem cropped up on either end, we could always reach each other by phone. We wouldn't pester Berry about every little thing, but he was there if we needed him.

Our first big blowout with Berry occurred in January 1968, right after the U.S.S. *Pueblo* was captured by the North Koreans. A tour of Japan was set, but the *Pueblo* incident raised the possibility of some heavy trouble between Communist China and the United States. Some people even thought it might escalate into something worse than Vietnam. Traveling anywhere over there always entailed some risk, but after a group meeting we decided that this was an exceptional situation, and we were not going anywhere near it until things cooled down. We made our position clear, but no one at Motown would take our no for an answer. All the executives—Taylor Cox, Esther Edwards, Don Foster—tried to convince us to change our minds. When that failed, they turned it over to Berry, thinking he would be able to sway us. A couple days after we'd told Motown no for what we thought was the last time, Berry phoned me at the Century Plaza Hotel in Los Angeles.

After exchanging pleasantries, Berry got to the point. "I hear you guys are worried about the *Pueblo* thing," he said. "Why don't you go on? Nothing is going to happen to you there." I restated our case, but Berry persisted. "Go on over. You know those Oriental women, they love black guys. You guys will be able to get all the action you want."

"Hey, Berry," I answered, "we get enough of that here. We ain't got to go way over there for that. Now, we made a group decision that we are not going, and that's that."

Finally Berry relented. "Okay, man," he said. "I'm sorry you feel that way, but okay."

I've always taken the fact that no Temptation was ever drafted as another sign of God looking out for us. Considering how many brothers ended up over there, we were very lucky. They didn't give deferments to guys who weren't in school, and many, for whatever reason, chose not to dodge the draft. Each of the Temptations was personally touched by the war. Lots of our friends went, and many were hurt or killed. Although we were opposed to the idea of the war, our support for the men and women who served never wavered.

I've never understood why we, as Americans, gave those guys so much hell for going to fight. They answered a call and have suffered for it ever since. They were made to go. It just didn't seem right for us to send them to so much pain and then refuse to treat them with respect because we didn't like the reason they went or because we didn't win the war. Over the years we've been touched by the many vets who've told us that whenever there was a lull in the fighting, they'd put on a Tempts tape. It is such a small thing, but we consider it a great honor.

The war was just one of many controversial things going down in the late sixties. We were living smack-dab in the middle of the age of Aquarius. Music, clothes, hairstyles, language—everything, it seemed—was changing, and not all of it for the better. During this period nobody thought too much about new dangers. We didn't even see them as dangers back then. Getting high was the just thing to do, and for too many it was the beginning of the end. I was no saint, but I was lucky in that most of my experiments ended so unpleasantly that it only took one try for me to decide not to mess with something.

My first cocaine experience took place during one of our record-breaking runs at the Apollo. The demand for tickets was so great that when we came out the stage door to go to eat after the show, we would see the line of people waiting for the next show winding all the way around the block. Fame was still new enough that certain scenes struck me as unreal, and this was one I'll never forget.

At the time we were hanging with some guys whom we still see today. We were between shows, and one of them said, "Man, you motherfuckers are killing them down here. Come on, take a hit of this here." In his outstretched hand he held a nice quantity of white powder—cocaine.

I declined. "Coke ain't my thing. Thanks anyway."

"Come on," he persisted. "Celebrate just this one time." He kept at me, and in a moment of weakness and, to be honest, out of curiosity, I gave in.

"All right, give me a hit." I hit it, and was surprised to find that it felt a lot better than I expected. I felt this beautiful surge of energy. So I hit it again. And again.

We finished the show and went back to our hotel to rest up for the next day. This run was scheduled so that we did four shows a day then, which is grueling no matter how young you are. It was exhausting, or at least it should have been. Back in my room I crawled into bed, closed my eyes, and waited to doze off, but I couldn't. Then I felt my eyes pop open—*boing*!—like in a cartoon. They would not close, and I felt jittery. I got up and walked the halls for hours, from two in the morning until ten the next day. By the time I'd finally worn myself down enough to sleep, we were due back at the Apollo.

Dragging my butt onstage, I tried to do my best, but from the first downbeat I knew it was all over. Everything I did or sang came out either too fast or too slow. My timing was totally off, and people definitely noticed that something was up. I looked out into the first few rows and saw people whispering to each and pointing at me. It broke my heart. I was never so ashamed of myself. Only God was going to get me through this one, so I said a silent prayer right on the stage: "Lord, if you let me off, I will not do that anymore." Sure enough, I never did, and I never forgot that. I couldn't stand the idea that something was controlling my mind and my body. That's probably why the whole drug scene today upsets me so. Lord knows I've seen my share of it firsthand, and I still can't comprehend why anyone would willfully submit himself to the tyranny of drugs.

With drugs all around, you couldn't help noticing the toll it was taking on other performers as well. Backstage at the Apollo one day I spotted a familiar-looking young guy. If you glanced at him, you wouldn't think anything about him, but up close you could see in his eyes that he was pretty far gone. When I got near enough, I realized I was looking at none other than my childhood idol, Frankie Lymon. We chatted for a few minutes, and he said that he liked the Temptations very much. Coming from him, the compliment meant quite a bit. We said good-bye, and I headed back to the dressing room. Once inside, I said, "Hey, guys, guess who's downstairs. Frankie Lymon." Everyone's face lit up at the mention of his name, and they ran down to see him. When they came back, though, it was obvious that they'd seen the same haunted look in his eyes. Barely a couple months after, Frankie Lymon was found dead of a heroin overdose. It was such a waste.

That spring of 1968 was rough. It was as though a black cloud was hanging over us, but we tried not to let it ruin everything. After a March date at the University of Delaware, Eddie and I broke away together for a night out. Footloose and fancy-free, we took off for Cleveland, to party and see some young ladies we knew. Of course, David took his limo back to Detroit, and Paul and Melvin flew home. We took the group's big silver-and-black Cadillac stretch limousine with our driver, John O'Den. John was a great guy. He must have been in his fifties or so, and had worked at Motown for a few years as a bodyguard and chauffeur. You always felt safe with John around. Years before he'd been heavyweight champ Joe Louis's sparring partner. He was strong and powerful, but also a sweetheart and lots of fun to have around.

We were driving along the Pennsylvania Turnpike, just outside of Pittsburgh. Around two or three in the morning, I roused myself from a nap and looked to see where we were. Eddie was fast asleep on the other side of the backseat. Judging by the road signs, there was a couple hours' ride ahead, so I sat back and closed my eyes. As I started to drift off I was shocked awake by the sound of tires crunching on gravel and the car body shaking like we were riding on a bumpy dirt road. Sitting up, I heard John scream, "I think we're going to hit!" Straight ahead loomed a huge eighteen-wheel semi that was jackknifed clear across the road. We were traveling at sixty, maybe seventy miles an hour, so there was no way to stop. I knew this was going to be the end, if not for Eddie and me, then certainly for John.

The limo smacked into the truck with such force that the metal partition dividing the front and back seats buckled from just the pressure of my shoulder hitting it. I heard Eddie groaning, and from John silence. We expected the worst, but John had ducked from behind the steering wheel and thrown himself across the floor just seconds before impact. An ambulance took us to the hospital, and except for some bruises and contusions, all three of us were fine. The limo, however, was squashed up like an accordion, and the state police told us that if we'd been riding in anything smaller, we'd have checked out for good. We signed a bunch of autographs at the hospital, and that night Walter Cronkite reported the story on the evening news. After a little time off, it was back to the road.

Years of constant touring and performing dull the details of specific nights, so that there end up being only a few you can recall in great detail. One particular show stays with me, though, and always will. It was in Charleston, South Carolina. Just hours before the gig we got the shocking news that a white man had shot the Reverend Dr. Martin Luther King, Jr., to death on the balcony of the Lorraine Motel in Memphis.

That night the whole world seemed strange. I remember saying, "I don't know if we want to go out." There was concern that King's assassination would spark racial violence, and it went without saying that nobody was going to be in the mood to have a good time. We ended up going ahead with the show anyway. The five of us made our best effort to be professional about it and give it a good try, but from the moment we stepped off our bus and onto the stage, you could tell it was hopeless. An atmosphere of shock and disbelief overwhelmed everyone. We didn't even bother saying anything about King, because what was there to say? They all knew about it; in fact, no one could think of anything else. It was like the entire world stopped. Our attitude was, Let's just do the show and get the hell out of here. It was one of the handful of times that we went through the motions and didn't get any flak for it.

As soon as we could, we boarded the bus for the long ride back to Detroit. I don't recall one word being spoken; it was total silence all the way. People stared out the windows into the black of night and did a lot of thinking. What I remember about those first few days after King's death was an intense feeling of personal loss. We'd lost President Kennedy a few years before, and what with the riots, it seemed like the country was moving toward the brink. Many people thought that King's death would touch off a bad scene all across America. Luckily, it didn't come to that, but it could have because there were many brothers ready to go to war over it despite the fact that King advocated nonviolence.

I was more angry than anything else, because King wasn't doing anything but trying to bring people together, preaching equality not only for blacks and whites, but for everyone. He was a great man, a man of peace. It's a sad commentary on the times, but it seemed just then that any man who stood up for what was right, for what he believed, would be shot down, and right when it seemed he was on the verge of achieving the most.

The next day, when I saw the news photo of King lying on the balcony, I realized that he had been standing right near the room that I used to stay in whenever we came to Memphis. It was a very eerie feeling.

Several weeks later, Berry arranged for us to go down to Atlanta with a number of other Motown acts to do a benefit for King's widow, Coretta Scott King, and the Poor People's March on Washington. Even though we did nothing special, just our regular show, it felt good to be supporting Mrs. King and the cause, and giving back something to her husband's memory. He'd meant so much to us.

King's death prompted a number of riots around the country, including in Detroit, and fueled the more radical elements of the Black Power movement. For some segments of the public, where an entertainer stood politically got to be an issue. I remember the boos and hisses Sammy Davis, Jr., received once because he'd been photographed with his arm around President Nixon. We were at an Operation PUSH benefit, and the crowd had Sammy in tears.

The only thing that stopped it was Jesse Jackson coming out and asking people to be polite. I know that when we'd play the Regal in Chicago during these years, a political group called the Blackstone Rangers would sit down in the first three rows and check us out. Unlike some other black entertainers of the time, however, we were never challenged by any political group. Our involvement was restricted to doing fund-raisers and appearing at benefits. On the whole, though, we avoided making political endorsements and just let our music do the talking.

Looking back on those days, I suppose a certain amount of radicalism was needed to raise the nation's consciousness about the plight of black Americans. Still, I never stopped believing that prejudice and hate go hand in hand, and having been the target of that crap, I don't believe in or support anyone who preaches hate, no matter who they are.

I must have been eighteen or nineteen when I was working for the Jackson Contracting Company in Detroit. It was menial labor, refurbishing and restoring broken-down homes. As I was taking out the trash I heard a little child saying to his playmate, "Oh, look! A nigger!" He couldn't have been more than five or six years old. I looked at him, shook my head, and walked back inside. I faulted not the child but the parents—for instilling in their son that kind of hate and lack of sensitivity. But regardless of where it came from, the results of those attitudes are the same. It has to stop somewhere.

No matter how you measure it, the lineup of Melvin, Eddie, David, Paul, and I had a special magic that can never be re-created or recaptured. Although a lot of my conviction about that came with the passage of time, even as we were living it we felt it in our bones. To be up there singing like angels, and moving so that you felt like it was you and four mirror images, then bringing audience after audience to its knees—we felt that power, and we knew how rare it was.

Knowing that made our situation with David all the more painful. Things kept going from bad to worse, and we knew something was going to shake, and probably sooner than later. It wasn't as if we didn't realize what David meant to the Temptations and our fans. Let's face it: Ruffin was a standout. When David stepped out, you always knew something great was going to happen. He was a fantastic singer and performer, and no one, from that time until today, does what he did. He was an original.

That said, his general attitude was still forcing us to think about who we were and what we were about. I agree with Berry's philosophy that no single person is ever greater than the group itself. The whole always exceeds the sum of the individual parts. I admit to holding my breath every time the thought of David leaving crossed my mind, but we couldn't be frightened into not doing anything about it, either. If he left, it was going to be a heavy change, maybe one our fans wouldn't like. That was a chance we had to take and just hope that our fans would continue to support us. Without meaning to, David had given us plenty of time to turn all this over in our minds, so that the day the shit hit the fan, we were prepared.

The other shoe finally dropped during a ten-day engagement at a Cleveland hotel supper club called the Versailles. One afternoon before a show, David's driver delivered a message to us: David says that you should carry on and do the show without him. At the time David was involved with one of Dean Martin's daughters, and she was opening her own show at the Latin Casino in Cherry Hill. He obviously felt that catching her act was more important than doing ours.

"There it is," I said when I heard the news, "the handwriting is on the wall. Ruffin's got to go." Melvin, Paul, Eddie, and I met in one of our rooms and agreed that David had gone too far and would have to leave the group. He'd been letting us know in little ways that being a member was not part of his plan. People at Motown, including Berry and Shelly, had kept tabs on the situation but didn't interfere. We drew up a legal document, which Melvin Franklin, Eddie Kendricks, Paul Williams, and I signed. It basically stated that David Ruffin was being relieved of all further responsibilities to the Temptations. With the passage of time and shifts in alliances, some people have claimed that I alone fired David. It's simply not true. In David's case and that of any other member, the personnel decisions always came down democratically. Not one person spoke up that day to keep David in the Temptations.

Toward the end of June, Don Foster gave David the bad news. For a guy who acted like he wanted to be away from us, he took it very hard. David's reaction was great shock; he could not believe it. In his mind, I guess, he was the key to the Temptations, so much so that the four of us would put up with anything. His inability to accept that it was all over with us was a sad thing to see, and we hadn't seen the last of it.

Everyone remembers it a little differently, but I believe we personally invited Dennis Edwards to join the Temptations. He was out of the Contours then and was working with his group, the Firebirds. Dennis was born in Birmingham, Alabama, in 1943, where his father was a minister. Dennis's family moved to Detroit while he was still a kid. Like the rest of us, he started singing in church—at two—but he was the only one of us with any formal musical training. At the Detroit Conservatory of Music he had studied piano and composition, and belonged to a gospel group called the Crowns of Joy. Our friend James Jamerson got Dennis an audition with Berry. At the time, Dennis was looking for a solo career, but Motown put him in the Contours for a time, and he cut a record with them called "Your Love Grows More Precious Every Day."

We were happy that he accepted our offer, and we got right to work. Of course, he had to learn the songs and the steps and get used to our schedules and so forth, but it seemed to be working out. The public got its first look at our new singer in July 1968 at the Forum in Los Angeles. Fans and reporters greeted us at the airport, and the excitement kept on building. We did the first half of the show with Eddie, Melvin, Paul, and me, then brought Dennis out for the last half. At the time, it was a theater in the round, and security had a particularly hard time keeping the girls back. Also adding to the excitement was the fact that we'd broken the Supremes' record for ticket sales there. The Forum seated about 20,000, and the Supremes had had a sellout just before. The way we topped them was that Shelly got the Forum people to put in a few extra folding chairs and sell tickets for those seats.

Dennis was in, but David didn't seem to want to go away. In July we were appearing at the Valley Forge Music Fair, outside Philadelphia, which was then just a tent. David was sitting in the audience, and in a sort of weird déjà vu of our early days, he tried to jump up on the stage with us. He tried this stunt a couple more times, and for a short while we hired extra security guys to keep him off.

Motown exercised its option to keep David on the roster as a solo act. In early 1969, they released his single, "My Whole World Ended (the Moment You Left Me)," a tune Johnny Bristol originally wrote with the Temptations in mind. It was a big hit, and David's solo career seemed to be getting off to a good start. We wished him the best.

But David *still* wasn't gone. For some reason I've never quite figured, David's leaving prompted a change in Eddie. We weren't hanging out socially so much anymore, and our communication starting dropping off. Even though he had agreed to let David go, once Ruffin was out officially, Eddie and he started picking up an alliance. Eddie actually began mentioning bringing David back. Eddie seemed to have a more or less perpetual attitude about something. Those days of him making us laugh and being a good buddy were on the wane. If Eddie disagreed with a group decision, he'd jump on Melvin for siding with me. Defending his position, Melvin would say, "Eddie, you know I'm on Otis's side.

Not all the time, but this time I think he's right." That would only make Eddie angrier. Eddie decided that I was the enemy, and it got to be a no-win situation.

"You're just hanging behind everything Otis said," Eddie would snap.

It got to where I was watching everything said, especially when the subject was Motown and Berry, to whom Eddie thought we weren't standing up enough. He let us know he thought we were ass kissers more than once.

Part of the problem wasn't just Eddie, but a general reaction on everyone's part to some changes in the weather at Motown. In late 1967 Holland, Dozier, and Holland left the label over a financial dispute with Berry. They wanted to split publishing, and they weren't the only ones. With greater success Motown became a less pleasant place to work. Maybe ignorance was bliss, because it wasn't until many of us learned through a wider circle of acquaintances in all areas of the business that our contracts with Motown were substantially below industry standards. Acts who sold tons of records and consistently pulled in crowds made enough to cope with it. In addition to success, you also got the benefits of Motown's attention and support. But for those who weren't in the same league as, say, the Supremes, the Tempts, and the Four Tops, the money thing got to be a very sore point. A couple years before there was some talk of Motown acts and producers uniting together to negotiate for better deals, but Motown got wind of it, thanks to certain snitch babies, and put a stop to that.

No matter how much money we were making, Eddie thought that Motown was giving us a raw deal. He wanted something to be done about it, and soon. He became impatient with my analytical, methodical approach. I saw his point; after all, we split the group's income equally, so we were each getting the short end of the same stick. But I felt it my responsibility to examine the situation from all angles and make sure that a piece of solid ground was waiting if we decided to make a major move. Eddie's solution was much simpler: the Temptations would go on strike—no more tours, no more records.

"I don't think that's going to get it, Eddie," I explained. "I think we should keep on recording, try to get as strong as we can and get in a much better financial position so that we can really do something. Motown's got too many acts around just dying to take our place. Ultimately, we'd be hurting ourselves."

The point Eddie wouldn't see and that the rest of us were all too aware of was that Motown considered no one indispensable. Berry Gordy, the eternal optimist, believed the label could weather any defection or dismissal, and judging by the record up until then, at least financially speaking, he was correct. Eddie saw the Temptations as crucial to Motown, just as David Ruffin viewed himself as essential to the Temptations. They were both wrong.

Melvin and Paul agreed with me, but Paul's friendship with and deep loyalty to Eddie made it awkward. This was another instance where Paul was torn, in this case between Eddie and what he knew what was best for the Temptations. Several times Paul said, "Otis, you know Eddie don't mean that in his heart. He's just hotheaded. Just trust me, Otis, I'll keep him under control."

But how the hell was Paul going to do that? His health kept sliding, and he was well on his way to to drinking two or three fifths of Courvoisier daily. Melvin, Eddie, Dennis, and I, along with some of our road guys, tried to be vigilant, discovering Paul's stashed bottles and pouring them down the drain, but our efforts were easily negated by the hangers-on who kept on his good side by replenishing the supply.

Dennis was still new enough that he didn't want to make anybody mad, so he kept quiet. That wasn't the answer, either, and I would get on his ass and say, "You can't be neutral all the time. You've got to stand up and say what you feel—be it right or wrong. We have to know where you stand." Ultimately, though, Dennis flaked out, and what with Paul falling deeper into his problems, it fell to Melvin and me to hold the line with Eddie.

Our final decision not to strike against Motown didn't mean we were totally happy, though. In addition to the contract thing, we started thinking more about writing and perhaps even producing for ourselves. In the seven years since we'd first signed with Motown, the whole industry had changed. For the first time in history the majority of top hits were written by the artists who performed them. We weren't saying we could whip out Top Ten hits or top any of the Motown staffers, but we did think that when we had time off we should be allowed studio time to work on things. Around the same time, Marvin Gaye and Stevie Wonder also began their struggles to write and produce themselves, which Motown fought at every step.

Even though we weren't writing songs, we made sure to get in our two cents when we recorded. We usually devised our own vocal arrangements, or refined the ones producers presented to us. Our feeling was, and is, no one has a greater stake in the continued success of the Temptations than we have. You can't expect to last if you don't make some changes with the times. We tried listening to everything and keeping abreast of what other acts were doing. I always loved the Beatles, for example, for their great songwriting, and Jimi Hendrix. But what really grabbed me was Sly and the Family Stone's first hits, especially "Dance to the Music." He brought forth something truly fresh, with more prominent electric guitar, multiple lead vocals, and a funkier sound, and I loved it. I remember being in New York and talking to my friend Kenny Gamble, one half of Philadelphia's famous Gamble-Huff production team, and he agreed with me. Back in Detroit, Norman Whitfield, Ann Cain, and I were standing outside a club called the Casino Royale, when I said, "Norman, have you heard Sly and the Family Stone?"

"Yeah," he replied, "I heard it."

"Maybe we should try that kind of thing for our next record," I suggested. We were riding a moderate hit, "Please Return Your Love to Me," a very sweet ballad that Eddie sang.

"Man, I don't want to be bothered with that shit," Norman said. "That ain't nothing but a little passing fancy."

"I don't know, Norman. I think it's gonna catch on."

It didn't seem that I'd convinced Norman, so we were surprised when we came into town a few weeks later, and Norman played us the tracks for the next thing he wanted us to record, "Cloud Nine." I remember listening to it and thinking, "Oh, so this is the passing fancy." Norman must have read my mind because he said, "So you were right. Let's go on and make the record."

"Cloud Nine" was the first song of what critics like to call our "psychedelic phase." A tremendous departure from our earlier work and anything to come out of Motown, it was Dennis's first lead vocal with us, and the tune fit his voice to a tee. Contrary to popular belief, the song is not about drugs—Norman didn't do drugs—but about changing your attitude internally, no matter how impossible that might seem. The lyrics even admit that the "world of love and harmony" is "a million miles from reality." To Norman's and Barrett Strong's credit, "Cloud Nine" minced no words talking about life for inner-city blacks. Musically speaking, Norman set a mood that was worlds apart: dark, threatening, even hostile. His choice of instrumentation was also radical for Motown: heavy electric guitars using effects like wah-wah pedals, different rhythms, and background-vocal arrangements where each of us sang different lines and parts, rather than doing the monolithic "aah" and "doo" patterns. While our debt to Sly Stone is pretty obvious, and would be more so on future tracks such as "Masterpiece," Norman incorporated those elements into a new sound that was, I believe, uniquely our own. We were excited by "Cloud Nine" but wondered how it would go over with our fans. Again, we got their full support, pushing "Cloud Nine" up to number six in early 1969. The biggest thrill came later when it brought home our and Motown's first Grammy award, for Best R&B Performance by a Duo or Group, Vocal or Instrumental.

Coming off that triumph, we were eager to make our Las Vegas debut at the Flamingo in October. It seemed safe to assume that the Vegas audience would be similar to the crowds we'd drawn at the Copa and other clubs. But we were way off on this one. The Vegas audience, which was then more middle-American and a little more conservative, just didn't buy the heavier stuff like "Cloud Nine." Adding to our problems that night, Paul came onstage obviously inebriated. Let's just say it was rough. Word about things like that spread all over town, and as a result we weren't invited back to Vegas until the early seventies, when we worked with Dionne Warwick and Bill Cosby.

Nineteen sixty-eight had its ups and downs, to be sure, but we ended it on a strong note with the *TCB* television special with the Supremes. From the beginning of the year, we'd been recording tracks with them. That fall Motown put out *Diana Ross and the Supremes Join the Temptations* and a number-two hit single, "I'm Gonna Make You Love Me." Following one of our appearances with the girls on Sullivan's show, NBC offered us our own hour-long television special. It took about ten days to tape and featured us doing both hits and standards, both straight and in a couple of production numbers. It was a challenge, and we were excited making it and pleased by its reception. *TCB* was a top-rated program, and one critic called it "the first major black television special in history."

Though we enjoyed working with Diana, Mary, and Cindy Birdsong (who replaced Flo), it was apparent that Berry favored them. We all knew that Berry and Diana had something going on, and that was cool. Later, however, when we heard through the grapevine that Berry gave them special gifts for doing such a great job on the show, while we didn't rate a simple thank-you, we weren't pleased. But, what the hell. These things were ceasing to be surprises. We'd do our job, and pick up the check.

Our final show of the year was at the sold-out Cobo Hall in Detroit. We were backstage when who should I notice standing by the stage door but Elbridge Bryant. I hadn't seen him in a while, and was taken aback by his appearance. His hair had grown long and unruly, and there were big dark circles around his eyes. His skin was the color of ash.

"Hey, Bones," I said, calling him by his old group nickname. "What's happening?"

"Hey, my brother," Al answered, "not a thing, you know. Just hanging on."

Though he was trying to be cool and carry on, a deep sadness seeped into just about every word. He talked about seeing us on television, and hinted that he wished he could have been there, too. He'd put together a little group, but nothing ever happened for them. About a decade later, Al died in Florida of cirrhosis of the liver. Even though he'd left us very early on, I always thought of him the same way I think of any guy who's been with us, as a Temptation. Back then I thought that if Al had stayed with us, his life would have turned out better, but looking back today, I don't know.

The main reason I say that is what happened to Paul. He was drinking and partying all the time now, and human leeches come with the turf when you're living that kind of lifestyle. Instead of being friends to Paul, they only encouraged his worst impulses. One by one, each of the guys in the group would take him aside for a little heart-to-heart and encourage him to pull himself together. Eddie, for one, often told Paul how much the group cared about him and how much he meant to us. "Stop it, Paul, you don't need this shit," Eddie would plead, but to no avail. Like anybody that deeply into the bottle, Paul had his defense mechanisms running on overtime and would take everything you said wrong. By now, the drinking had begun to affect us all. He was not a cool drunk; if he had some in him, everybody knew it.

In spring 1969 Paul opened the Celebrity House West, a beauty salon, with his girlfriend Winnie. This only increased the emotional and financial pressures bearing down on him. As bad as the drinking might have been, though, Paul's real problem was his health. He wouldn't see a doctor until 1971, so there was no telling what was wrong. Basically, though, I saw a general physical breakdown. Onstage, he started having trouble keeping up until it reached a point where he would be gasping for breath. Even so, he kept smoking cigarettes. Eventually, we traveled with a tank of oxygen, which we kept in the wings for Paul.

Finally we had no choice but to bring Richard Street aboard. Richard was working at Motown and had recorded a couple of records with his group, the Monitors. With us, he stood behind the curtain and sang all Paul's parts, except, of course, for Paul's special numbers. It was painful to witness the deterioration of such a talented, intelligent man. Understandably, the ordeal was uncomfortable for Richard. There was an unspoken understanding that if Paul ever left the group, Richard would take his place. It was getting to be only a matter of time.

Norman kept coming up with more "message" songs: "Run Away Child, Running Wild," "Don't Let the Joneses Get You Down," and "Psychedelic Shack." The last tune was pretty far out, but that was just Norman. Listening to those tracks you'd think that maybe Norman did a lot of drugs or had a driving social conscience, like Marvin Gaye expressed on *What's Going On*, but in fact he was merely following the "psychedelic soul" trend.

These were all sizable hits in the United States, and in several cases England, too, but the big number-one for 1969 was "I Can't Get Next to You," a love song, so to speak. We each had different lines to sing; for example Paul sang the first line ("I can make the gray sky blue") and Melvin sang the second ("I can make it rain whenever I want it to"), and so on. Eddie devised the choreography for it from this stiff-legged dance he saw his kids doing around the house.

In May President Richard Nixon's elder daughter, Tricia, invited us to perform at her Masque Ball at the White House. She said that we, along with the Turtles, were her two favorite groups. It was quite an honor for us, and afterward we got a guided tour through the White House. I'm an avid reader of history, so I was excited to be standing where great events had taken place. The Secret Service was extremely thorough and checked everyone and everything out. Before the ball, they destroyed a suspicious object they heard ticking in the Turtles' drummer's box. It turned out to be a metronome that got switched on in shipping.

Just when it looked like we'd made it, something else came along, and we kept moving up. That year we taped our own syndicated television special, *The Temptations Show*, which co-starred comedian George Kirby and actress Kay Stevens. The Supremes made several more records with us—"I'll Try Something New," "The Weight," and *Together*—and we taped a second well-received late-year special, *G.I.T. on Broadway*, for NBC.

Inner Detroit had changed, and so that year Ann and I moved from a northwest suburb to the predominantly white suburb of Southfield. I fell in love with that home the first time I saw it. It was a gorgeous ranch-style house with a circular drive, big yard, marble floors, and skylights throughout. Walking through it the first time all I could say was, "Put together the papers." Ann went to work redecorating and made it into such a showplace that *Architectural Digest* wanted to cover it.

At the same time, Smokey and Claudette Robinson were house hunting, too. I told him about my place, and he soon found a house nearby. After he'd decided to move to Southfield, he asked me, "Oak,"—that was his nickname for me—"aren't you afraid to be out here with all these white folks?" To be honest, it never occurred to me. In fact, when Ann and I moved in, several people from the neighborhood dropped by to introduce themselves and give us gifts. They were all happy to have us there. I had some wonderful times in that house, and even today people will tell me what a great place it was. Whenever we play Detroit, I still drive by, just to see that whoever lives there now is taking good care of it.

By this point, Motown had been our home for over eight years. Things had been changing little by little, but it was still Hitsville to us. That ended in the late sixties, when part of the daily operations were moved from Hitsville on West Grand Boulevard to a regular, cold, ugly office building on Woodward near the Fisher Freeway, and the recording began taking place in other studios. It was also then that Berry installed a more conventionally corporate upper-management staff made up of people whose business was business, not music. They commissioned a Big Eight accounting firm to do a time study. Motown spent a couple hundred thousand dollars to have these guys analyze who was doing what, how much it cost, and how much profit could be squeezed out of every position and department.

The guys who did the study knew only about books. Their whole outlook was based on the premise that two plus two always equals four. Talent, style, class—these didn't figure in their equations. The first department to go was Artist Development, probably the one part of the company most responsible for making Motown acts Motown acts. They didn't, or couldn't, see how Artist Development gave a performer greater confidence and polish or made an act look different or sound better.

Berry began spending more time in Los Angeles and less at his desk. Rumors started circulating that he might be moving the whole operation out there. I like the West Coast well enough (I live there now), but back then Motown outside Detroit was unthinkable.

As much as we might have lamented all this "progress," the charts didn't lie. There was no drop-off in the number or quality of the hits. In addition to Smokey and the Miracles, Jr. Walker and the All Stars, the Supremes, the Four Tops, Stevie Wonder, Marvin Gaye, Tammi Terrell, David Ruffin, and us, Motown had added Gladys Knight and the Pips, Edwin Starr, and the Jackson 5, a phenomenal group of brothers with an eleven-year-old lead singer named Michael. What suffered was morale. The old friendliness and camaraderie that had supported all of us in the beginning was replaced by a general air of businesslike formality. By moving the operation off West Grand, Motown took the first step away from its roots, not only geographically but spiritually. Things got a little too sophisticated and specialized for my taste. Every time we came back in from the road and stopped by Motown, there seemed to be a little bit less of Hitsville there.

Even in the studio, things were shifting. For all intents and purposes, the Temptations were Norman's group now, which was fine. He had great material and really exploited our potential as singers by trying out different things on us. Trouble was, as time became more precious to us, Norman got more loose about it. If we were scheduled to record at eight o'clock, we were there and ready at eight. Norman, however, might drag in half an hour, an hour later. And it wasn't just a matter of time. As singers, we'd be mentally prepared to go at it. Nothing takes the wind out of you like sitting around in a studio twiddling your thumbs.

This happened more often than not, and several times we had words with him about it. Sometimes Norman would strut in, making no apologies for his lateness, and launch into a rap about how much money he won at the track that day. When I'd tell him we'd didn't give a damn about his gambling adventures, he'd get into a snit and ask us if we wanted to cancel the session (which he knew we couldn't do), then start riding our asses because we weren't jumping on the tune.

"Hey, Norman, you're the one who started it," we'd say, then he'd apologize, and it would go on and on. And Norman wasn't the type that you could let slide, because he'd walk all over you. To our way of thinking, it's the producer's job to cope with the temperamental artist, not the other way around. Finally, we got to feeling, "Why are we always going through this shit?" The answer: we were selling records, Norman's records, and that was the glue that held things together. All we could do was refuse to pay for the booked studio time that he was late.

So there was a little tension between him and us, but overall the relationship was still solid and productive. Generally, Norman was good at keeping costs down. He worked quickly once he got to it and had cut deals with the musicians, so that even an album as complex as *Cloud Nine* could be recorded in a little over a week for about $80,000. With us selling at the rate we were then, the real cost to us was minimal. Another good thing was that Norman didn't have us recording a bunch of stuff that he stuck in a can and didn't get released because Motown charged us for those tracks, too.

Motown's attitude was that the Tempts and Norman and Barrett Strong made up this little machine; so as long as the machine worked, it was left alone. That's probably why we could put tracks on our albums that were not from the Jobete catalog, like the Beatles' "Hey Jude," which we loved. It also gave Norman leeway as far as the content of our songs, some of which, like "Message from a Black Man," were quite direct and maybe a little too politically outspoken for some people's tastes. Though we never sang it live, it got a lot of airplay.

Even with the world on a string, we couldn't seem to keep things together inside the group. It was a puzzle to me how five guys who in so many ways had it made couldn't keep their personal stuff straight. One night after a show at the Westbury Music Fair on Long Island, Melvin and Eddie started going at it over something someone had done onstage that night. Whatever it was, it was probably blown out of proportion, but Paul and I had to pull them apart and make them cool out.

Later that night Melvin and I took a walk. We were standing behind our hotel, looking up at the heavens with tears rolling down our faces. We weren't ashamed to admit that we couldn't understand what was happening to us, or what might happen to us if things didn't straighten out. The fighting always upset me, because you could never predict where it was going to end. This night was one of those rare times when I thought that maybe we'd done everything we were supposed to and maybe it was time to pack it in. Melvin and I talked about it for a long time and determined that neither of us wanted to quit. We promised each other we'd keep it going, no matter what, even if we had to do it without Eddie or Paul. Don't misunderstand: we didn't want to lose them, but we felt very strongly that things were moving in that direction.

We prayed together and thought about what our success really meant. When you stop to think about the millions and millions of talented people on earth who will never get even one break, you can't help appreciating what you have. The two of us resolved to hold on. We had a precious thing. Strangely, after that talk things seemed to calm down for a stretch. I look back on that night and like to think it was a test to see how much faith we could muster. Twenty years later Melvin and I are still together, so we must have passed.

In London in 1970 I had another of those experiences that proves my theory that women are fascinating. We were appearing at London's Talk of the Town, and during our stay met and hung out with many celebrities, including the Beatles and Nancy Wilson, in the city's most exclusive clubs, like Tramps. One of those we met was a famous actress who was very popular at the time. She invited us up to her apartment, where we met some other actors, including Roddy McDowall, and had a generally enjoyable evening. Whenever I'd seen this actress in the movies or on television, I found her very attractive, so imagine my amazement when she started coming on to me very blatantly. She sent me a large bouquet of roses. She was very nice, but at the time I was married to Ann and not interested.

The night before we left to come home, I was in my hotel packing when the phone rang. It was her. She asked me what I was doing, and I said, "I'm packing, because we have an early flight back to the States."

"You're packing?" she asked, as if she didn't believe me. "That's not all you're doing! Who have you got there? Who are you fucking?"

"Whoa," I thought. This was a twist. I collected myself and answered, "There's no one here but me. And I'm not doin' nothing."

"Bullshit! You've got some bitch over there. I know you're fuckin' . . ." and so on and so forth. Finally she said, "Well, if it wasn't for the press, I would come on over there and check you out, but I think the publicity would be adverse."

"Yeah, I think so too. Good-bye." I hung up.

The next day one of the guys brought a copy of a London tabloid onto the plane. In the gossip section was a little item that named the actress and said she'd been seen with "a member of a very popular famous black group." And that was from just going to her place, so I dread to think what would have happened if she'd come over.

Also during that trip we met with the Archbishop of Canterbury, who commended us for setting such fine examples for youth. Back in the States on March 26, Congressman John Conyers, Jr., cited our music and our work as "ambassadors of goodwill and understanding" in the *Congressional Record*. He spoke of our community work and the fact that we each owned local businesses in Detroit. (At the time, I co-owned a clothing store with Pete Moore of the Miracles and Melvin; Eddie had a restaurant.) We were very proud to have been so honored for our accomplishments outside the music business and the time we had contributed to charitable causes.

In 1970 we had a Top Five hit with "Ball of Confusion," a very upfront political statement that was as relevant when Tina Turner covered it in 1984 as it was then. When Norman first showed us the lyrics, we were wondering how we were ever going to get all those damn syllables in one line. It reminded me of one of Bob Dylan's songs, "Subterranean Homesick Blues." Of course today lots of people know the song by heart, but the first time we looked at "evolution, revolution, birth control, sound of soul, shooting rockets to the moon, kids growing up too soon," we stopped in our tracks. Fortunately, Dennis had a real fast tongue.

Norman's big streak with us hit a bump with the next release, "Ungena Za Ulimwengu (Unite the World)." In case you wondered, the title is Swahili. It was our first record in six years not to go Top Thirty. Coincidentally, around then, Norman produced a big hit for Edwin Starr, "War," a tune we recorded first. This was only one of many tunes Norman recorded with more than one act. I think Norman was experimenting with different approaches, using us, Gladys Knight and the Pips, Edwin Starr, and later the Undisputed Truth, to record the same tunes. That said, I also think it was a good way for Norman to fatten his income, too. I've read where some people believe that this was a source of conflict among the various acts, and the fact that Norman was spreading his material among so many of us did cross our minds. But this was the way Motown had always operated.

Through it all I'd stayed close to my family. A few days before we were set to go to the Copa in 1970, Haze found out she had to have an operation. It was a routine thing. Haze had always been healthy, and except for her asthma, there was no reason to think she wasn't going to come out of it just fine. When I stopped by the house to see her before leaving for New York, we chatted, then she said a funny thing.

"Well, son, when you get back, I won't be here."

"Aw, come on," I said. "You're going to go in there, and you'll be all right." As I said it, it was impossible for me to think it would be any other way.

"No, son," she said gently. "You're never going to see me again."

I flew to New York, and we'd done a couple of days when Ron Wakefield from Motown called me. I answered the phone, and from the minute Ron said hello he sounded like he was about to cry.

"What's wrong with you?" I asked.

"I have some bad news for you, Otis. I just got a call that your mother passed."

I was numb with shock. Ann and I sat on the bed, and she cried. I still couldn't comprehend it. God must have come to her and told her that he'd be taking her. How else could it have been?

Needless to say, I was grieving. I went to Detroit, then returned to New York to finish up at the Copa. We were singing "War" one night, and my voice cracked. Right onstage Eddie shot me the meanest look I'd ever seen. Even people in the audience later remarked on it. I knew right then that if we got together backstage, we were going to lock ass, and I didn't want any part of it.

The best thing to do, I figured, was move my clothes from our upstairs dressing room to the room the Copa Girls used. During an intermission I instructed our valet, Bucky Smith, to bring my stuff down, and when Melvin heard what was happening, he did the same. We had some time between shows, so after the first one, Melvin and I changed and split. When Eddie found out that we left, he got madder than hell and took off. After we came back for the second show, Don Foster said, "Otis, Eddie doesn't look like he's going to make it." He offered to talk to him, but I told him to forget it. This was something that had been just waiting to happen. There were only a couple of days left, and so the four of us finished the last shows.

This is when we decided, or were forced into deciding, that Eddie would be leaving the group. Even though according to our press release, he left on his own, it was really a little more "mutual" than that. We didn't try to stop him from going and he didn't want to stay, so that was that.

One day before Eddie left us, he and I were walking around and I said, "Eddie, I've known you for over ten years now, but I feel like I never really knew you at all."

"Yeah, I guess that's true," he answered. "You never really did know me."

As fate would have it, Eddie left us with one of our biggest hits, "Just My Imagination (Running Away with Me)," a romantic ballad that Norman and Barrett had worked up a couple years before but never got around to cutting on us. We loved the song with just the basic tracks, but were totally knocked out when we heard the finished record, with all the strings. Arranger Jerry Long, who studied in Paris and scored movies, did a wonderful job capturing the song's magical, dreamy sadness. It was, I think, Eddie's finest moment.

We were up half the night recording the song, and when I left at six in the morning, Eddie was still putting down his vocals. Things between us were very bad, but I called him the next day to let him know I was concerned about how hard he worked and appreciated his efforts. Basically, I wanted to reach out to him. It was hard to accept the fact that our old vow was being broken for a second time. The song hung at number one for a couple weeks in the spring of 1971, but by that time Eddie was gone.

7

E ddie officially left the Temptations in March 1971. We
hustled to find his replacement, knowing it would be a
difficult task.

Through the years we had worked countless times with the
Vibrations, the Los Angeles quintet known for their outrageous
dancing and showmanship. One of their members was Ricky
Owens, a tall, nice-looking first tenor who had been with them
since the beginning. During his tenure with the Vibrations, he
became known for a couple of special numbers, "Misty" and
"Cindy," which never failed to drive the girls crazy.

The word out was that the Vibrations were splitting up, so we
asked Ricky to come to Detroit and audition. His singing was
great, as we expected, but for some reason he wasn't moving that

well. He appeared awkward, and his timing was off. Figuring it was something we could work on, we enlisted him anyway. We usually toured less in the spring and spent that time recording. That summer Motown released the second single from *Sky's the Limit*, "I'm the Exception to the Rule," backed with "It's Summer," songs we'd recorded after Eddie and before Ricky with just the four of us.

The scene of Ricky's public debut with the Temptations was the Carter Barron Amphitheater in Washington, D.C. Of course, the shows were all sold out, and on opening night the place was jam-packed. Everything was running smoothly, but the moment of truth arrived when Ricky started singing "Just My Imagination." Instead of singing the first line, "Each day from my window, I watch her as she passes by," he sang something like "Each window, my day . . ." A loud hush fell over the audience, then the booing started. It was a nightmare. The next night the Carter Barron was so empty you could have shot a cannon from the stage and not worried about hitting a damn thing. The word spread all over town: New Temptation Ricky Owens can't sing, and the Tempts are in trouble. We knew we'd have to let him go right away.

We didn't imagine that we'd have to start looking for another tenor so soon, but the trouble with Ricky persisted. A woman we knew told us about a guy she'd seen in Baltimore named Damon Harris. According to her, not only could Damon sing very much like Eddie, but he was also good-looking, a fact that was always a consideration. We got in touch with him and asked him to come over to meet us the next day.

Damon, whose real name is Otis, was quite a bit younger than we, only about nineteen years old when we met. In a funny twist, he had sung in a group called the Tempos, which he'd patterned after the Temptations. A fellow member of the Tempos was Billy Griffin, who later replaced Smokey Robinson in the Miracles. Damon seemed in awe of us. He'd brought along a little list of songs to sing, and he sang a few. While I didn't hear anything particularly outstanding, everyone else seemed to like him a lot.

"I think he's good," Dennis said.

"And I vote that we put him in," Richard added.

"Hey, I think we should keep looking," I said. "Besides, I think the age gap is a little too wide for us. We're twenty-seven, twenty-eight, and he's just nineteen or so. It's going to be hard for him to deal with some things we take for granted."

"He'll learn," Dennis said.

"Yeah, give him a shot," Richard said.

So, the Tempts being a democracy, I relented. Looking back, I probably spoke against Damon more out of frustration with the way things were going generally than out of any feeling toward Damon himself. Damon stuck with us for nearly four years, and for most of that time, he was all right. In the beginning he kept addressing us as Mr. Street, Mr. Edwards, Mr. Franklin, and Mr. Williams, which was nice, but after a while I couldn't stand it. One day I took him aside and said, "Hey, just call me Otis. You make me sound like I'm part of the Over-the-Hill Gang."

If only Paul's problems were as easily solved as the group's. I remember earlier that year going into Paul's room to wake him. As usual, it was in some hotel somewhere, and he hadn't gotten up. Lying in his bed he looked to be in a sleep so deep and heavy that you could think he was dead. I walked to the side of the bed and gently shook him as I called his name. He saw it was me and slowly pulled himself up, then turned to sit on the edge of the bed.

"I feel bad, Otis," Paul said wearily, shaking his head. "You just don't know how bad I feel."

I don't know what prompted that remark, but Paul sounded like he was carrying the weight of the whole world. I didn't know what to say. His general condition, from his failing health and his drinking, had been sliding in recent years, but during the past couple months the change had been unbelievably swift. In addition, it was affecting the group adversely. Even though Paul felt much worse physically, he made no move to stop drinking. As always, we harped on him, mixing messages of concern with dire warnings, but he'd heard it all before. "Man, I can handle it," he always said. "I'm cool. Don't worry about it. I'll be at the show on time." He was missing shows, though, and the ones he did were not always so great anymore. It ate us up inside to see this great performer surrender to his darker side.

Several times Don Foster mentioned that Paul should see a doctor, but Paul always managed to put it off. Maybe he feared that a doctor would only confirm what he felt deep inside, that something in his body had gone terribly wrong.

I don't have any specific remembrance of Paul's last performance with us because there was no such thing as a planned "farewell." We never knew when a show might be his last, but we all felt the day drawing closer. We couldn't face that prospect, and yet as Paul got sicker we knew someone would have to tell him. He was our soul, our creative leader, and the thought of having to go on without him killed us all. Just imagining the look on his face when he heard the news was enough to stop me.

As it happened, though, we never got to that. Someone finally convinced Paul to see a doctor. After examining Paul, the doctor told Don Foster that Paul had no choice but to come off the road. I have heard from several sources that the doctor found a spot on Paul's liver, but I don't know that to be a fact. Whatever it was, though, Paul got the message, and he left the group, although he stayed on the payroll and helped us work out new routines until the end.

Paul's departure meant that within just three years, the group had lost three guys. Only two original Temptations remained: Melvin and I.

Richard came in officially as Paul's replacement and has been with us ever since. Melvin and I always liked Richard's voice a lot.

You'll remember that he sang lead on two of our first tracks as the Distants: "Come On" and "Alright." For some reason, though, certain people at Motown thought that Richard's voice lacked something, so producers never gave him the number of leads we always felt that he should have. From this point on, the overwhelming majority of the leads went to Dennis, simply because Norman's material called for that rough, churchy style.

One of those songs was our fall 1971 release, "Superstar (Remember How You Got Where You Are)," a hard-driving, multipart lead that Norman and Barrett had written with Ruffin and Kendricks in mind. And I don't mean that they wrote it for either of those guys' voices. I hesitate to say that Norman and Barrett were poking fun at Eddie and David or their attitudes, but they were dropping a less than subtle hint. Also on the *Solid Rock* album was "Take a Look Around," the next single and another of Norman's heavy message tunes. Although most of our early-seventies singles were still topping the R&B, or black, charts, they drifted around in the twenties on the pop chart, which was unusual for us. Part of it was that the music business was changing, and the Motown product, the polished entertainer, was being pushed aside by audiences favoring the looser, wilder, more daring performers of the day. We felt the change, and there were times when it hurt us.

The next single, "Mother Nature" backed with "Funky Music Sho Nuff Turns Me On," only went to number twenty-seven on the R&B chart and number ninety-two on the pop, a very disappointing showing. Somewhere along the way things had gotten off track. In the spring of 1971 a new trio Norman produced, Undisputed Truth, scored a huge hit with "Smiling Faces Sometimes," the song that would have followed "Just My Imagination" had Eddie stayed. We'd done the song in 1971 for *Sky's the Limit*. It's been said that we felt Norman was neglecting us by "giving away" material we'd recorded to other acts. In truth, we never objected to Norman recording stuff with other groups. However, we did believe that he was not paying as much attention to the records we released as he should have. In addition, he continued turning up late for sessions and then giving the lead singers hell if they didn't sing a song right on the melody. Norman was a firm believer in one of Motown's formulas for success: "K.I.S.S.," which stands for "Keep it simple, stupid." For example, a producer or a singer might love a great, elaborate vocal riff, but we rarely put them on our records because we knew that most people who bought the records wouldn't be able to sing along to those parts, especially not white folks.

As Norman's stock at Motown rose, he became maddeningly meticulous to the point where we might spend all day and all night in the studio without completing even one song. At one point we met with Berry and expressed our opinion that we'd probably gone about as far as we could with Norman, and that the public's boredom with the same old sound was keeping the singles down on the charts. No one else took our complaints seriously or made any moves to fix things, so we continued with Norman for another couple years, growing less and less happy about it all the time.

For the *All Directions* album Norman gave us a truly strange mix of tunes: a few ballads, including Ashford and Simpson's "Love Woke Me Up This Morning" and Ewan Maccoll's "The First Time Ever I Saw Your Face," an Isaac Hayes tune, "Funky Music," and "Mother Nature," and two songs we fought tooth and nail to not record, "Run Charlie Run" and "Papa Was a Rollin' Stone." The first concerned a relevant and worthwhile subject, white people fleeing the newly integrated neighborhood, and we had no objection to the lyrics. What we hated were the lines Norman made us speak on the chorus. After we sang "Run, Charlie, run," we had to say, "The niggers are comin', the niggers are comin'" in the incredulous tone of voice Norman must have thought white people would use. The first time Norman explained how the song went and what he wanted, I said, "Wait, Norman, you have got to be kidding."

"No," he replied in all seriousness. "We went through this. This is how it goes."

"Man," I said, "we don't want to be singing no shit about 'the niggers are comin'.' It's too much."

Norman, being Norman, wouldn't hear of it any other way, so we recorded it, though we never ever sang "Run Charlie Run" onstage. And we caught some hell for it being on the record.

"Papa Was a Rollin' Stone" was a song we started out hating but eventually learned to love.

Norman put down the instrumental tracks to "Papa Was a Rollin' Stone" while we were out, and when we heard it, we thought it would make a fantastic song—for somebody else. We were just so damned sick of this kind of song. We begged to go back to ballads, but nobody was listening to us. Adding the icing to the cake were the opening lyrics—"It was the third of September, the day I'll always remember, 'cause that was the day when my daddy died." They didn't sit too well with Dennis, since his father had died on the third of September. The whole time we were recording it, we were five very angry guys, and Dennis sang it through clenched teeth. We walked out of the studio that night furious and certain that "Papa" wasn't going to do anything. Once it flopped, we figured, they'd have to let us go back to singing about romance.

Several weeks or so later, coming back from some dates in Hawaii, we stopped at a disc jockeys' convention in Philadelphia. As we made the rounds, stopping in the different record companies' suites, all we heard was "Papa Was a Rollin' Stone" being played over and over and over. The next thing, that sucker zoomed straight up the chart, and in December it became our fourth number-one record, selling over two million copies. The following year, it netted us three Grammies: for Best Rhythm & Blues Vocal Performance by a Duo, Group or Chorus; Best Rhythm & Blues Instrumental Performance; and Best Rhythm & Blues Song. Like I said, it kind of grew on us.

This was the last of our albums on which Norman collaborated with Barrett Strong. I'd known Barrett since we were kids; we used to race each other when he lived across the street from me. I'm not sure what went down between those two, but we didn't see Barrett around much after that. From this point on Norman took his role as writer-producer more and more seriously. On our next album, *Masterpiece*, Norman's picture on the back cover was bigger than ours, and with each album, there were fewer but longer (and longer) songs. By the time we put out our last album with Norman in the early seventies, *1990*, which had only two songs on the second side, we felt more strongly than ever that our fans were being ripped off. People complained to us about it, too. On some tracks our singing seemed to function as ornamentation for Norman's instrumental excursions. When we started reading articles where writers referred to the Temptations as "the Norman Whitfield Choral Singers," we got really mad. Of course, no interviewer who valued his health would call us that to our faces, but the way they talked sometimes, we knew it was what people were starting to think. If there was ever any thought given to us trying something new, "Papa"'s success nipped it.

Shortly after the *Masterpiece* album we made our first trip to Japan. Knowing we had thousands of fans over there, we looked forward to the tour. We enjoyed visiting other countries and learning about their cultures. After so many years, we'd become accustomed to hearing applause when we came onstage, after each number, and—on a good night—a little in the middle here and there. In Tokyo we gave it everything. I mean, we were struttin' it, singing our butts off, really doin' it. For some strange reason, though, the Japanese sat there like they were in a lecture hall. Pretty soon they had us thinking, "What the hell? Damn, maybe we better get out of here and go back home, because we ain't getting it here." We didn't give up, but by the latter part of the show we pretty much accepted that we'd bombed.

At the end of the last number we got ready to walk off, when suddenly we were overwhelmed by thunderous applause. Every single person in the audience stood and yelled at the top of his lungs, and it went on and on. We took more bows than I could count. It was only after we got offstage someone finally told us that this was a typical Japanese response. They believe that it's rude to applaud until the end of a performance.

Even though Paul no longer sang in the group, we saw him regularly whenever we were home. Melvin, Richard, and I kept reaching out to him any way we could, and I know that he and Eddie maintained close ties. Keeping Paul off the road didn't really improve his health; it just kept it from worsening. He still drank, so there were some rough times. As to what was going on in his personal life or with his business, those weren't things we spoke of in any great detail. I know only what I saw: Paul seemed to have lost his spirit.

Looking to branch out, Melvin, Cornelius Grant, and I started our own production company, D.O.C. Productions, Ltd. Our goal was to scout out fresh talent and develop it—write songs, set up recording deals, produce them, and so on. As we learned, it's a very time-consuming job, but before we gave it up we landed a contract with RCA for a trio called Swiss Movement, who recorded our "Take a Chance on a Sure Thing." We were all very excited about it, and one day I played the track for Paul. I guess I was looking for his opinion or his congratulations. Out of nowhere he said, "Hey, Otis, why don't you cut that track on me?"

"Paul," I said, "I don't think we can do that, because it's already committed to RCA. They've paid the money and all."

It was a very awkward, painful moment for us both. Everyone knew that Paul wanted very much to be back in the studio, if not with us, then as a solo. I suppose that in light of David's solo success (Eddie's was still a year or so away) Paul figured that he deserved his break, too. I assume that Motown had the same option to retain Paul as a solo as they exercised with David and Eddie. The fact was that they weren't interested. There was no doubt in anyone's mind that Paul was still a talent, but he was sickly and could no longer perform. By then everyone knew of Paul's problems, and Motown probably didn't see any point in investing in him. Without anything to that effect being said, I think that Paul understood, and it was eating him up. One day out of the blue Paul said, "Man, sometimes I feel like saying fuck it and committing suicide."

I was stunned. "Paul, don't talk like that. Come on, now. It's going to be all right. Don't you even start thinking about no mess like that."

"Well, hell," Paul said. "I'm just tired of sitting around here. You know me, I'm used to being out there onstage. I love it. I miss it."

Although I tried to calm Paul down, I took what he'd said very seriously. I didn't doubt for a second that he meant every word. It struck me then just as clear as day that Paul's mental attitude had gone over into something else.

There was nothing else to say. He was my friend, but a friend who wasn't taking care of himself, who wouldn't or couldn't stop drinking or resolve his personal problems. It broke my heart to see this happen to a warm, wonderful, talented guy like Paul. We later learned that Motown did record Paul on two songs. One of the titles was "I Feel Like Giving Up." Neither was ever released.

We all traveled to New York in mid-August 1973 to attend Damon Harris's wedding. The reception was held in a restaurant on the grounds for the 1964 World's Fair, in Queens. It was a joyous occasion, and we were all happy for Damon and his bride, Tina. After the festivities we returned to our hotel in Manhattan and weren't in an hour when Richard called my room and said, "I just called home. You heard about Paul?"

"No. What's wrong?" I asked.

"They found him dead, lying in the street, near Fourteenth and West Grand," Richard replied, very upset.

"Are you kidding?" It didn't seem possible.

"No, Otis," Richard answered softly. "I'm not."

We were set to fly back to Detroit the following day, but we switched our reservation and left immediately. There's no other way to describe our feelings except to say we were all in total shock, especially when we learned that Paul's death wasn't an accident. The official cause of death was a self-inflicted gunshot to the head.

In those first hours after I heard the news, and countless times since, I flashed back on the last Copa date Paul did with us in 1970 or so. No matter how he felt, usually once he was onstage he gave it his all. It was like the stage was a magic place for him. The one night that I recall especially vividly, he was doing "For Once in My Life," and as he sang it, you could hear that he was squeezing every note for all it had. It was like he was saying, "I may not be here too much longer, but I'm going to do it while I still can." As he came up to the bridge, Adam Clayton Powell, Jr., a former United States Congressman, stood at his table, applauding and crying. The next thing you knew everyone in the place was standing, and the applause kept coming. Pretty soon we were all crying. The ovations just washed over us in waves, and Paul accepted the cheers graciously, like a prince. I remember thinking to myself, "So this is what all the rough times are about. This is what makes it all worthwhile." And Paul was so proud. That's the image of him I treasure: standing on the Copa stage, holding a whole audience in the palm of his hand, looking so happy.

On August 24, exactly one week after Paul killed himself, we attended his funeral at the Tried Stone Baptist Church. Over 2,500 people viewed his body in the days before, and the church was filled with friends and family, his wife Mary and their five children, people from Motown, and as many fans as could get in. Of course, Paul's death brought us together: Melvin,

Eddie, David, Dennis, Cornelius, and I were the pallbearers. During the service David rose to sing one of Paul's special songs, "The Impossible Dream," but partway through he was so overwhelmed by grief that he couldn't continue and Eddie, Melvin, Dennis, and I walked to the front of the church to help him finish. Standing near the head of Paul's open coffin we couldn't make it through either, and after a few moments, we all returned to our pews, in tears.

After the service we carried Paul's coffin to the hearse and took that last ride with him to the cemetery. At the gravesite, they opened the casket again, and before it was closed for the last time, Eddie bent down and kissed Paul gently on the face.

Shortly after Paul died, I was lying in my bed one night reading. For some reason I felt compelled to look up, and standing at the foot of my bed was Paul. He said, "I'm all right where I am, Otis. I just want to let you know." And then he was gone. Talking to Eddie later, I said, "Man, you know, I saw Paul."

Eddie replied, "Yeah, he came to me, too."

Funny thing was, it wasn't scary at all. I believe it was Paul, perhaps not Paul as we knew him here on the earth, but his spirit. And I also believe that what he said was true.

When someone you love commits suicide, you can't help but wonder what, if anything, you could have done to prevent it. I went through a period of deep soul-searching, replaying our conversations in my mind, but what bothered Paul was no mystery. He was a very complex man with many problems and conflicts. By the time he died, I guess he believed there was nothing left for him, and that's the shame. Paul was our pillar of strength, and even today we try to approach things as he would have, with that confidence and sense of pride he instilled in each of us. I've always said Motown, Shelly, Cholly, Maurice King—all those people—as much as they refined and polished us, it was Paul who gave them something to work with.

Now, over fifteen years after Paul's passing, there are still people who believe that his death wasn't a suicide but a case of murder and that somewhere along the way something's been hushed up. I can't believe that. For one thing, except for a few weeks before his death, when people who saw him frequently said that he was in very good spirits, Paul was an unhappy man. He spoke of suicide to me and to several others. It's true that Paul left behind some tax problems, but I can't imagine him being involved in something someone would kill him over. I sometimes wonder if people don't continue speaking of Paul's death as a great mystery because they can't accept the fact that such a wonderful, well-loved person might have suffered so that he couldn't see any other way around his problems. After all, if it could happen to him, it could happen to any of us.

All I know about Paul now is that if he had straightened out his life and were still living today there is no question that he would be a major force in the music business. He had a good heart, he was a good person, and he knew so much. He so often said, "You're only as good as your last show," and we still take it to heart. Every time we pray, we think of Paul. Sometimes when I look back at all that he gave us it's easy to forget that he was about the same age as we were. He always struck me as someone with a very old soul. We still miss him.

Toward the end of 1973 Ann and I decided to end our marriage. The two of us had been drifting apart for a while, and during our time together she had become a Jehovah's Witness, something I didn't join her in. Traveling constantly, I'd often left her at home, and before long jealousy and suspicion took us over. I didn't learn until after we were separated that Ann and my family never got along, so my relatives stayed away. Walking through my home in Southfield, I'd think to myself, "What's the point of having a good life if your family isn't there to share it with you?" I wasn't around enough to keep close tabs on what was really going down, and had no idea about it until my grandmother Lucinda told me. After we separated, Ann went back to working for Ike and Tina Turner.

In February 1974 Motown released "Heavenly" from the *1990* album, a song Richard sang and we all had very high hopes for. It took off up the charts, and from every indication, this was going to be a winner. Unfortunately, it got snagged on music-business politics. Today people claim that some radio station playlists are dictated by consultants, which may well be true. In contrast, back then the disc jockeys ruled the roost and picked what they played. It was the Temptations' good fortune to have always enjoyed the full support of the jocks, especially the black guys. This time it all backfired.

At the same time "Heavenly" was scaling the charts, we were booked for a stand at Bachelors III in Fort Lauderdale, Florida. I'll never forget those shows because Jackie Gleason always came to see us. From the stage I could look down, and right in the front row would be the Great One cheering us on.

Because of our commitments, we couldn't be in Los Angeles for the American Music Awards ceremony, so Ewart Abner, who was then president of Motown, accepted our award for Best Vocal Group. In his acceptance speech, supposedly made on our behalf, he not only failed to acknowledge the jocks' continued support of the Temptations, but went out of his way to thank Dick Clark for always being there for us. We like Dick Clark a great deal, but to cite him, or anyone, really, without thanking those who deserved to be thanked was wrong. We just about died watching Abner give his speech on television that night. We knew it wasn't cool and expected there'd be hell to pay.

Sure enough, when we got to Memphis some disc jockeys said, "We saw the AMAs, and we're happy that you brothers won, but we did not like that speech that Abner gave. We're sorry that we've got to take it out on you, and it's not directed at you personally, but we've got to teach Motown a lesson. We're not playing your record." And they didn't. Despite some gracious gestures toward the jocks on Motown's part, "Heavenly" nosedived and was on and off the pop chart in nine weeks. It was quickly followed with "You've Got My Soul On Fire," a hell of a song that also failed to do as well as it should have.

We were hitting one of those slumps nobody can avoid if you stick around long enough. It seemed that we could do no right. Not to say everything was miserable; it wasn't, but those songs weren't moving like they would have a year or two earlier. It was very obvious to us that people had had enough of hearing the *kung*, *whacka-whacka, chung* sound Norman was noted for. Traveling the world, we heard people's reactions and opinions. We had a tighter grasp of the situation than the people at Motown who were sitting at their desks. The time for a change was long overdue as far as we were concerned, and so we met with Berry about it again. "You all know what's happening," I said. "Our records are dropping off. People are tired of hearing us sing about the world's woes. We need to get back to the ballads." There was no arguing with the numbers, so Berry decided to team us with James Carmichael, who had produced the Commodores.

In the midst of this we also told Berry that we wanted our own publishing company. We were writing songs, which we knew that if the Temptations ever recorded at Motown would be published by Jobete. We called a big meeting, and we stated our case: Basically, we were grown men, and artists, and felt that if we did write anything we should have our own publishing. Berry, who was there with his brother Bobby, clearly didn't like what he was hearing.

"What are you going to do with publishing?" Berry asked. "Who's going to administer it?" He continued running down all the details, and as he got angrier, we could see spittle forming at the corners of his mouth. We looked at one another as if to say, "Whew! We really touched a nerve with this!" We'd never seen him so angry.

The meeting wore on, with the upshot that Berry did not give an inch on the publishing. We left the office furious. Damn it, we weren't kids anymore, and the very least he could have done was meet us halfway. Maybe it wasn't always the case, but by this point he must have known that we knew what was going on, who was getting what size piece of the pie. It was insulting.

In early 1974 or so we all moved out to Los Angeles. As had been rumored, Berry did move the operations out west, and Motown in Detroit all but ceased to exist. It was only a matter of time before we joined him, but it was strange to be so far from our relatives and friends. Los Angeles was worlds away from Detroit, and for some guys the adjustment was rough. Dennis moved first, followed by Melvin and me, and later Richard and Damon. At first Melvin and I had our apartments in Hollywood, on South Doheny Drive. It seemed that moving to L.A. prompted many changes in different guys' behaviors, and for some reason an increase in drug use.

Also that year I met my present wife, Arleata. We were playing the Apollo, and Arleata was brought backstage to meet us, entirely against her will, by a girlfriend with a thing for Dennis. The first time I saw her I thought she was very pretty, and I started a conversation by asking her about her astrological sign, which was then the hip thing to do. We started dating on and off, then after one night we spent talking until dawn, I knew I'd found the one. She still lived in New Jersey, so we kept up a bicoastal romance until she moved out to live with me in L.A. in 1976. We married in 1984.

We turned all of our attention to the new record. We started working on *A Song for You* out at Berry's beach house in Malibu, where we met along with Suzee Ikeda, a former Motown artist who was our project manager, Berry, James Carmichael, and Ron Miller, who had written many hits, including "For Once in My Life," and a few other people. While selecting material, we came across "Glass House," a tune Berry wrote with Ron Miller. We recorded a version of it with Carmichael producing, which Berry played for Jeffrey Bowen. Back in 1967 Jeffrey coproduced the

Mellow Mood album with Frank Wilson before leaving Motown to work with the Holland brothers and Lamont Dozier at their Hot Wax and Invictus labels. There he had worked with Freda Payne, Chairmen of the Board, Honey Cone, and some others.

Jeffrey told Berry he liked the idea of "Glass House" but heard it differently. Berry, being the fair-minded guy he is, said, "Well, you go do a track and let me see what you come up with."

When we heard Jeffrey's take on it, we were very impressed. Not being a learned musician, as Carmichael was, left Jeffrey a little freer to experiment. His version had that elusive punch and directness our latest records had been lacking. Berry decided to give the production assignment to Jeffrey, and we set to work.

Back when we'd worked with Jeffrey on *Mellow Mood* he was in his early twenties but had good ideas and was a pleasure to work with. Before we got too far into recording *Song for You*, however, our relationship with him was so bad that I now consider those sessions some of the most miserable moments of my career. Not to take anything away from Jeffrey as a producer; he has fine ideas and knows what he's doing. His problem is that he cannot handle people, and before long we started noticing a bad attitude on his part.

Everything came to a head one night when we were recording the vocals on one of the album's most beautiful songs, "Memories." Some parts of it called for a very subtle, wistful style of background singing that must be done in perfect unison. We were trying our damnedest to get it just right, and were coming close, when Jeffrey exploded.

"Naw, man," he yelled. "I mean, shit, you all just ain't doin' it." He chewed us out like we were school kids and generally acted like an asshole.

We kept saying, "Just give us a little time. We're going to get it. Don't worry." But Jeffrey wasn't hearing any of it. He didn't view his role as helping the artist but bullying him, which simply doesn't work.

One evening we were in the recording studio, and Jeffrey was in the control booth. There's an intercom between the two rooms so that whoever's in the booth can talk to people in the studio, and apparently Jeffrey didn't know that he'd left it on. The next thing I know I hear Jeffrey's voice coming over the speakers saying, "Shit, if I was still working with the Chairmen of the Board and not these guys, I wouldn't have to put up with this crap!"

I could not believe my ears. I expressed my intention to kick Jeffrey's ass then and there, but the other guys in the group talked me out of it. Not surprisingly, things weren't flowing, so we called it a night and all went home. Exhausted, I lay down to rest but my body kept racing. When I turned over on my right side, suddenly my whole body broke into shaking like nothing I'd ever felt before. When it kept getting worse, I phoned Steve Martin, a brother who was working for us. "Steve," I said, "there's something wrong. I can't stop shaking. Please come over."

Steve and his wife got there within minutes and took me to Hollywood Presbyterian Hospital, where I saw a doctor. He examined me and asked some questions, then said, "Look, whatever it is that's bothering you is not worth it. Your nerves are shot. You better stop whatever this is about, or you're going to get yourself in very bad shape."

He prescribed some tranquilizers, but I took only a couple and threw the rest away. I couldn't stand that heavy, lethargic feeling. There wasn't anybody I was jeopardizing my health for, least of all Jeffrey Bowen.

When Berry heard what happened, he called for a big meeting between all of us, Jeffrey, and some Motown executives. Berry was concerned about what had gone down, and the gist of his message was that things shouldn't have got to that point to begin with, and this is not how recording should go, and so on.

When Berry was finished, I said, "Hold it, we are not through here. I really want to emphasize that what I went through last night is not something I'm ever going through again. I'm gonna let you know right here, Berry, and you know I don't mince words. This kind of thing happens one more time and I'm gonna kick this little motherfucker's ass." I glared across at Jeffrey.

"No, man, I didn't mean it," Jeffrey said, backtracking.

"Well," I said, "everybody else sitting here, when six o'clock comes, you all go home, while we, the Temptations, are up all hours recording and God knows what. And the last thing we want to hear from anybody is those kind of unnecessary nasty-ass remarks."

"Well," Berry said, "we hope it doesn't get to that."

"It better not," I replied, "because I'm the one whose body was shakin' last night, and I don't want any of you to get the idea that just because we sat here today and ran everything down that it's all hunky-dory. Here's the period after the sentence: Jeffrey, if you ever do anything like that again, I'm gonna clean your plow."

With that the five of us left. Of course, recording the rest of the album was somewhat strained, but Jeffrey kept in line most of the time.

The next problem on the agenda—and there always seemed to be at least one—was Damon. Like any guy who joins the group, Damon went through a year-and-a-half probation period on straight salary. During that time Damon was respectful, easy to work with, and a generally great guy to have around. Once the probation ended and the big money started coming in, things changed.

Berry happened to be sitting in the control room while we were recording "Glass House," and when it came time for Damon to sing his line, he was very lackadaisical about it. "Now, come on," Berry said to Damon, "give me some *ummm!* You know, sing it like you mean it. Give me a little gusto."

Damon sang the next take the same lazy way.

"What's wrong, man?" Berry asked. "I want that thing. Give me some fire."

Damon said, "I'm tired."

Berry shot me a glance, then said, "I do not like his attitude. You all get rid of him." This was the first time Berry ever interfered with the group personnel. Damon was stupid because anybody who knows Berry will tell you that he won't stand for that kind of nonsense. We had an engagement that evening, so we let Damon finish his singing, figuring we'd deal with it later.

This wasn't Damon's first time acting up, though. During a group discussion he gave me some lip, which I didn't like. The change that came over him was caused by the usual thing: the inability to deal with suddenly having money and being a star. A couple of times we tried to talk to him, but nothing seemed to penetrate.

The most outrageous incident spawned by Damon's budding ego happened onstage at the Apollo. One of Damon's featured numbers was "Love Woke Me Up This Morning," and after the song we'd vamp a little so that Damon could cut loose. Melvin, Richard, Dennis, and I were behind him doing our steps, when Damon starts talking about what a pleasure it was for us to perform, and so on. Then he announced, "And we, the Temptations, would like to thank you all for making it possible for us to buy these fine mink coats and beautiful cars and homes and diamonds . . ." The boy would not shut up. The four of us couldn't believe our ears, but we kept on stepping, and gritting our teeth. Nobody wants to hear that kind of nonsense down in Harlem, and you could see it was going over like a ton of bricks with the crowd.

Back at the hotel we decided that he'd crossed his last line with us. He had to go. When we got back home to Los Angeles we called a meeting at Melvin's apartment and that's where we told Damon that he would have to leave the group. We told him that neither we nor Berry liked his attitude, and that whatever he was up to doing was doing him more harm than good. Damon was shocked; he had no idea it was coming. Several times we had tried to talk to him, but to no avail. We were sorry to have to drop him, but, again, no one man is greater than the group.

Despite all that went down while we were making *A Song for You*, it's still my favorite record and one of our biggest commercial successes, with two R&B number-one hits—"Happy People" and "Shakey Ground," and a third R&B Top Ten, "Glass House." It also included the first Tempts-penned song since "The Girl's Alright with Me," "I'm a Bachelor." The only track on the record I wasn't crazy about is "The Prophet," a tune with lyrics based on the work of the Lebanese poet Kahlil Gibran. With all due respect to Kahlil's fine work, the song just didn't cut it. We had recorded "Soulmate," which was very beautiful and had the same feel as "Memories" and "Firefly," but Suzanne De Passe and Jeffrey felt it wasn't strong enough. It was later included on the *25th Anniversary* collection.

We had planned to come off the road for a while to freshen up the act, work out some new staging, and get ready for an appearance on *The Midnight Special*. All we needed was our first tenor. Back when Melvin, Cornelius, and I were working with the Swiss Movement, we met Tony Silvester, who was then a member of the Main Ingredient. He'd left the group and was producing, having just hit with former Drifter Ben E. King's hit "Supernatural Thing." We happened to be talking one day when he mentioned a singer named Glenn Leonard. We stopped by his house in New York and picked up a tape of Glenn singing, which knocked us all out. Tony knew how to contact Glenn in Toronto, where, as it turned out, Glenn's group, True Reflection, had just broken up. When we got back to L.A., we called Glenn and arranged for him to meet us.

Melvin and I went to the airport to pick him up. Our longtime friend Yvonne Fair came along to check out Glenn from a woman's point of view. She stood apart from us in the terminal, and after Glenn arrived she gave us the high sign meaning that he'd passed that test. We all climbed into the car for the drive to Motown vice president (Creative) Suzanne De Passe's apartment, and Melvin and I started singing. Glenn jumped right in and sounded great.

At Suzanne's we introduced Glenn to Berry, Lon Fontaine, and some other people from Motown, and they all seemed to like him. It was in many ways a perfect match. We had dates coming up, so we worked him to death getting ready, but he hung in there.

He took his new job quite seriously and was very excited about being in the group, maybe too excited. The day of his debut, Glenn had so psyched himself out that he broke out in hives. He soon recovered, though, and stayed with us for nearly eight years.

In September of 1975 we traveled to Manila to give a concert and see Muhammad Ali's big fight with Joe Frazier, the famous Thriller in Manila. We had met Ali before, in New York, when we spotted his bus and he invited us to come in and hang with him. We boarded his bus and had a nice talk with him. He was busy changing clothes, since, as he explained, he was chasing some girl, but he was kind enough to tell us that he was one of our biggest fans.

The fight took place in the Philippine Coliseum, a big, tin-roofed building with no air-conditioning, and it was hotter than hell inside. Everybody, it seemed, thought that Frazier had it sewn up, but we felt differently. The five of us sat together in one of the rows closest to Ali's side of the ring. All around us people chanted at the top of their lungs, "Frazier, Frazier, Frazier!" We figured, screw this mess, and started screaming, "Ali, Ali, Ali!" There was a while to go before the actual fight, and as we were sitting there, Ali's friend Drew "Bundini" Brown came to take us backstage. He said that Ali wanted to see us.

Back in the dressing room, Ali was sitting as his trainer Angelo Dundee bandaged his hands in preparation for the fight. "The Temptations," he said, greeting us. We made a little chitchat, then Ali said, "Man, do me a favor. I'm kind of nervous. Why don't you all sing 'Ain't Too Proud to Beg' so I can have a little fun now."

We broke into it and gave it our all. When we finished, Ali gave us a smile, and all of his helpers and handlers broke into applause. We wished Ali the best of luck and returned to our seats to watch the match. Of course, Ali won on a technical knockout after fourteen rounds, and later Bundini told us that our singing really soothed Ali, and maybe even helped him beat Frazier. We heard that there were a couple of minutes before the bout when Ali seriously considered not even coming out.

That evening we attended a dinner at the presidential palace, where we were guests of President Marcos and the First Lady, Imelda. When we got to the palace we went up to Ali to offer our congratulations, and he said, "Don't shake my hand too hard," so we shook his fingertips. After a while the music began and people got up to dance. I may dance onstage, but almost never out in public otherwise. When it comes to that I'm the same wallflower I was in junior high.

I was sitting there, enjoying myself, talking to the other Tempts, when suddenly Imelda Marcos approached our table and took my hand.

"I want to dance with you," she said, smiling.

I shot a glance at the other guys, and somebody whispered, "You can't turn down the First Lady, Otis. Get up."

So Imelda and I took a few turns on the dance floor, and the whole time my mind was off in one of those dazes. What was I doing here, dancing with the First Lady of the Philippines? I wanted to pinch myself. I don't know what went down with the Marcoses, politically speaking, but she was a very nice-looking, pleasant lady then, and not a bad dancer.

The country had been under martial law since February, and our flight barely made it out to Hong Kong before they closed the airport. I thought that Hong Kong was one of the most beautiful places I'd ever seen, situated as it is up on a mountaintop. On the drive to our hotel we saw little kids practicing their t'ai chi ch'uan. Having always been a big fan of the martial arts, I found it exciting to be in Bruce Lee's hometown. One of the wealthiest cities in the world, Hong Kong was in many ways quite amazing. Before we left our hotel to walk over to a nearby disco, though, a promoter warned, "Watch where you step."

"Why?" I asked.

"You might step on someone's home," he answered matter-of-factly.

Sure enough, we crossed the street and found poor people living in their "homes," dirty little mattresses thrown down in the gutter. It was one of many, many sights that I have seen and not quite ever been able to believe.

8

The tremendous success of *A Song for You* was a great boost, and we knew that even though Jeffrey Bowen was not our favorite person, he was a good producer for us. It only made sense to follow up with Jeffrey again. The problem was that Motown didn't have Jeffrey under contract and we couldn't wait until he was before we started the next album. While we were on tour in Europe, Motown issued what I consider a totally bogus album, *House Party*. The only decent tracks on it were "Keep Holding On," which the Hollands wrote and produced, and two of our compositions: "Darling, Stand by Me (Song for My Woman)" and "What You Need Most (I Do Best of All)," a tune I came up with after being inspired by the sight of a woman I knew. When I received a telex in Holland listing the *House Party* tracks, I was furious. Here we were coming off one of our best records, and Motown was slinging out a mismatched collection of, pardon my French, shit. It seemed in character with Motown's philosophy that some people will buy anything. Not to say that we were happy when the record flopped, but we were secretly hoping that Motown had learned a lesson: the public expects the Temptations to uphold a certain standard of quality.

We got right down to working on *Wings of Love,* but before too long it was obvious that there would be problems not only with Jeffrey but with Dennis too. Before we were too far into it, we'd catch Jeffrey taking Dennis aside and saying things like, "You don't need to be with them guys. I can cut you into things, Dennis. You could be bigger on your own." It was the same old story.

The real proof of the pudding was in the record, where Jeffrey either didn't bother to record our background vocals or, where he did, mixed them so far down that we might as well not have bothered. Jeffrey was trying something "different": a big, smooth choral sound that, good as it was, didn't suit us. When he wanted to record Dennis alone, we relented; anything to get the thing finished. We were surprised that he took that approach, considering how well he'd captured our rougher side on *Song for You,* but by then I'd given up trying to figure out Jeffrey. The only track released as a single was "Up the Creek (Without a Paddle)," which Jeffrey cowrote with a couple other guys, one of them being Sly Stone. When Sly came to the studio, we told him how much we admired his work, and so on. But it was obvious that Sly's day in the sun had come and gone. Because of some legal complication, Sly is not credited on the song, but it is his.

We knew for sure that this one wasn't going to make it either. I was up at Berry's house listening to it with him, and he seemed quite pleased. When I said, "It ain't going to do nothing," it threw him for a second.

"Why are you saying that?" Berry asked, surprised.

"You've got only Dennis on those tracks, and people aren't going to go for it. You can't have a Temptations record without the Temptations' harmonies and carryin' on or without Melvin's bass. I think releasing this is going to be a big mistake."

Berry immediately picked up the phone and called Jeffrey. "Otis don't believe the album is going to amount to anything," Berry told him before handing the phone to me.

"Jeffrey," I said, "it's not going to work." After I explained why I felt that way, he made some excuses about taking us in a new direction, a new sound, blah, blah, blah. Sure enough, it was one of our poorest-selling albums in years. About the only positive things I can say about the experience is that we weren't going to be working with Jeffrey anymore, and Berry finally saw that we should have a crack at producing ourselves.

We were in the process of recording *The Temptations Do the Temptations* when our contract came up for renewal. It was 1976, and Motown was a totally different place. For one thing, most of the original artists had defected or faded—the original Marvelettes broke up in the late sixties, the Four Tops moved to ABC in 1972, Martha and the Vandellas parted ways in 1973, Gladys Knight and the Pips moved to Buddah the same year, and the Miracles left the label in 1976, a few years after Smokey went solo. Around this time, though, Berry's biggest loss was the Jackson 5. The boys' father, Joe, negotiated a handsome deal with Epic Records. Only Jermaine Jackson, who was married to Berry's daughter Hazel, stayed behind.

In Motown's eyes, it wasn't the artists' frustration or anything the company did that drove us away but the evil influence of "outsiders," like outside managers, outside accountants, outside attorneys. They made it seem as if we weren't smart enough to see for ourselves what was happening. In the case of the Miracles and the Jackson 5, Motown held an attorney named Abe Somers responsible. Beginning in 1970 or so, we started taking care of our own business. One result was that our accountant discovered $300,000 in "missing" royalties, and that is when Abe became the

Temptations' attorney. We trusted him implicitly and took for granted that he would represent us in our negotiations with Motown.

Though we still had two years left to go on our current contract, we met with Barney Ales, Suzanne De Passe, Tony Jones, Suzanne's assistant, Ralph Seltzer, Motown's legal counsel, and Suzee Ikeda, our project manager, to discuss their ideas and our feelings. It was a general sort of feeling each other out. Barney then casually asked, "Well, tell me, who is you guys' attorney?"

I'd no sooner got the words "Abe Somers" out of my mouth than Barney jumped out of his seat and slammed his fist down on the conference table.

"Get rid of him!" Barney screamed like a man possessed. "The sooner you get rid of him, the better things will be for you all."

Everyone was stunned. We'd known and liked Barney for a good while and never saw him carry on like that. Then he pointed at Ralph and shouted, "And you! If he calls you, don't you respond. Do not return any of Abe Somers's calls. I'm sick of this Abe Somers!"

After a moment, I said, "Is there any other business here? Because we are not getting rid of our attorney. You can just forget that. We have nothing else to talk about." The five of us got up and left.

Later that day Suzee called me to talk about what had gone down. "Sue," I said, "what happened today is just not right, and this could easily be the straw that breaks the camel's back. What gives Barney or anybody there the right to tell us who to have as our attorney? We've spent years having our careers and our money handled by people we didn't like. If we give up our attorney, we're screwed. Then where does it stop? They can forget all about it."

"No, you're right," Suzee said. "I'm surprised at Barney. I'll call Berry."

Berry was vacationing at La Costa, a luxury resort, but he

called me the next day and said, "Otis, I am truly sorry that it went down like that. I will call Barney. He owes the Tempts an apology for that."

"Well, Berry," I said, "that's all fine. But we are not getting rid of our attorney." We hung up and I waited for Barney's call.

The next morning Barney was on the line, rambling on and on.

"Barney," I said, "it's just not right what you said. And we are not leaving Abe."

"Well, you know that's you guys' decision. If I offended you guys . . ." and so on. I listened and listened to this yacking, but never once did Barney apologize for what had happened, and I could tell that he had no plans to either.

Finally I said, "Well, I guess there's nothing else for us to say. Good-bye."

Berry didn't call me again, and after discussing it with the other guys, we decided to finish our album and start shopping around for a new label. After fifteen years on the roster, we felt many twinges of sadness at the thought of leaving "home," but what was going down was part of something bigger than just Barney not liking our attorney.

Suzee later told me that after our meeting with Barney, Marvin Gaye was in to discuss his upcoming contract. Now here was Marvin, one of the most talented men in the business, who had made Motown God only knows how much money. No one knows for sure what was said behind closed doors that day, but when Marvin stormed out of the office, Suzee saw tears in his eyes. Something was going terribly, terribly wrong.

When I notified Suzanne De Passe that we would be leaving Motown, she told me that we still owed Motown some things in terms of records and time on the contract. "Whatever it takes to work it out," I said, "work it out. We've got to go, because the way we're being treated is just not right."

Next thing I knew Lee Young, Jr., another Motown executive was on my line saying, "Mr. Gordy asked me to call you guys. Mr.

Gordy said that whatever it takes to keep you guys here, let me know. He doesn't want to lose you. So what will it take? What kind of money are you talking about?"

"Lee, you know it's not about money. Listen, I have a son, and I would not be able to look him in the eye and deserve his respect knowing the way Motown is treating us. We're not kids anymore. We're grown men, seasoned artists. It's about respect and dignity. None of us is a multimillionaire, you know, so there's always room for more money. But money isn't going to solve it. And as long as that attitude is there, we don't want to be."

"Okay," Lee replied. "I'm sorry it has to be this way. We'll get to work, and I'll get back to you."

The first problem that cropped up was the matter of our name. Back in 1966 someone suggested that it would be a good idea for us to write to Washington, D.C., and register a copyright on the name the Temptations. I filled out the forms and mailed them off, feeling good that we were protecting our interests, even in a small way. A couple weeks later I got a letter from the copyright office informing me that our application arrived two weeks late: a Mrs. Esther Gordy Edwards had already applied and was granted ownership of the name the Temptations. Unlike some other acts, we'd never signed a contract with a provision granting Motown those rights.

In our case, when we found out what they'd done behind our backs, we were upset. At the time, though, we were on the rise. It didn't seem worth creating a fuss over. But by 1976 those days of being grateful and accepting were long gone. We fought, and Motown eventually relented and reversed the rights to our name to Melvin and me. Lee Young, Jr., signed a special document to that effect, which I took home, framed, and still have hanging up in my house. Just like an invitation I received to dine with President Jimmy Carter in the White House, it hangs as a reminder of how far we'd come.

All the while this was going down, we were finishing our album. Producing ourselves was quite a challenge, but we enjoyed having the chance to prove we were more than just singers. We worked with our friend Benjamin Wright, a producer who also writes and does a lot of work with Gladys Knight and the Pips. Having to wear so many hats—writers, producers, singers—was exhausting but ultimately rewarding. *The Temptations Do the Temptations* remains one of our favorite albums, and it got some wonderful reviews.

With us leaving, though, Motown had no incentive to promote the new album. It was focusing most of its efforts on Jermaine's latest solo effort, which ended up not doing that well, while ours peaked in the fifties. Traveling around the country we met lots of disk jockeys who told us that they loved the record and couldn't understand why Motown wasn't pushing it. Even without the label's backing, the single "Who Are You (and What Are You Doing the Rest of Your Life)" made a respectable showing on the black chart, so we felt somewhat vindicated. But our time with Motown was over, and we began to look ahead.

Abe was considering offers from CBS, Warner Bros., Polydor, and Atlantic. We were especially attracted to CBS because it had the muscle and the machinery to break and support records. The Jacksons were doing well there, and our friend Kenny Gamble had cleaned up with CBS distributing his Philadelphia International label. I'll never forget one day when Melvin and I were sitting in the office of Ron Alexenburg, a CBS executive. A call came through saying that some I.R.S. guys were in the building to attach the income of a member from a famous and well-respected black group for failure to pay taxes. As I sat there, Ron called down to the accounting department and instructed them to cut the government a six-figure check. The government guy came up to the office, and after Ron handed him the check, he said, "Here. Now get the fuck out of the building." Of course, this was before the record industry as a whole hit a big recession. But it wasn't even the money, though; the act in question certainly sold enough records to warrant that kind of loyalty. Just the idea that a label looked out for its artists like that impressed us.

The longer we negotiated with different labels, the clearer we saw how pitiful our deal with Motown really was. Here we'd fought for years to get the privilege of sharing our songwriting income with Jobete, and none of these other labels wanted even a penny of our publishing. To say it was an eye opener is an understatement.

Unfortunately, in the midst of what seemed to be a new beginning, we had to let Dennis go. His troubles were getting out of control; his attitude was generally intolerable. A couple years later, when his mother confessed to me that she had spoiled him rotten because he was an only kid, I said to myself, "Aha!" We loved Dennis; he's a good brother, but we just couldn't take his nonsense anymore, and at the same time he felt the urge to try it solo, so he went back to Motown.

We seriously considered adding Ollie Woodson at that point because he was a tremendous singer, but the chemistry wasn't right then, and for some strange reason he had orangish hair, which was a little rough on the eyes. We weren't sure that he would blend in with the Tempts' visual image, so we passed on him.

Dennis's replacement came to us on the recommendation of one of the Impressions, Sam Gooden. He sent us a tape, and we liked what we heard, so Louis Price became the twelfth Temptation. Louis, who was born in 1953, was considerably younger than the rest of us, but he worked hard and could really sing. Louis's voice was a very smooth, fine baritone, like Jerry Butler's, and worlds apart from that gritty sound Ruffin and Edwards had. Louis could be innovative with his singing, which seemed like a good direction for us at the time. We realized we were taking a chance toying with our sound, but it seemed worth the risk. We felt the need for a big change and were looking forward to making a fresh start, but the question was, doing what?

CBS courted us, but their signing the Tempts was contingent on being able to get Kenny Gamble and Leon Huff to produce us. The prospect was very exciting, and we felt that Kenny and Leon and the Temptations would be a match made in heaven. Kenny and

Leon Huff's Philadelphia International label was super-hot then, producing Harold Melvin and the Blue Notes, Teddy Pendergrass, MFSB, the O'Jays, Lou Rawls, and the Jacksons. Kenny was finishing the Jacksons' *Goin' Places,* after which we were going to discuss him producing us. We waited several months, continuing to tour, but when we finally got to Kenny he said, "I'm really sorry, but once I finish this Jacksons thing for Epic [a CBS label], I'm not doing any more outside projects. It's just not worth it to me. I'm going to have to stick with concentrating on my own acts."

That was a pretty big blow, and we were disappointed, of course, but through our friend Benjamin Wright we met Hillary Johnson, a top executive at Atlantic Records. Atlantic, which always had a good track record with black music, made us a fantastic offer, so we signed with them in the fall of 1977, nearly a year after leaving Motown. Neither of our two albums with the label, *Hear to Tempt You* and *Bare Back,* did as well as we hoped, though neither was a total loss. Working on the first album we met a songwriter named Ron Tyson. He'd written and produced for the Four Tops, the Dells, the O'Jays, Harold Melvin and the Blue Notes, and Curtis Mayfield. He cowrote seven of the album's nine tracks, and his scratch vocals on the demo tapes were impressive. He was a fine first tenor who sounded a hell of a lot like Eddie Kendricks. Making the record was a lot of fun. But unfortunately, the Ron Baker, Norman Harris, and Earl Young production team couldn't quite get a fix on us. They'd done a lot of disco, and combining that style's strong percussion and swoopy strings with Louis's smooth, mellow-sounding voice resulted in an odd mix.

Bare Back was a Holland brothers production, so it was kind of like old-home week. Among the guys we worked with for that were Eddie "Bongo" Brown, the arranger Paul Riser, and, of course, Eddie and Brian. The tracks sounded hot enough, and the tunes were all solid, but while it did better than the previous record, it couldn't compete on the disco-dominated charts.

Between the two albums' disappointing showings and the fact

that Hillary Johnson, our chief corporate ally at Atlantic, split after the first one, we were cast adrift. A third album, produced by Ron Kersey, was recorded, and I feel it is the best of our Atlantic efforts, but it's in a vault somewhere. We started thinking that perhaps Atlantic wasn't the place for us, but our contract still had some time on it. In the midst of this crisis Kenny Gamble called, saying he wanted to talk about working with the Temptations, and asking if Melvin and I could fly out to meet him in Philadelphia.

Thinking he wanted to talk to us about leaving Atlantic for Philadelphia International, Melvin and I flew into Philly. Everything was very pleasant; then Kenny got a little more specific about what he had in mind when he mentioned working with the Temptations: not Melvin and I with Glenn, Richard, and Louis. What Kenny was proposing was a reunion between Melvin, me, and Dennis and David and Eddie. It wasn't what we expected.

Melvin and I looked at each other, surprised. "Well," I said, "I don't think so. There's a lot of stuff that's gone down between us, and while I don't harbor any bad feelings myself, I don't know if all these wounds are healed enough for something like this." Frankly, Melvin and I didn't think that David and Eddie, who by then had strong solo careers going, would be interested.

"If I could make it happen," Kenny said, "what then? Just tell me, would you do it?"

"That's fine, Kenny," I said, "but what are we to do with Glenn, Richard, and Louis? These guys have been good to us, and they have families. We can't just cut them off like that, so you'd better be prepared to make some restitution."

Kenny understood, and we left things like that. In the meantime, we were still touring and getting ready to perform in Europe that fall.

Of all the places we've visited, perhaps the most fascinating and memorable was Africa. That summer we traveled to South Africa to perform a series of concerts, on the condition that we would appear only before integrated audiences. Although every place we

played the sight of whites and blacks sitting, even dancing together, warmed my heart, one show in Johannesburg really stands
out in my mind. From the stage we could see people in the crowd
starting to move a little, then to get up and even to dance together,
probably for the first time in their lives actually interacting socially
and peacefully with someone outside their race. And the looks on
their faces were something to see. It was as if for those fleeting,
precious moments the human spirit transcended the government's
repressive and inhumane apartheid laws. When we saw several
blacks and whites hugging one another, I cried and thought to
myself, "God, music does it again."

In some ways it was similar to countless scenes we witnessed
across America in the early sixties. But there was no fooling
yourself: this was not America. Blacks in South Africa have
virtually no civil rights whatsoever. Though blacks comprise
seventy percent of South Africa's population, they cannot vote,
own land, travel without permission, or work without special
permit. All blacks are confined to separated areas called *ban-
tustans*, which cover only fourteen percent of the land. The words
and the figures are appalling in themselves. If you come from the
United States, though, it's impossible to truly understand the black
South Africans' plight without seeing it for yourself.

While we were in Johannesburg we arranged to travel the ten
miles south to Soweto, a group of segregated townships where over
850,000 blacks live in tin-roofed houses and shacks. Only a
quarter of them have electricity; medical care is shamefully inade-
quate. During our day there we were surprised to learn how many
of the people knew who we were; some even brought out copies of
our records for us to autograph. Several people told us that they
were happy that we had come, and that because of the government's policies, they were essentially cut off from the rest of the
world and felt that blacks in America had forgotten about them.
They wanted people to see firsthand how they were living.

Toward the late afternoon the sky grew black with coal-oil

smoke so thick the fumes could knock you out. Our hosts told us to go inside, knowing that the fumes would make us ill since we weren't used to it. Inside we were served a wonderful meal of meat and a cooked-grain dish called poi, which is not the same thing as the Hawaiian food of the same name. It was very tasty, and we quickly caught on to their dining customs. Most everything is eaten with the hands, and everyone shares, eating from one another's plates.

I left South Africa with a sense of anger and pain unlike any I'd ever felt before. Until the day South Africa emerges as a democracy that includes the black majority I will never set foot there again. At the same time, though, I do not regret having gone and seen for myself what goes on. While there I visited the home of the great Zulu king and warrior, Shaka Zulu. Until his assassination in 1828, Shaka galvanized the native Africans and successfully held off the advances of the Boers, the early white settlers. Among the many books in my library are two biographies of Shaka Zulu, which never leave my home. The continent of Africa is the motherland of my forefathers. I have no way of learning exactly where my great-great-great-grandparents were taken from, but I brought back a single stone, perhaps the only tangible reminder of my own roots I will ever possess.

Shortly before we were set to depart for Europe that fall, Melvin was shot by a car thief. Melvin had just finished having his hair done and had gotten into his car and started it. For some reason he left his car running while he walked a woman he knew from the salon to her car. In those few short minutes, a stranger got into Melvin's car and started to pull away. Melvin ran back, jumped in on the passenger's side, and tried to pull the car keys out of the ignition. It was only after he got into the car that he realized that the man was armed with a gun. The thief was driving and shooting at the same time, and before it was all over, Melvin had been hit twice, in the hand and the leg. As the gunman aimed, Melvin pleaded for his life, and when he recognized Melvin, he pushed him out of the car and sped away. He told Melvin that the only thing that kept him from killing him was that he knew he was one of the Temptations.

I was home that night when I got the call that Melvin had been shot. I went numb with fright. It took a while, but Melvin did recover. Every day I thank God that he wasn't taken from us. Unfortunately, Melvin wasn't able to go with us to Europe, so we had to make the trip without him. It was just me, Richard, Glenn, and Louis.

Because Shelly still worked for Motown at the time we left, we had been forced to find a new manager. For a while we were with Sid Seidenberg. A few months before the European tour Sid Bernstein, the promoter who brought the Beatles to Shea Stadium in 1964, told Seidenberg that when he asked people in Poland which American acts they would like to see, our name came up most often. The prospect of visiting a foreign country under Communist rule was certainly fascinating, so we agreed, and a one-date "tour" of Poland was arranged.

From the moment we set foot on the plane that would take us to Gdansk it felt like we had stepped into another world. The Polish-run airline was the same one that the U.S. Olympic boxing team was flying when they crashed in 1980. Looking around inside the cabin of the old, creaky plane, we could see that the whole thing was coming apart. The takeoff seemed to take hours, and it felt like we weren't ever going to get off the ground.

The moment we landed officials took away our passports, leaving us at their mercy. It's hard to appreciate what having your freedom means until you're put in a situation where every move you make is determined by someone else. Once we got to our hotel, we were informed of other rules. None of the doors had locks, and if two unmarried people wanted to hang out together after ten at night, it would have to be in a public area, like the hotel lobby. You might wait days to be able to make a call to the United States.

The next day, as we were standing out in front of the hotel waiting for the car to take us to the show, dozens of strangers walked up and began touching our clothes. We're all very clothes-conscious, so we were dressed pretty spiffy, but the way these people looked at us and oohed and aahed, you'd think we were wearing suits of platinum. I'll never forget the looks on their faces. They appeared totally amazed that such things could even exist. They couldn't seem to touch us enough. On the way to the show we passed what we were told was the best clothing store in the city, and the clothes were the ugliest, drabbest things I'd ever seen. It was pitiful.

The show was part of a music fair, and although we have no idea how those people had gotten ahold of our records, they sang along to every song and waved copies of our album jackets in the air. The applause wouldn't stop, and we almost didn't get off the stage. It was probably one of the most appreciative audiences we'd ever played for. They hung on every single note and were so into the music, you'd think they'd never heard anything like it before. I realized how much we take for granted in America. I couldn't imagine living in a society where pop music was only available through the black market. What did that government think it was protecting its people from?

We were so hyped up after the show that we looked forward to hanging out in the hotel lobby and maybe getting to talk with some of the people. We noticed one girl sort of hanging to the side and looking us over. One of the guys noticed her immediately and was very interested in getting to know her better. She seemed to have the same thing in mind, and several times she made tentative moves to approach us. The first time, a man who worked for the hotel, maybe in security, said something to her in Polish and she backed off. A few minutes later, though, she was back, and the man spoke to her again, but in a much nastier tone. Seeing the way the man spoke to the girl was getting Glenn a little hot under the collar, and I could see that this could easily turn into the kind of situation you didn't want to be in with somebody else holding your passport. After the man spoke to her the last time, the girl glanced at us with a shocked expression, then walked out into the night. I casually strolled over the desk clerk, who spoke English, and asked him what the security guy had said. He explained that she'd been told that we all had VD and that she would catch it from us. It was just one indication of how low some people would stoop to keep us more or less isolated from the citizens.

The next day we were waiting at the airport to catch a flight to Amsterdam. We were hanging out with our road crew when somebody put on a tape of L.T.D.'s song "Holdin' On." I guess the tension got to us, because we started acting silly, lining up single-file, holding the guy in front of us by the shoulder, doing this funny little walk up the stairs, and singing at the top of our lungs. At first the Poles didn't know what to think, then they started smiling and laughing, and finally they just broke out, like, "Yeah!" What struck me as strange about it was that they had to think about responding and smiling, almost like they couldn't be too happy, or smile too much, or show too much emotion. It made me very sad.

Shortly after this, the Soviet government invited us to perform in Russia. Even though the money they offered was just okay, it would have been another of those once-in-a-lifetime experiences and, naturally, we did feel some sympathy for people living under Communist rule. It's been said before, but it's true: Music is the universal language. Around that time, though, B. B. King had some trouble leaving the U.S.S.R. after a tour and, just thinking about the tension in Poland, I said, forget it. Perhaps everything would have been fine, but it didn't seem worth the risk.

We were looking forward to Amsterdam because our road manager, Ralph Garcia, promised he would take us to the Street of Dreams, a red-light district unlike any other in the world. Prostitutes there sit "on display" in picture windows, usually in lounging outfits, and we learned that many of them have husbands and boyfriends, and this is just considered their job. We strolled around, fascinated, until one of our guys saw a woman he wanted to get next to. He walked over to her, she said something to him, and he came back, shocked. She'd turned him down, saying something about black guys being too big, taking too long, and not paying enough money, but in much more colorful language. We couldn't believe it and almost died laughing right there on the street. Passersby looked at us like we were crazy.

Since things didn't look too promising on the Street of Dreams, we kept walking until we came to a theater with a live sex show. Curious, we walked in. There on a regular stage was a big bed and behind that was a little band. As we walked to our seats we heard, "Da, da-dum, da-dum-dum," and I thought to myself, "No, this can't be happening." But after a few more bars, there was no question—the performers were doing their very live, no-doubt-about-it sex act to "Papa Was a Rollin' Stone."

In March 1979 Atlantic released the last single from *Bare Back,* and shortly after we agreed to terminate our relationship. It was a friendly parting, with neither side casting blame and all of us accepting that things just had not gelled. Suddenly we were label shopping again. On top of that, Louis was fading out of the picture. It never came down to us telling him he was out of the group; there was an unspoken understanding that this wasn't the best situation for him or us. He and I still keep in touch and have a good relationship today. Around then, coincidentally, Dennis started calling. His solo career hadn't happened, Motown dropped him for not taking care of business, and he was making noises about coming back to the Tempts. After many long discussions we agreed to bring Dennis back, although we made it clear to him that we weren't going to tolerate any nonsense. Dennis holds the official record for being fined more than any other Temptation. But for all the trouble he sometimes got in, we loved him; it was good to have him back with us again. Career-wise, too, it made sense; after so many years and hits, it was Dennis's voice people expected to hear.

We considered offers from Warner Bros. and Polydor, but Kenny Gamble pursued us most avidly. During the initial discussions, his offer was very attractive, but as we got closer to fixing it in writing, things changed. Nothing was happening except for some talk that we might try to do a gospel album. We were as far from a deal as we'd been in a long time.

We were still touring, of course. One day I went to Melvin's apartment for a rehearsal and found Glenn looking like he'd been hit by a truck.

"Damn, bro," I said. "You look like you had a hell of a night out."

Glenn didn't say much back, then Melvin grabbed my arm and said, "Come here. Let's take a ride. I have something to tell you."

As we drove around Hollywood, Melvin told me that Glenn called him the night before, asking him to come get him. Apparently Glenn got his butt kicked in some seedy after-hours club. The guys who'd beat on Glenn told Melvin that if he hadn't been one of the Temptations, he'd have gotten it even worse. After everything that had been going on, this was too much to handle. Glenn was having personal problems and had been drinking.

"Okay," I said. "I'm sick of this crap. We're trying to hold everything together, and these guys are always up to something. I never know what to expect anymore. Let's just call up Kenny, and if he can get the reunion together, we'll go for it."

I hadn't seen David or Eddie since Paul's funeral. Things between us weren't strained because we didn't really have a relationship. Everything was incommunicado. If we saw one another in a club or on the street, it was just "Hi, how are you doing?"

Melvin and I flew into Philadelphia again, Dennis came from Cleveland, Eddie from Birmingham, and David from Detroit. Kenny put the five of us up in a nice hotel and paid us a per diem. He meant business.

▲ The Temptations shortly
after Dennis joined us in
the summer of 1968. *(Left
to right)* Melvin, Paul,
Dennis, Eddie; *(seated)*
me.

▲ From our not-so-great debut at the Flamingo Hotel in Las Vegas, October 1968.

▲ Our big fashion show at the L.A. Forum (we also sang there). *(From left)* Dennis, Melvin, Eddie, me, Paul. *Don Paulsen*

▲ Ever the fashion plates. *(Left to right, standing)* Dennis, Eddie; *(kneeling)* me, Melvin, and Paul. *Courtesy George Schlatter Productions*

▲ Celebrating another one of my twenty-ninth birthdays, at the Flamingo Hotel.

▲ Who are these masked men? And why? It's still my birthday. *(From left)* Melvin, me, Paul, Dennis, and Eddie.

▲ Our first engagement at the Los Angeles Forum and one of the highlights of our career. *(From left)* Eddie, Melvin, Dennis, me, and Paul.

◄ Dennis and Paul.

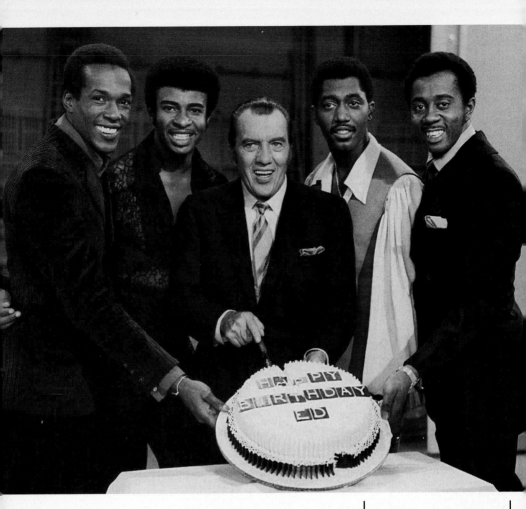

▲ Helping Ed Sullivan celebrate his birthday.

▶ At Tricia Nixon's Masque Ball at the White House, May 1969. *White House Photo*

▶ Music knows no political bounds: shortly after with Edward and Joan Kennedy *(far left)*.

▲ Going gold.

▲ Me visiting with two members of the Lovin' Spoonful. *Don Paulsen*

▲ Doing what we do best.

▲ Here we are in Europe, proving that we worked just as hard on our civilian threads as on our stage uniforms. *(From left)* Paul, me, Eddie, and Melvin.

▲ With my second wife, Ann Cain.

◄ With our friend Elton John.

▲ Here we are with former world heavyweight champ and great fan Muhammad Ali, many years after we sang "Ain't Too Proud to Beg" for him in Manila.

◄ Believe it or not, I was quite proud of these horsehide pants—at the time, that is. *Courtesy Motown Record Corporation*

▲ The party at New York City's Studio 54 commemorating our signing to Atlantic Records in 1977.

▲ Another birthday bash, during the Atlantic period. *(From left to right, standing)* Jamey Miller, a former road manager, Glenn Leonard, Richard Street, me, Louis Price, Sid Seidenberg; *(seated)* Cholly Atkins, our choreographer, and Melvin. *Courtesy Sidney A. Seidenberg.*

▲ As ever, on the road.

▲ After we appeared with Cybill Shepherd and Bruce Willis on *Moonlighting*, Bruce asked us to sing on his album and perform with him at the Palace Theater. *(Top, from left)* Bruce, Melvin, me, Ali Ollie Woodson, Ron Tyson. *(Bottom, from left)* Melvin, me, Cybill, Bruce, Ron, and Ali Ollie on the *Moonlighting* set.

▲ Here we are with our manager and friend, Shelly Berger, celebrating our twenty-fifth anniversary with dinner at Le Dôme, Los Angeles. *(From left, back):* Richard, Ali Ollie, Melvin, me, *(front)* Ron, Shelly. *Photo © 1986 Michael Jacobs/MJP*

▲ Shelly, Melvin, Ron, myself, Bill Tannen, Richard, and our good friend, Billy Dee Williams.

The day the five of us met at Kenny's office was a little tense. You could feel that everyone was uncertain and supercautious. There wasn't any anger or hostility, but that old warm feeling was never rekindled. I expected to feel a little sadder about it than I did. I found myself thinking that if Kenny could pull it off, it would be great, if not for us, then certainly for our fans. Over the years probably hundreds of people had pulled up alongside my car or stopped me in the street to ask when we were all getting back together again, so there was no question that, at least financially, a Temptations reunion would be a success. On the other hand, if it didn't pan out, Melvin and I would have to make our own situation work better. As it turned out, Kenny couldn't deliver, and after one thing and another, it all fell apart.

During a group meeting that fall I said to the guys, "Don't be surprised if we start hearing from Motown soon." I don't know what made me say it; I just felt it. Sure enough, Smokey called and we arranged a meeting. Even though he was living right down the street from me, I'd seen him only at social things. We hadn't really sat down to talk for quite some time, so when we set this meeting, I knew what was coming.

"How do you guys feel about discussing coming back to Motown?" Smokey asked.

When he said that, the other four guys turned toward me and looked, waiting for my answer. It was no secret that our leaving Motown had left a bitter taste in my mouth, and in Motown's as well.

"Well, Smokey," I said. "You know it's about business. We're willing to listen to anybody and we're trying not to be closed-minded."

"Good," he answered. "I'll set up a meeting at Motown, and you guys can come in and talk."

It's important to remember that Smokey wasn't offering us a

deal, or even the possibility of a deal, just a meeting. Since we'd left Motown, they'd hired a man named Don Ellis as head of the Creative department. One day we found ourselves back at Motown, in a room with Berry, Don Ellis, Lee Young, Jr., and some other higher-ups. Why Berry wanted us back was probably partially sentimental. He'd managed to hang on to Stevie, Diana Ross, Marvin Gaye, and, of course, Smokey, and I think it was important to him to have back as many of the old mainstays as he could. Smokey also seemed to want us back. Don Ellis, on the other hand, made it clear that he didn't want us at all. He felt that the old days were over and that Motown should be moving on.

Berry gave us a speech about why it would be good for us to re-sign with Motown and all about "the Motown spirit." Melvin, for one, responded to that. After Berry finished, all eyes turned to me again. Melvin, Richard, Glenn, and Dennis had been listening to me go on about Berry and Motown so many times. But it's one thing to speak your mind to your buddies and another to let it be known to everyone else, especially the person whom you feel is most re-sponsible. They were staring dead at me with a look that said, "Okay, Otis, you're so good at shooting your mouth to us, let's see you tell Berry."

"Berry," I said, "before we get into anything else, I've got to let you know how I really feel about this thing."

"Sure," Berry answered, "go ahead."

I took a deep breath and blocked out everyone else in the room. Looking Berry straight in the eye, I said, "Well, as artists we need to be freed from hassles and games in order to excel. We've got to feel that people are behind us, and personally, I have felt from time to time that you did not like me." Everyone listened quietly as I ran down all of my complaints about the way Motown had treated the Temptations over the years.

When I finished, Berry was chewing his tongue, a little habit he has, and said, "You articulated that very well. So let me run it down to you. First, I do like you, and I've never said that I didn't like you." And then he continued talking for a while, giving us his side of the story.

When we'd both finished, I felt like someone had poured cool water over me. The tensions eased, and it did feel like we were home again. Later that day Suzee Ikeda called and asked me what I'd said to Berry, because he told her that he liked and respected me for being so honest with him. It seemed that we had turned a page.

The next day we got together to start rehearsing songs. The five of us were sitting in Berry's conference room, a large space dominated by a huge table surrounded by chairs, waiting for Berry to arrive. Suddenly the sliding oak doors at one end of the room opened, and there stood Berry, making his dramatic entrance. He stared at me, then smiled and said, "Come into my office."

We followed Berry through the oak doors into his office, where he sat down in his chair. After a couple more minutes he looked at me, made that little smacking noise with his lips, and said, "Maybe one day, Otis, you would like to have this here seat."

"No, Mr. Gordy," I replied. "Thank you, but I have a lot to learn before I sit there. That's the hot seat. But thanks for the compliment."

"Okay," Berry said, "let's get to work."

Berry had a song he wrote for DeBarge but decided against recording with them because it was too hard-sounding for them. He told us he held on to it because he knew that we'd be back. In terms of the sound, lyrics, and general mood, "Power" was classic Tempts, the kind of track we'd been dreaming of. We started work on recording, even without a contract, something Berry usually never did. But he had faith that it would all work out.

Not surprisingly, during the contract negotiations, though, the ghost of old Motown reared its ugly head. During our time with Atlantic, we'd formed our own publishing company, Tall Temptation Music (ASCAP), which we were not about to give up. We had every intention of continuing to write and record our own songs, as we had on our last Motown album. Abe Somers was working things out, and, for our protection, told Motown that we wanted only a one-album deal. This drove Berry, who likes to work multialbum, multiyear deals, crazy. When Berry couldn't change Abe's mind, he called me.

"Otis, I just got off the phone talking to your attorney, and he only wants to give me a one-album deal. I want you guys back.

"Now, let me tell you about lawyers," Berry continued in his best father-knows-best tone. "Your attorney works for you, you know. You listen to what he's saying, but bottom line, you have to make the decision and tell him what you want to do."

The whole time Berry was talking, I was listening, calculating, thinking, "Now, is he telling me this to get me to go along with him, like in the early days, or what?" Berry kept talking, saying, "So, I'm telling you that I don't want no one-album deal, and I want you guys back. Now, how do you feel about that?"

"Well, Berry, we want to be back."

"Well, what I think you have to do, Otis, is call up your man and tell him to work it on out."

"Okay," I said. "Now, Berry, what about our publishing company?"

Berry sort of stuttered and stammered for a minute, and I could hear Lee Young, Jr., who was in on the conference call, chuckling quietly. "Publishing company?" Berry exclaimed like he'd never heard of such a thing. "I mean, you guys ain't had no hits. What do you need a publishing company for?"

"Berry, it ain't always going to be that way. Jeez, if everybody had that kind of pessimistic attitude, there wouldn't be very much getting done, would there?"

I heard Lee Young, Jr., stifle a giggle. After a second, Berry gave in.

"Well, all right. Lee, work it out with them. We'll do a split deal with them."

"Thank you, Mr. Gordy," I said.

"Okay, man," Berry replied, like he always did. We were back on the Motown roster.

It was 1975, and we had just finished a show at Shady Grove, near Washington, D.C., when one of our security guards brought me a note. It read:

"My name is Sherry Hanes, and I just spoke to your father, Sonny One."

I was stunned; this was no prank. Nobody knew about Sonny One but me. I told the security man to find Sherry Hanes and bring her backstage. When she came back, we talked, and she said, "My folks live right up the street from your father. In fact, I talked to Otis just the other day. He talks about you often, and he said he would like to see you." I took down her number and address.

I wasn't sure what to think. In the twenty-five years since I'd left Texarkana, I'd only been back once and had totally lost contact with Sonny One. Not that I had anything against anyone there, but I had a new life in Detroit. Deep in my heart, though, I knew that I was living off my memories of Texarkana. As I got older I would find myself thinking back to those days at Sunset Elementary School, learning to ride my bike, finding out about girls—all those wonderful things. Now and then I thought about my father. A father myself, I had learned how important a child's love is. I promised myself I would go to Texarkana the next time we had some days off.

Of course, like everybody else when it comes to this kind of potentially heavy thing, I put it off. It was never the right time, it seemed. Finally in 1980, I decided to go, and Melvin, being his wonderful self, said, "Well, I'm going to go along with you, Otis, to see your daddy." Even though Melvin and I have had our rough times, he's a real friend I can count on.

Of course, everything in Texas was different from what I remembered. The population of Texarkana had doubled, and many of the people and places I'd cherished were gone. My cousin

Calvin had drowned years before; the haunted house had been demolished. It was thirty years later. The first day we were there my cousin Delores prepared a big dinner for us, and my father came. Everyone called him Otis, and so did I. Initially everything was very awkward. He was seventy-five years old, a retired carpenter and fix-it man who'd made a decent living for himself and his wife. We sat out in the backyard and talked. I never really knew him as a kid, except to look at him and say, "Yeah, that's my old man." Looking at his face, I could see the resemblance. It was strange, but comforting in a way.

I gave him a Temptations tour jacket, and we embraced. I tried to tell him that regardless of how things were between us, I had no resentment. I didn't really know him and he'd never really done anything to me. I know a lot of people would hate having a father who was like Sonny One, but I didn't and I told him that, which seemed to make him happy.

I ended up doing most of the talking because Otis was extremely shy, and, I think, had some regrets about the past. No matter what I said, it seemed that he'd reply with "yep, yep, yep" and kind of look down in his lap or off into the distance. As I was talking, I'd catch him looking at my face as if he couldn't quite believe it was me, but when our eyes met, he'd fix his gaze off somewhere else again. Melvin sat there with us the whole time.

One day we went over to see his house. It was a nicely kept, quaint little place that he'd done a lot of work on. When we walked inside I saw that all along the walls my father had put up pictures of the Temptations. It almost took my breath away. Later some of my relatives told me that he was so proud of me. He just couldn't express himself. When I told him that I was touched that he'd kept those pictures, he replied, "Yep."

During the course of our talking he asked about my mother and I told him that Hazel died a few years back. He said, "I often wondered how you and her were getting along." That was about all he had to say on it, but I guess that was okay. After all, it happened so long ago. You could see that he had deep feelings about many things; he just didn't know what to say. The day we left I called him and told him that it was great seeing him, that he was all right with me, and that I loved him no matter what happened.

A couple years after that Delores called to tell me that Otis had cancer. Foot surgery kept me from attending my father's funeral. But I look back on those few hours we shared and can say that there was no unfinished business between us, that he died knowing that his son loved him.

9

Within three months of our official re-signing to Motown, *Power* was in the stores. The title single got off to a hot start, but in the wake of the Miami riots so many pop stations pulled it from their playlists that it died. These things always work like a mile of falling dominoes, and less than a few weeks later "Power" was gone. The ironic thing about it is that the song tells people to be informed, to think, to vote, and not to follow self-appointed leaders blindly.

Next out were "Struck by Lightning Twice," then "Take Me Away," a theme song from the movie *Loving Couples*. While we were still selling out shows all over the country, our records were stalling out, and even those that had scaled the black charts weren't matching that success on the pops. Radio formats were becoming so specialized and tightly focused that the playlists became segregated, just as they had been before the sixties.

Time for another change. For years we'd been interested in working with Thom Bell, a former protégé of Kenny Gamble and a successful producer in his own right. When the opportunity arose, we grabbed it. Thom, Linda Creed, and some other writers composed some truly beautiful songs. We loved working with Thom and we were happy with the album, but lacking that trademark Tempts sound, it was doomed to a so-so run, and didn't even crack the Top 100. Every shift in direction or attempt to move ahead entails some risk, but if we hadn't taken on new sounds, we'd have been gone long ago.

The rumors that the "classic" Temptations would be reuniting kept bubbling up in the press and around the industry. Nine times out of ten, there was nothing behind it, but as the years wore on and old Motown came into vogue, producers began grasping just what a goldmine such a reunion might be. Jimmy Bishop, a promoter who years before had been a top-dog disc jockey at WDAS in Philadelphia, knew of Kenny's attempts to put us back together again and thought he could pull it off. Every now and then I'd get a call from Jimmy telling me that he could get the money and the backers, and so on. I heard him out the way I'd listen to anyone, but I couldn't decide how I felt. Even in the few hours Melvin and I spent with Eddie and David in Philadelphia, we were egg-shelling it, making special efforts not to say the wrong thing, use the wrong tone, or do anything that would be misinterpreted.

One day Jimmy called to announce, "I think I can pull the reunion tour off. I talked with David and Eddie; they are of a mind to do it."

At the time David and Eddie were not recording as frequently as they had been in the early to mid-seventies. They still performed, but it was safe to say that their commercial peaks were years behind them. Jimmy said that David and Eddie were both basically receptive to the idea, but they, especially Eddie, wondered how we felt about it.

"Well, Jimmy, tell them we will sit down and talk about it. If we can make some money and enjoy ourselves, sure."

After having worked with other managers during our time away from Motown, we were very pleased to be back with Shelly Berger. When he left Motown to start his own management firm in 1981, we made the jump with him. Since we'd left Berry in 1976, the label had become less of an all-purpose record company/management firm and basically given up trying to wear every hat. We made a handshake deal with Shelly, which remains in force today.

After one of Jimmy's calls, I talked to Shelly about the reunion idea, and he agreed that it was worth pursuing. We arranged for Jimmy to bring David and Eddie to Lake Tahoe, where we were appearing at Caesar's. Things among us were a little tense, especially with Glenn, who had to be wondering how far this reunion thing might go and if it meant he'd have to leave. One night we were finishing the show with "Power," and when we got to the last verses, we introduced David and Eddie. There we stood together for the first time in over fourteen years, and it was like someone had cast a magic spell over the crowd. Even in our peak, at our prime, we'd never gotten a reaction like this one. People were so excited, and it wasn't like they were on some nostalgia trip. They really loved us. And I have to admit that for a few minutes I felt myself falling back in time to those old days. I was very happy to see that, and thought everyone sounded good together. Motown worked out all the details for us to record a reunion album and then kick off a national tour. It wasn't discussed too much early on, but I believe most people around Motown, and perhaps David and Eddie as well, were looking at the reunion not as a special thing unto itself, but maybe a test to see if they might be able to join us on a permanent basis.

First thing we did was start recording. Rick James wrote "Standing on the Top," setting the tone for the occasion. The lyrics were upbeat, positive, and confident, and the melody, complete with Rick's trademark punk-funk backing, rocked. We'd worked with Rick on his *Street Songs* albums and admired his work. Between his long braided locks and lyrics that celebrated sex and drugs, he was everything you couldn't have been at Motown a decade before. We liked Rick and thought highly of him as a producer, but he was wild.

Motown got some great press mileage out of the reunion idea, and expectations for the record ran high. But aside from "Standing on the Top," the album was disappointing. It seemed to us that the situation called for something considerably better thought-out than a collection of different songs recorded by a variety of producers. At the time we were recording, though, we had fun. In many ways, it was good to be back with David and Eddie.

When it came time to shoot the *Reunion* album cover photo, the photographer had the seven of us all decked out in classic black tuxedos and getting out of a yellow Checker cab. A Checker cab? If you asked me, the reunion called for something more along the lines of a Rolls-Royce Silver Shadow.

We rehearsed with Lon Fontaine in a space that belonged to a local church. The church rented it out to other performers, television series, and movie studios. We spent a good month and half working our butts off, getting those old steps down and learning new ones. Sure, we were all breathing a little harder, but we were still doin' it, and that's all that mattered. It was a good time for all of us. I sent for my son, Lamont, to come out and stay for a while. During breaks in rehearsal, we'd play basketball. Lamont had become a good athlete, and he could shoot some baskets. He'd grown up to be a good-looking boy; girls loved him. I was very proud of him.

Being together with Eddie and David gave us the opportunity to talk about things. It rarely got too heavy, but in the course of our conversations I learned some things. One day after rehearsal I was driving Eddie and David back to their apartments when Eddie said, "Otis, man, you should never have changed."

"Yeah," David agreed, "you should have never changed. You

should have been more disciplined, because when we knew you were going to be on our asses, you had us going. Guys like us need that kind of discipline to keep it together."

That's something I never expected to hear. It made me think back to what a hard-ass I'd been early on and how I'd slacked off in the later years. As much as I took my responsibility seriously, after a certain point it just wore on me, and I guess I got tired of being the class monitor. Of course, I'd still chew somebody up for being late or slacking off, but I didn't approach it with the same vigor as before. And I never in a million years dreamed that someday David and Eddie would thank me for fining the hell out of them and jumping on their asses for all kinds of infractions. I just said, "Thank you," and kind of smiled to myself.

So in many ways we were happy to be working with David and Eddie again, but we couldn't escape our past, and while some of the bitterness might have been forgiven, I don't honestly believe all of it was forgotten. During rehearsals one day Eddie said, "I felt as though when David and I left the group, the group should have stopped. You all should have just quit singing after we left."

I really couldn't believe my ears. "Man, are you kidding me? We live in a world that's lost kings, queens, and presidents, and the world is still going."

Eddie didn't say anything else about it. It never occurred to me that he regarded the fact that Melvin, Richard, Dennis, and I had carried on—and were still carrying it on, although admittedly with some interruptions—as some kind of betrayal or personal affront. It opened my eyes.

Despite this, Eddie was fine to work with. He never missed a rehearsal or a show, and did his job beautifully. The problem, again, was David. The tour kicked off early that spring and closed in early November. At the beginning, everything ran smoothly. I think we were each on our best behavior, trying to keep things cool. Whatever happiness the reunion brought us started unraveling when we hit Detroit. I felt that I was watching a rerun of a bad movie: the riffraff, the hangers-on, the leeches seemed to be materializing out of thin air, and, as in the old days, they all gravitated to David. Our fee was contingent on all seven of us doing the show; for every man who didn't go onstage, the group was docked thousands of dollars a night. David missed the first three shows at the Premier Center in Detroit, and the promoter was on our case. We were letting down the fans and losing money. During all our talks about getting together, this was what I feared. It was one time I was sorry to be right.

There was no talking to David, but because he was still tight with Eddie, I took Eddie aside and said, "Man, we are out here to make money, not lose it. I'm riding it out, Eddie, but please believe me, if David don't get his act together, you guys can forget this reunion going on after this tour. We're not putting up with this shit."

Eddie understood, but he knew as well as I did that David wasn't about to change his ways for anybody, least of all us. Over the years I'd talked to him until I was blue in the face, and Eddie did try. The infuriating thing was that we knew David knew he was hurting all of us. He just didn't, or couldn't, care. By the time fall rolled around, I regarded the reunion not as a once-in-a-lifetime dream come true but an exercise in torture. I had decided early on that if it came to this, I was fading out. I wasn't getting myself all worked up and sick trying to straighten out Ruffin. There wasn't any percentage in it. And besides, Dennis wasn't exactly toeing the line, either.

How David and Eddie felt toward us and Motown was made crystal clear during a meeting between the seven of us and Jay Lasker, who was then Motown's president. Jay just wanted to have a talk with us and discuss Motown's plans for us—the usual stuff. As we were sitting around a table, David walked in with a takeout breakfast and sat down on the floor. Being polite, Jay said, "David, here, sit at the table."

"No," David replied, "I'll be all right here on the floor."

Then Jay made some remark about Detroit, which David took the wrong way and responded to by raising his voice and carrying on as if he'd been insulted personally. Right after that, Eddie hopped out of his seat and started saying, "Later for this shit. I'm a grown man, and you're not going to treat me like a kid, like you did before."

"Well, Eddie," Jay said, trying to cool him out, "please sit down and we'll talk it all over."

Eddie said something truly rude, then he and David stormed out of the room. Melvin, Richard, Dennis, Glenn, and I sat there looking at each other. Later that day Jay called me and said, "We aren't working with them after this." I understood, and agreed. Looking back and knowing how Jay felt about us, I should've joined David and Eddie in cussing him out.

The strain of disagreement left each of us with frayed nerves. But our ties to one another ran deep, even in the face of conflict.

I remember boarding the bus while on tour in Chicago. David came on after me. Tension was running sky high. He pointed an accusing finger at me. "And you!" he shouted. But then he broke down. "Ah, buddy, buddy." He sat in one of the front seats and started to cry. I was speechless, so I just stood there beside him, rubbing his shoulders, trying to let him know that I cared about him.

"Oh, Otis, Otis, man," he said, sobbing. "I just don't know what's wrong with me. I don't know what's wrong with me, man. Please somebody help me."

"Yeah, Ruffin, yeah," I said softly. "It's going to be all right."

But it wasn't. As much as I tried to reach out to him, time and bitterness had created a shell, and David lived inside it. Every once in a while we'd have a moment like the one on the bus, where he'd open up and drop that damn belligerent attitude. But just as quickly, he'd close up again. David was far beyond my reach. Back in June he'd pleaded guilty to a tax-evasion charge, and he had a date for sentencing in early November, right after the reunion tour ended. A judge sentenced him to six months and a day and slapped him with a $5,000 fine. Even if everything with the tour had run beautifully, Ruffin's legal troubles would have quashed any plan for something more permanent.

By the time we finished our last date, I'd had it. In one of those twists of fate, the tour ended at the Westbury Music Fair, the very same spot where, so many years before, Melvin and I resolved to stick together. The important thing was that we were still sticking together. As for David and Eddie, I'm not sure what they wanted. An apology? For what? Here time had changed everything and nothing.

Right after Christmas I called Eddie to tell him that it was official: we were going back to the current Tempts lineup. He wasn't happy to hear it, but I don't think it came as a big surprise, either.

Toward the end of 1982 we started work on *Surface Thrills*, another of our more adventurous albums. Produced by Dennis Lambert and Steve Barri, it was dominated by what I call the "white rock" sound—lots of synthesizers, drum machines, out-front guitar breaks. It made for an interesting detour, but a detour nonetheless. The next record, *Back to Basics*, while not a blockbuster, marked several important changes, the arrivals of Ron Tyson and Ollie (later Ali Ollie) Woodson (who appears on one track), a battle of the groups with our old, dear friends the Four Tops, and a "reunion" with Norman Whitfield, who produced five of the eight tracks. He wrote the album's hit single, and one of my favorite ballads, "Sail Away," which was Ron Tyson's record debut as a Tempt.

We'd noticed Ron for some time, and when Glenn started falling out on us during the reunion tour, we resumed what was threatening to become a perpetual search for the first tenor.

One day, out of the blue, Ron phoned me. "Man, I hear you're looking for a tenor," he said.

"Yeah, we are. Do you know one?" I asked.

"Yeah, I do," he replied.

"Oh, yeah? Who?"

"Me!" he answered, laughing.

"Wow, Ron. I would have never guessed that you would say that. Are you really serious?"

"Of course I am," he said.

"Well, Ty, I'll keep that in mind. We're going to Fort Lauderdale, and I'll call you then." We all liked Ron, who is one of the sweetest, most easygoing guys in the world. Of course, we knew of his writing projects and him having little groups, but for some reason his name just never came to mind when we thought of replacements.

I called him from Fort Lauderdale, and after a few delays, he flew down from Philly to audition. We almost knew before he sang for us that we wanted him, but we went through the motions anyway. He agreed to join up with us after the reunion tour ended.

Bringing Ron in was one of our better moves. Not only is he a great tenor, one I'd rank right up there with Eddie Kendricks, but an excellent songwriter. Plus, having been in the business for so many years, Ron knew the lay of the land. He'd been around the big time, so it wasn't something that was going to work any changes on him. He had his head screwed on right.

Probably the biggest event of 1983 was the *Motown 25* special, commemorating the label's first quarter century. During the days of rehearsal and the final taping I saw people I hadn't seen in years, and everywhere I turned I seemed to be facing another memory. More than once I caught myself tripping back into the past, thinking about how it was when we were all young and ambitious, starting out together.

Walking around backstage I ran into Marvin Gaye. We'd hardly seen him at all since 1976. We heard that he'd split to Hawaii, then Europe, where he wrote the material for his comeback album, *Midnight Love*. I regarded "Sexual Healing" as one of the most wonderful things I'd ever heard. I remembered driving along a

Detroit street one day in 1971 when "What's Going On" came over my radio. It so amazed me that I had to pull over and park my car until it was over.

As well as I'd known Marvin from before, I was somewhat in awe of him this day. Of course, after he was shot to death by his father in April 1984, just over a year later and one day before his forty-fifth birthday, the press portrayed him as a tormented genius on his way back, but it was only half true. As long as I'd known Marvin, he always seemed to be haunted; a beautiful man, a genius, but truly tortured. Shortly after he died, his closest friend Harvey Fuqua stopped by Shelly's office and took me aside.

"Otis, I want to tell you something," he said. "Marvin was on a death wish. He wanted to die. He was tired."

That may have been so, but when I last ran into him, he seemed in good spirits.

"Where the hell you been?" he asked as we embraced. We couldn't talk too long because we had to get ready. While I was getting my makeup done, my mind drifted back to twenty-some years before, to me and Marvin sitting at the piano in the old Hitsville studio. You'd often find him sitting down there, just playing whatever came to his mind.

"Sit down here," Marvin said. "Let me see how good your ear is."

I sat down on the bench, and Marvin ran down some notes and chords, and I'd sing whatever he played. "You have a good ear," he said. He was a talented and sweet, wonderful man.

Mary Wells, the Miracles, Martha Reeves, Jr. Walker, Stevie, Smokey, the Supremes, the Jacksons—the whole "family" was there. Even though no acknowledgment of them made it onto the final program, those who'd passed, like Paul and Flo, were deeply missed. How proud Paul would have been to see us there. Maybe he did. For some it was less like a homecoming than a little visit. Motown's old guard had continued to dwindle; even Diana Ross had left Motown for another label back in 1981.

Most people regard Michael Jackson's appearance as one of the show's highlights, and it was. I couldn't look at him without remembering the first time we met. Being out of town so much, we'd just heard rumors about these five little dynamos. When we finally met face-to-face, which is a funny way to put it, since my face was about three feet up from his, he and I formed an instant mutual-appreciation society.

I'd always known Michael to be a sensitive, kind person. One time we coheadlined an Operation PUSH benefit for Jesse Jackson in the late sixties with Michael and his brothers. The crowd got so wild that security hustled us off the stage and into a paneled U-Haul truck, slammed the doors, and drove us to safety. It was pitch-dark inside, and there were no seats, so we had to hold on to the metal bars running up the inner walls. I heard Michael's little voice asking, "Where's Otis? Where's Otis?"

"He's in here, Michael," someone said.

A second or two later the light came on, and Michael looked up at me as if to say, "Okay." Like everything was cool, because I was there. I was touched by his concern. There's not much I can add to all that's been said about his records. They're great, and I'm very proud to see that Michael's done so well.

Another guy we hadn't seen in years was Bill Cosby. In the sixties, he'd tell people about us and get them to check us out. His friend and *I Spy* costar Robert Culp came to see us at the Whiskey-a-Go-Go in Los Angeles, and after the show he said, "I like you guys, but all the Cos talks about is the Temptations, the Temptations." Cos gave us an even bigger compliment once when he told Berry, "You can make a whole lot of changes to your company, but do not mess with the Temptations."

In those years he and I played tennis together, and Melvin and I would sit in on his recording sessions. He was every bit as witty and funny in real life as he is onstage. We were hanging out at his house in Beverly Hills when he announced that he and his family were moving to Boston. Having just discovered California's wonderful climate, I asked him why. He replied that making love is better when it's cold outside.

For the *Motown 25* special, someone thought it would be cute to present the Tempts and the Four Tops together in a little battle, like the ones we did back in Detroit. We switched off between medleys of our respective hits, then they'd sing parts of ours and we'd do parts of theirs. In the middle of the taping, though, Dennis and Levi Stubbs really got into it, and seeing Dennis singing, "I can't help myself, I love you and nobody else" to a gloating Levi was pretty funny by itself. We got such a good response that after the show I said, half-kidding to Duke Fakir, "Maybe we should take this out on the road."

"You're right," he replied. "We should sit and talk about that."

"You serious?" I asked.

"Yeah."

"Then let's get our managers on it," I said, thinking this would be good for a few dates. By the time it was over, the T 'n' T tour ran for nearly three years and went all over the world.

Now, being cooped up with your own guys can be tough enough, let alone somebody else's, but we all truly loved one another. And being pros, we knew how to keep little things from getting in the way. One thing about hanging with those guys, you had to know how to cap or your ass was grass, especially with Levi around. Each of their guys has a close friend in one of our guys. My personal favorite is Levi, who's a wonderful guy, but almost untoppable, pardon the pun, when it comes to being a wit. One day in New Zealand I tried to crack on an outfit he was wearing— red and green, if you can believe it—by addressing him as "Christmas," when without missing a beat, he turned around and said, "Yeah, and Otis, and when that shit you're wearing comes back in you'll be in style."

I remember seeing them back in the fifties, when we were still the Distants, or whatever. They were very hot, and sort of like the Primes in that their style was very sophisticated and refined without being stiff. They often played the Flame Show Bar, and every now and then I'd work up the courage to stick my head in the door, just to see what was happening. Of course, someone at the door always chased me away because I kept trying to peek. There were fine women there, too, but that's another story.

We once appeared with Duke, Levi, Obie Benson, and Lawrence Payton in the early sixties at a little club, and they did a routine with Ray Charles's "What'd I Say" where they'd all go down to the floor and jump up into these fantastic moves. It was something to see. I couldn't believe how well they were moving then and hoped we'd get to be half as good.

The Temptations are still dancing onstage, despite the ravages of time, but the Tops are very open about their less exhausting presentation today. As I write this, the Tops have been together without a single personnel change for over thirty-five years. As one of them told me, "We're too old for that shit now. We just get out there and sing." But that's enough. Back in Detroit, we considered them hot competition, and during the T 'n' T tours it was clear that they hadn't lost their touch. We love their records, and with the exception of maybe one other group I know, we think the Tops are the greatest.

Right after the *Motown 25* taping, we got down to completing *Back to Basics*. We'd started having trouble with Dennis during the *Reunion* sessions, with his showing up late or being messed up from partying. All I could think was, "Oh no, not again. He can't be blowing it a second time." But he was, and we knew from experience to start lining up a replacement rather than wait for the inevitable.

Melvin's mother, Momma Rose, was good friends with a Bobby Goodnews, Ollie Woodson's father. Melvin, who's always been very close to his mother, had kept her up to date on our problems with

Dennis, and she offered to talk to Goodnews and put Ollie in touch with us.

We were in Atlanta when we decided that Dennis had crossed the line one time too many and was going to be leaving. The whole situation made me absolutely furious. That a great talent like Dennis would let distractions make him stray struck me as the dumbest thing in the world. To earn good money making yourself and thousands of people happy was, to me, a dream come true. That guys like Dennis couldn't grasp this never fails to confound me. But, what the hell, he blew it.

We met Ollie in Atlanta, and he auditioned for us. He'd done something with his hair, so he looked much better. Richard asked him to squall for us, and he squalled; the audition was over. We told him to be packed and ready to leave for Los Angeles, where we were recording *Basics*.

Ollie came with us to Florida, where Cholly was rehearsing us for the next show. The rehearsal space was a big room on the second floor of a building that you entered from an exterior staircase. All along the wall were windows, so you could see right in. This one day, the five of us—Melvin, Ron, Richard, Ollie, and I—were working when Dennis came up the stairs. We saw his face in one of the windows for just a second, then he turned around and left without saying a word. He knew it was over.

Like Ron, Ollie was a songwriter, so when Melvin's interest in writing with me declined, I paired up with Ollie. His strong suit was melodies; he played several instruments in addition to being a fantastic, flexible singer. Unlike Ron, Ollie hadn't gotten that many breaks, and he expressed his frustration over the fact that no one would listen to his stuff. It's hard to say why, because when we heard his songs, we thought they were very good. We'd sit together in the music room at my house and cook up new tunes. One of our first collaborations, "Treat Her Like a Lady," became one of our biggest-selling hits of the eighties, and the album it came from,

Truly for You, is one of our best. On the three albums we recorded with Ollie—*Truly for You, Touch Me,* and *To Be Continued*—eleven of the twenty-seven tracks were written by one or more Tempts, another thing we were very pleased with.

Through the years, except for visits with me, my son Lamont lived with his mother Josephine. Jo and I remain friends, and kept in touch about Lamont. We were in Atlantic City, appearing at Trump Plaza. Just a short while before, I'd sent Lamont some money so he could get a car he wanted, and decided to find out if he'd received it and check in. When I called, he mentioned something about not getting along with his mother, and I just listened. Being away so much, I saw my role as a sympathetic ear, a shoulder for Lamont to lean on. It wasn't my place to interfere between him and his mother. I advised him to keep cool, and so on. It was a generally nice talk, and, as always, I told him I loved him.

The next day we were rehearsing with Maurice King. He was teaching us a song called "I Want to Know What Love Is," when Ken Harris, our road manager, came in with a very troubled look on his face.

Kind of kidding, I said, "Damn, Ken, is it that bad?"

"Yeah," he replied.

"Well, what's wrong?" I asked.

He hesitated for a minute, then said, "Otis, Lamont is dead."

I heard the words, but they didn't register, and I stood there a minute looking at him as he spoke.

"We just got a call, and you'd better call Detroit."

I was totally numb as I walked back to my suite. All the guys—Melvin, Richard, Ron, Ollie, Maurice—came up to try to comfort me, hug me, rub my shoulder. The only thing I could say was, "I just talked to him last night." It was so unbelievable. You expect your parents and your peers to pass in your lifetime, but not your child. Never your child. It was one of those freak things. Lamont was working for a construction business and had fallen from a roof. He was just twenty-three.

It's impossible to describe how I felt. Lamont was my only child, and every time I see any of the other guys with their boys, it still hurts deeply. Several years later, when my grandmother Lucinda passed at eighty-eight, Josephine said, "Otis, don't worry. Everything will be all right. God doesn't give you more than you can stand. There's a reason for all of that." I often remember and find comfort in Jo's words. We cannot question God's work.

Beginning in 1985 we started branching out, doing other things in addition to recording and touring. We made a bunch of commercials and were invited to make cameo appearances on television shows, including *The Fall Guy, The Love Boat,* and *Moonlighting.* Bruce Willis is a great fan, and after the taping we gave him and Cybill Shepherd Temptations jackets and agreed to appear with Bruce on his album. He said that one of his dreams was to sing with us, so we did "Under the Boardwalk" with him on *The Return of Bruno.* We were offered parts on *Webster,* but when we couldn't fit it into our schedule, they gave our lines to the Four Tops. Having to act a little was a big departure from our previous television experience. We'd done little skits here and there, played members of the French Foreign Legion on *Laugh-In* and Sonny and Cher's show and the deacons in Flip Wilson's Church of What's Happening Now, but never "acted." We quickly learned that it was a whole different thing, lots of fun but a challenge, too.

When you and your friends have some degree of fame, you have to make a conscientious effort to separate what you know about them as people from what you read in the press. There's probably no one who gets more bizarre press than Michael Jackson, most of which I cannot believe. I'd heard rumors that Michael Jackson had been spotted around wearing a Joker's mask, modeled after the Cesar Romero character from the *Batman* TV series, but felt that they were not true.

About three years ago, I stopped at a newsstand on Ventura Boulevard in the Valley. When I first got out of my car, I noticed someone standing nearby wearing a San Francisco 49ers football jacket. Suddenly I heard a voice saying, "Otis?"

I took a closer look. "Michael?" I asked. Sure enough, he was wearing the Joker mask.

"Yeah," he answered softly.

"Well, I'll be damned."

We embraced and I congratulated him on the success of *Thriller* and told him how much I liked it. He thanked me politely in that soft voice, and asked how the Temptations were doing, what we were up to. After several more minutes of conversation, he said, "Well, I have to be going," got into his Rolls-Royce with a buddy and drove away.

A minute later the guy at the newsstand came up to me and asked, "Wasn't that Michael Jackson?"

"Yeah," I answered.

"That's a shame," he said, shaking his head, "that poor kid's gotta go around in a mask just so he can go down the street."

"Yeah," I said.

"Hey, why did he come up to you?"

"Oh, we shared a few stages together."

"Oh. Okay." We said good-bye, and I left.

It was about time for another personnel change. Things with Ollie were breaking down, and had been ever since he'd passed the eighteen-month probation period. It was the same tired story. After his lateness almost cost us a guest shot on a television show, I laid into him but good.

"Ollie," I'd say time and again, "you cannot do it like this. You've got to have some discipline. I've been around some singing-ass brothers, and you can hold your own with the best of them, and I'm including David Ruffin and Dennis Edwards. But if you don't get your act together, you're going to be sorry."

These pep talks would take place in hotel rooms, usually, and he'd say, "I appreciate that," and so on, but he'd slide back into that old thing again.

The stupidity of it got to me. I couldn't see why someone would say, "Well, I've got a bunch of shows to do, I've got to be on time and look sharp. I guess I'll stay up all night doin' whatever."

The killer was that Ollie knew exactly what he was doing. We were doing a show in Baltimore in November 1986, and Ollie showed up with just minutes to spare.

As we stood in the wings and awaited our introduction, he said, "I know you want to cuss me out, don't you?"

"Ollie, what you're doing is going to cost you," I said. "I've seen this happen to guys too many times, and I know what the end result is going to be. Sooner or later, it's going to catch up to you, Ollie, and that's going to be it."

We took the month of January off, and Ollie drove his Maserati down to Birmingham to visit his mother. He hadn't been gone but a few days when we started getting calls from friends and former employees down there that he was bad-mouthing all of us to anybody who'd listen. One guy told me, "The Temptations helped me put food on the table for my family, and I'm not going to hear some guy low-rate you." We weren't going to hear it, either, and Ollie left the group that month.

Coincidentally, Ron Tyson had been telling us about seeing Dennis's solo act in Philadelphia. Dennis had recorded an album for Motown in 1985, which hadn't done so well. Ron caught his act in a little club, but, he said, "Dennis was looking good and singing great. People were really going for him."

"That's great," I said. "But—"

We talked it over, and Shelly thought it was worthwhile to have Dennis out, just to talk. The four of us, with Shelly, sat down and discussed things with Dennis for quite some time. It was an intense, emotional meeting, because he wanted to be back, and we still loved him, but just the thought of having to go through the same crap all over held us back.

"Just trust me," Dennis said. "I know I've been wrong, and yes, what you guys are saying is right. But just trust me."

So we did, and it's been great having him back. He still holds the record for fines, and I know he looks for us to get on his case about things. One time after he showed up late for a private-party appearance for Yankees owner George Steinbrenner, he knocked on my door and said, "Otis, please don't put me out of the group. I need to be in the group. You've got to help me get it together."

"Jesus Christ, Dennis, what am I? Your surrogate father?" Like I didn't know the answer.

In 1987 we renewed our contract with Motown and completed our first album with Dennis back (for the second time), titled, appropriately, *Together Again*. For our first single we released "I Wonder Who She's Seeing Now," a gorgeous ballad that features a harmonica solo by none other than Stevie Wonder. It may have taken over twenty years, but we finally got something back for all those sleepless nights we spent on the bus listening to little Stevie perfect his art.

The Motown that we knew in the sixties was a once-in-lifetime phenomenon, and everything has changed, even Berry. I've always respected and admired him, even when the business problems left me feeling less than loving toward his company. With time we've all mellowed, and it's much easier to separate what's business and what's personal, which saves a lot of wear and tear on your head and frees you to concentrate on your music. The one positive aspect of our struggles is that we blazed a trail for those who followed. The way things are today, there's almost no way that the next Berry Gordy could assemble a machine like Motown. Anything's possible, but the odds of us ever seeing Berry's like again are slim to nil. I truly believe that in his heart Berry still carries the same pure love of music and the unabashed enthusiasm of a fan. Without it, we'd all have disappeared years ago.

The Temptations have been through so many things, together and separately. I'd be lying if I said that everything between us was always smooth. Despite it all, I bear no malice toward anyone. The Temptations still stand today, not in spite of those who left us, but because of them. No matter what passed between us, there's still a place in my heart for anyone who's stood on a stage with us, and particularly David and Eddie. They will always be Temptations.

Wherever Paul is I hope that he knows how much we miss him and how great his contribution to us was. Eddie and David I can still talk to, even if the opportunities aren't as frequent as I'd like. Not long after we'd re-signed with Motown in 1987, Eddie paid us a surprise backstage visit. We were in the dressing room when we heard he was there, waiting out in the adjacent lounging area. I didn't even wait to change out of my uniform. I walked right up to Eddie, hugged him, and kissed him on the forehead.

"It's really good seeing you, you know?" I said.

"It's good seeing you, too," he replied with that mischievous grin. Just a couple years shy of fifty, Eddie still had that impish smile that got women fighting for the chance to cuddle him.

Back in the dressing room, I thought to myself, "Damn, I like that dude." Sometimes on impulse I call him or David, just to tell them that I'm thinking about them, that I still love them. Their reactions vary, of course, but that would never stop me from saying it. Life's too short not to say how you feel.

Richard, Melvin, and I have known each other for over thirty years now, and we've known Dennis for over twenty. We've all had our ups and downs, times when one of us has been less of a good friend to another than he should have been. In a crisis, though, we help one another and know that there are always four guys we can count on. I guess the key to our staying together decades beyond what most people expected we would is learning to live with one another and accepting our differences, personal quirks, and idio-syncrasies. I'll never forget when Ron started touring with us and tried to sleep on our bus in a bunk right over Melvin's. He couldn't do it, because Blue was, as usual, snoring like thunder. Ron was amazed that the rest of us barely heard it.

That's what time will do for you.

Not too long ago we returned to Hitsville to film a segment for a Showtime special we did with the Four Tops. I'd been back to Detroit many, many times since moving to Los Angeles. Whenever our itinerary took us to the area, I'd stop off to visit my family members and friends who still live there. I liked just to get in a car and drive past all the places I knew and loved—the house in Southfield, the old clubs, houses where special girls lived, the corners we sang on.

Many of the old places are gone but some remain. One that still exists is Hitsville, now a little museum filled with the relics of a sound, a style. When we got there, I was amazed at how small everything seemed. I haven't grown, and the place didn't shrink, so it was only in my mind that Hitsville loomed like a mansion. Maybe it was because the music we created there was so big. We used to joke that there must have been a ghost there who made the records sound so damned good, and as I walked through 2648 West Grand Boulevard, I felt its presence.

Walking back through the lobby, I spotted the same chaise lounge that David sat on and cried the day we found our first record on the chart. It wasn't far from the spot where Berry would stand when he acted out one of his funny stories or recounted for our amusement, blow by blow, one of his boxing matches.

"Yeah, man," Berry would say, "and then I ducked him." Berry would duck some invisible right hook, and we'd all laugh.

Then I thought of all those wonderful women. How did so many of them end up at Motown? And then Beans Bowles's sage advice: "Don't mess with any of Berry's sisters. That's all I'm going to tell you. Just don't mess with them." So we didn't.

Motown's not the same; we're not the same. Nothing is. I realize that the magic left Hitsville a long time ago. But the spirit still lives in all of our hearts, and, we hope, that whenever someone hears one of those records or chuckles at an overly literal piece of choreography on an old tape that a little bit of it flickers for a second somewhere. That's what we did it for.

As kids singing in the school cafeteria, we wanted something very badly: to be up there on a stage somewhere, anywhere, maybe the Fox Theater. That's about as far as my imagination stretched. I'd think about what we'd do, my little group and I. We'd put on the most beautiful midnight-black tuxedos, with every seam pressed and every button shining. Fine new polished black shoes, immaculate white shirts, sharp cuff links, and some sexy-smelling aftershave just in case singing worked as well on the girls as we hoped. Maybe somewhere between the Cadillacs and Frankie Lymon and the Teenagers, they'd announce us. In a little less than three minutes, we'd hit those impossible notes, sing a couple of dazzling harmonies, and with a couple of killer moves bring the house down.

I drive by the Fox whenever I can now and look at the big front doors we ran through and the yards of ornate brass that someone always seemed to be polishing whenever you went by. You can see nobody's put a rag to it in ages, but when I last looked it still seemed to glisten with a bit of the old shine.

Temptations
Singles Discography[1]

MIRACLE RECORDS

Lineup: Otis Williams, Melvin Franklin, Paul Williams, Eddie Kendricks, Elbridge Bryant

Date	Pop	R&B[2]		Title
7/61	—	—		"Oh Mother of Mine"
	—	—	b/w	"Romance without Finance"
11/61	—	—		"Check Yourself"
	—	—	b/w	"Your Wonderful Love"

GORDY RECORDS

Date	Pop	R&B		Title
3/62	—	22		"Dream Come True"
	—	—	b/w	"Isn't She Pretty"

Date	Pop	R&B[2]		Title
9/62	—	—		"Paradise"
	—	—	b/w	"Slow Down Heart"
9/62	—	—		"Mind over Matter"[3]
	—	—	b/w	"I'll Love You Till I Die"[3]
3/63	—	—		"I Want a Love I Can See"
	—	—	b/w	"The Further You Look, the Less You See"
6/63	—	—		"Farewell, My Love"
	—	—	b/w	"May I Have This Dance"

Lineup: Otis Williams, Melvin Franklin, Paul Williams, Eddie Kendricks, David Ruffin

Date	Pop	R&B[2]		Title
1/64	11	nc[4]		"The Way You Do the Things You Do"
	—	nc	b/w	"Just Let Me Know"
4/64	—	nc		"The Girl's Alright with Me"
	33	nc	b/w	"I'll Be in Trouble"
8/64	26	nc		"Girl (Why You Wanna Make Me Blue)"
	—	nc	b/w	"Baby, Baby I Need You"
12/64	1	1		"My Girl"
	—	—	b/w	"Nobody But My Baby"
3/65	18	3		"It's Growing"
	—	—	b/w	"What Love Has Joined Together"
6/65	17	4		"Since I Lost My Baby"
	—	22	b/w	"You've Got to Earn It"
9/65	83	15		"Don't Look Back"
	13	4	b/w	"My Baby"
2/66	29	1		"Get Ready"
	—	—	b/w	"Fading Away"
5/66	13	1		"Ain't Too Proud to Beg"
	—	—	b/w	"You'll Lose a Precious Love"
8/66	3	1		"Beauty Is Only Skin Deep"
	—	—	b/w	"He Doesn't Love Her Anymore"
11/66	8	1		"(I Know) I'm Losing You"
	—	—	b/w	"I Couldn't Cry If I Wanted To"
4/67	8	2		"All I Need"
	—	—	b/w	"Sorry Is a Sorry Word"
6/67	6	3		"You're My Everything"

Date	Pop	R&B[2]		Title
	—	—	b/w	"I've Been Good to You"
9/67	14	3		"(Loneliness Made Me Realize) It's You That I Need"
	—	—	b/w	"Don't Send Me Away"
12/67	4	1		"I Wish It Would Rain"
	—	41	b/w	"I Truly, Truly Believe"
4/68	13	1		"I Could Never Love Another (After Loving You)"
	—	—	b/w	"Gonna Give Her All the Love I've Got"
7/68	26	4		"Please Return Your Love to Me"
	—	—	b/w	"How Can I Forget"

Lineup: Otis Williams, Melvin Franklin, Paul Williams, Eddie Kendricks, Dennis Edwards

Date	Pop	R&B		Title
10/68	6	2		"Cloud Nine"
	—	—	b/w	"Why Did She Have to Leave Me"
11/68	—	—		"Rudolph the Red-Nosed Reindeer"
	—	—	b/w	"Silent Night"
11/68	2	2		"I'm Gonna Make You Love Me"[5]
	—	—	b/w	"A Place in the Sun"[5]
1/69	6	1		"Run Away Child, Running Wild"
	—	—	b/w	"I Need Your Lovin'"
4/69	25	8		"I'll Try Something New"[5]
	—	—	b/w	"The Way You Do the Things You Do"[5]
5/69	20	2		"Don't Let the Joneses Get You Down"
	—	—	b/w	"Since I've Lost You"
7/69	1	1		"I Can't Get Next to You"
	—	—	b/w	"Running Away (Ain't Gonna Help You)"
9/69	46	4		"The Weight"[5]
	—	—	b/w	"For Better or Worse"[5]
12/69	7	2		"Psychedelic Shack"
	—	—	b/w	"That's the Way Love Is"
5/70	3	2		"Ball of Confusion (That's What the World Is Today)"
	—	—	b/w	"It's Summer"
9/70	33	8		"Ungena Za Ulimwengu (Unite the World)"

Date	Pop	R&B[2]		Title
—	—		b/w	"Hum Along and Dance"
1/71	1	1		"Just My Imagination (Running Away with Me)"
—	—		b/w	"You Make Your Own Heaven and Hell Right Here on Earth"

Lineup: Otis Williams, Melvin Franklin, Paul Williams, Dennis Edwards

Date	Pop	R&B		Title
6/71	51	29		"It's Summer"
—	—		b/w	"I'm the Exception to the Rule"

Lineup: Otis Williams, Melvin Franklin, Richard Street, Damon Harris, Dennis Edwards

Date	Pop	R&B		Title
10/71	18	8		"Superstar (Remember How You Got Where You Are)"
—	—		b/w	"Gonna Keep On Tryin' Till I Win Your Love"
4/72	30	10		"Take a Look Around"
—	—		b/w	"Smooth Sailing from Now On"
6/72	92	27		"Mother Nature"
—	27		b/w	"Funky Music Sho Nuff Turns Me On"
9/72	1	5		"Papa Was a Rollin' Stone"
—	—		b/w	"Instrumental"
2/73	7	1		"Masterpiece"
—	—		b/w	"Instrumental"
5/73	40	8		"The Plastic Man"
—	—		b/w	"Hurry Tomorrow"
7/73	35	2		"Hey Girl (I Like Your Style)"
—	—		b/w	"Ma"
11/73	27	1		"Let Your Hair Down"
—	—		b/w	"Ain't No Justice"
2/74	43	8		"Heavenly"
—	—		b/w	"Zoom"
5/74	74	8		"You've Got My Soul On Fire"
—	—		b/w	"I Need You"
11/74	40	1		"Happy People"
—	—		b/w	"Instrumental"

Date	Pop	R&B[2]		Title
2/75	26	1		"Shakey Ground"
—	—		b/w	"I'm a Bachelor"
6/75	37	9		"Glass House"
—	—		b/w	"The Prophet"

Lineup: Otis Williams, Melvin Franklin, Richard Street, Glenn Leonard, Dennis Edwards

Date	Pop	R&B[2]		Title
10/75	54	3		"Keep Holding On"
—	—		b/w	"What You Need Most (I Do Best of All)"
4/76	94	21		"Up the Creek (without a Paddle)"
—	—		b/w	"Darling, Stand by Me (Song for My Woman)"
9/76	—	22		"Who Are You (and What Are You Doing the Rest of Your Life)"
—	—		b/w	"Let Me Count the Ways (I Love You)"

ATLANTIC RECORDS

Lineup: Otis Williams, Melvin Franklin, Richard Street, Glenn Leonard, Louis Price

Date	Pop	R&B[2]		Title
10/77	—	21		"In a Lifetime"
—	—		b/w	"I Could Never Stop Loving You"
1/78	—	58		"Think for Yourself"
—	—		b/w	"Let's Live in Peace"
9/78	—	42		"Bare Back"
—	—		b/w	"I See My Child"
11/78	—	31		"Ever Ready Love"
—	—		b/w	"Touch Me Again"
3/79	—	—		"I Just Don't Know How to Let You Go"
—	—		b/w	"Mystic Woman (Love Me Over)"

GORDY RECORDS

Lineup: Otis Williams, Melvin Franklin, Richard Street, Glenn Leonard, Dennis Edwards

Date	Pop	R&B[2]		Title
4/80	43	11		"Power"
—	—		b/w	"Instrumental"
7/80	—	55		"Struck by Lightning Twice"
—	—		b/w	"I'm Coming Home"

MOTOWN RECORDS

11/80	—	69		"Take Me Away"
—	—		b/w	"There's More Where That Came From"

GORDY RECORDS

8/81	67	36		"Aiming at Your Heart"
—	—		b/w	"The Life of a Cowboy"
10/81	—	—		"Oh, What a Night"
—	—		b/w	"Isn't the Night Fantastic"

Reunion Lineup: Otis Williams, Melvin Franklin, Richard Street, Glenn Leonard, Dennis Edwards, Eddie Kendricks, David Ruffin

4/82	66	6		"Standing on the Top (Part 1)"
—	—		b/w	"Standing on the Top (Part 2)"
7/82	—	82		"More on the Inside"
—	—		b/w	"Money's Hard to Get"

Lineup: Otis Williams, Melvin Franklin, Richard Street, Glenn Leonard, Dennis Edwards

12/82	—	—		"Silent Night"
—	—		b/w	"Everything for Christmas"
3/83	88	17		"Love on My Mind Tonight"
—	—		b/w	"Bring Your Body Here"
5/83	—	—		"Surface Thrills"
—	—		b/w	"Made in America"

Lineup: Otis Williams, Melvin Franklin, Richard Street, Ron Tyson, Dennis Edwards

10/83	—	67		"Miss Busy Body (Get Your Body Busy)"

Date	Pop	R&B[2]		Title
—	—		b/w	"Instrumental"
12/83	—	—		"Silent Night"
—	—		b/w	"Everything for Christmas"
2/84	54	13		"Sail Away"
—	—		b/w	"Isn't the Night Fantastic"

Lineup: Otis Williams, Melvin Franklin, Richard Street, Ron Tyson, Ali Ollie Woodson

Date	Pop	R&B		Title
10/84	48	2		"Treat Her Like a Lady"
—	—		b/w	"Isn't the Night Fantastic"
2/85	—	14		"My Love Is True (Truly for You)"
—	—		b/w	"Set Your Love Right"
4/85	—	81		"How Can You Say That It's Over"
—	—		b/w	"I'll Keep My Light in My Window"
10/85	—	14		"Do You Really Love Your Baby"
—	—		b/w	"I'll Keep My Light in My Window"
1/86	—	63		"Touch Me"
—	—		b/w	"Set Your Love Right"
5/86	—	63		"A Fine Mess"
—	—		b/w	"Wishful Thinking"
7/86	—	—		"Put Us Together Again"
	47	4	b/w	"Lady Soul"
11/86	—	25		"To Be Continued"
—	—		b/w	"You're the One"
3/87	—	45		"Someone"
—	—		b/w	"Love Me Right"

MOTOWN RECORDS

Lineup: Otis Williams, Melvin Franklin, Richard Street, Ron Tyson, Dennis Edwards

Date	Pop	R&B		Title
8/87	—	3		"I Wonder Who She's Seeing Now"
—	—		b/w	"Girls (They Like It)"
12/87	—	8		"Look What You Started"
—	—		b/w	"More Love (Your Love)"

Temptations Album Discography

GORDY RECORDS

Date	Pop	R&B	Title (producer)
3/64	95	nc[4]	*Meet the Temptations* (Berry Gordy and William "Smokey" Robinson) "The Way You Do the Things You Do," "I Want a Love I Can See," "Dream Come True," "Paradise," "May I Have This Dance," "Isn't She Pretty," "Just Let Me Know," "Your Wonderful Love," "The Further You Look, the Less You See," "Check Yourself," "Slow Down Heart," "Farewell, My Love"
2/65	35	1	*The Temptations Sing Smokey* (William "Smokey" Robinson) "The Way You Do the Things You Do," "Baby, Baby

Date	Pop	R&B	Title (producer)

I Need You," "My Girl," "What Love Has Joined Together," "You'll Lose a Precious Love," "It's Growing," "Who's Lovin' You," "What's So Good About Good-Bye," "You Beat Me to the Punch," "Way Over There," "You've Really Got a Hold on Me," "(You Can) Depend on Me"

11/65 11 1 *Temptin' Temptations* (William "Smokey" Robinson)
"Since I Lost My Baby," "The Girl's Alright with Me," "Just Another Lonely Night," "My Baby," "You've Got to Earn It," "Everybody Needs Love," "Girl (Why You Wanna Make Me Blue)," "Don't Look Back," "I Gotta Know Now," "Born to Love You," "I'll Be in Trouble," "You're the One I Need"

6/66 12 1 *Gettin' Ready* (William "Smokey" Robinson)
"Say You," "Little Miss Sweetness," "Ain't Too Proud to Beg," "Get Ready," "Lonely, Lonely Man Am I," "Too Busy Thinking About My Baby," "I've Been Good to You," "It's a Lonely World without Your Love," "Fading Away," "Who You Gonna Run To," "You're Not an Ordinary Girl," "Not Now, I'll Tell You Later"

11/66 5 1 *The Temptations Greatest Hits* (various)
"Beauty Is Only Skin Deep," "Ain't Too Proud to Beg," "My Girl," "Get Ready," "My Baby," "It's Growing," "The Girl's Alright with Me," "Since I Lost My Baby," "Girl (Why You Wanna Make Me Blue)," "Don't Look Back," "The Way You Do the Things You Do," "I'll Be in Trouble"

3/67 10 1 *Temptations Live!*
Introduction, Medley: "Girl (Why You Wanna Make Me Blue)," "The Girl's Alright with Me," "I'll Be in Trouble," "I Want a Love I Can See," "What Love Has Joined Together," "My Girl," "Yesterday," and "What Now My Love," Group Introduction, "I Wish You Love," "Ain't Too Proud to Beg," "Ol' Man River," "Get Ready," "Fading Away," "My Baby,"

Date	Pop	R&B	Title (producer)

"You'll Lose a Precious Love," "Baby, Baby I Need You," "Don't Look Back"

7/67 7 1 *With a Lot o' Soul* (various; Norman Whitfield)
"(I Know) I'm Losing You," "Ain't No Sun Since You've Been Gone," "All I Need," "(Loneliness Made Me Realize) It's You That I Need," "No More Water in the Well," "Save My Love for a Rainy Day," "Just One Last Look," "Sorry Is a Sorry Word," "You're My Everything," "Now That You've Won Me," "Two Sides to Love," "Don't Send Me Away"

8/67 13 1 *In a Mellow Mood* (Frank Wilson and Jeffrey Bowen)
"Hello Young Lovers," "A Taste of Honey," "For Once in My Life," "Somewhere," "Ol' Man River," "I'm Ready for Love," "Try to Remember," "Who Can I Turn to (When Nobody Needs Me)," "What Now My Love," "That's Life," "With These Hands," "The Impossible Dream"

4/68 13 1 *The Temptations Wish It Would Rain* (Norman Whitfield)
"I Could Never Love Another (After Loving You)," "Cindy," "I Wish It Would Rain," "Please Return Your Love to Me," "Fan the Flame," "He Who Picks a Rose," "Why Did You Leave Me Darling," "I Truly, Truly Believe," "This Is My Beloved," "Gonna Give Her All the Love I've Got," "I've Passed This Way Before," "No Man Can Love Her Like I Do"

12/68 15 2 *Live at the Copa*
Introduction, "Get Ready," "You're My Everything," "I Truly, Truly Believe," "I Wish It Would Rain," "For Once in My Life," "I Could Never Love Another (After Loving You)," Introduction of Band and Group, "Hello Young Lovers," "With These Hands," "Swanee," "The Impossible Dream," "Please Return Your Love to Me," "(I Know) I'm Losing You"

Date	Pop	R&B	Title (producer)
2/69	4	1	*Cloud Nine* (Norman Whitfield) "Cloud Nine," "I Heard It Through the Grapevine," "Run Away Child, Running Wild," "Love Is a Hurtin' Thing," "Hey Girl," "Why Did She Have to Leave Me (Why Did She Have to Go)," "I Need Your Lovin'," "Don't Let Him Take Your Love from Me," "Gotta Find a Way (to Get You Back)," "Gonna Keep On Tryin' Till I Win Your Love"
7/69	24	2	*The Temptations Show* (Jackie Barnett) with Kay Stevens and George Kirby. Selections include: "Get Ready," "I've Got to Be Me," "The Best Things in Life Are Free," "Life," "Ol' Man River," "Swanee," "Old Folks," "Hello Young Lovers," "Cloud Nine," "If I Didn't Care," "Run Away Child, Running Wild"
10/69	5	1	*Puzzle People* (Norman Whitfield) "I Can't Get Next to You," "Hey Jude," "Don't Let the Joneses Get You Down," "Message from a Black Man," "It's Your Thing," "Little Green Apples," "You Don't Love Me No More," "Since I've Lost You," "Running Away (Ain't Gonna Help You)," "That's the Way Love Is," "Slave"
3/70	9	1	*Psychedelic Shack* (Norman Whitfield) "Psychedelic Shack," "You Make Your Own Heaven and Hell Right Here on Earth," "Hum Along and Dance," "Take a Stroll Through Your Mind," "It's Summer," "War," "You Need Love Like I Do (Don't You)," "Friendship Train"
7/70	21	5	*Live at London's Talk of the Town* "Cloud Nine," "My Girl," "Ain't Too Proud to Beg," "I Can't Get Next to You," others.
9/70	15	2	*Temptations Greatest Hits, Vol. II* (Norman Whitfield) "Cloud Nine," "I Wish It Would Rain," "It's You That I Need," "I Could Never Love Another (After Loving You)," "(I Know) I'm Losing You," "I Can't Get Next to You," "Ball of Confusion (That's What

Date	Pop	R&B	Title (producer)

the World Is Today)," "Psychedelic Shack," "Run Away Child, Running Wild," "Don't Let the Joneses Get You Down"

10/70 — — *The Temptations Christmas Card* (Barrett Strong and Clay McMurray)
"Rudolph the Red-Nosed Reindeer," "My Christmas Tree," "Santa Claus Is Comin' to Town," "Silent Night," "Someday at Christmas," "White Christmas," "Let It Snow," "Silver Bells," "The Christmas Song (Merry Christmas to You)," "The Little Drummer Boy"

4/71 16 2 *Sky's the Limit* (Norman Whitfield)
"Gonna Keep On Tryin' Till I Win Your Love," "Just My Imagination (Running Away with Me)," "I'm the Exception to the Rule," "Smiling Faces Sometimes," "Man," "Throw a Farewell Kiss," "Ungena Za Ulimwengu (Unite the World)," "Love Can Be Anything (Can't Nothing Be Love But Love)"

1/72 24 1 *Solid Rock* (Norman Whitfield)
"Take a Look Around," "Ain't No Sunshine," "Stop the War Now," "What It Is?," "Smooth Sailing from Now On," "Superstar (Remember How You Got Where You Are)," "It's Summer," "The End of Our Road"

7/72 2 1 *All Directions* (Norman Whitfield)
"Funky Music Sho Nuff Turns Me On," "Run Charlie Run," "Papa Was a Rollin' Stone," "Love Woke Me Up This Morning," "I Ain't Got Nothing," "The First Time Ever I Saw Your Face," "Mother Nature," "Do Your Thing"

2/73 7 1 *Masterpiece* (Norman Whitfield)
"Hey Girl (I Like Your Style)," "Ma," "The Plastic Man," "Masterpiece," "Law of the Land," "Hurry Tomorrow"

MOTOWN RECORDS

Date	Pop	R&B	Title (producer)
9/73	65	5	*Anthology* [3 LPs]

"The Way You Do the Things You Do," "I'll Be in Trouble," "The Girl's Alright with Me," "Girl (Why You Wanna Make Me Blue)," "My Girl," "It's Growing," "Since I Lost My Baby," "My Baby," "Don't Look Back," "Get Ready," "Ain't Too Proud to Beg," "Beauty Is Only Skin Deep," "(I Know) I'm Losing You," "All I Need," "You're My Everything," "(Loneliness Made Me Realize) It's You That I Need," "I Wish It Would Rain," "I Truly, Truly Believe," "I Could Never Love Another (After Loving You)," "Please Return Your Love to Me," "Cloud Nine," "Run Away Child, Running Wild," "Don't Let the Joneses Get You Down," "I Can't Get Next to You," "Psychedelic Shack," "Ball of Confusion (That's What the World Is Today)," "Funky Music Sho Nuff Turns Me On," "I Ain't Got Nothin'," "Ol' Man River," "Try to Remember," "The Impossible Dream," "I'm Gonna Make You Love Me" (with the Supremes), "Just My Imagination (Running Away with Me)," "Superstar (Remember How You Got Where You Are)," "Mother Nature," "Love Woke Me Up This Morning," "Papa Was a Rollin' Stone" Note: The compact disc version of *Anthology* (released in 1986) includes, in addition to the selections listed above: "Masterpiece," "Shakey Ground," "Power," "Sail Away," and "Treat Her Like a Lady"

GORDY RECORDS

12/73	19	2	*1990* (Norman Whitfield)

"Let Your Hair Down," "I Need You," "Heavenly,"

Date	Pop	R&B	Title (producer)

"You've Got My Soul On Fire," "Ain't No Justice," "1990," "Zoom"

1/75 13 1 *A Song for You* (Jeffrey Bowen)
"Happy People," "Glass House," "Shakey Ground," "The Prophet," "Happy People" (reprise), "A Song for You," "Memories," "I'm a Bachelor," "Firefly"

11/75 40 11 *House Party* (various)
"Keep Holding On," "It's Just a Matter of Time," "You Can't Stop a Man in Love," "World of You, Love and Music," "What You Need Most (I Do Best of All)," "Ways of a Grown Up Man," "Johnny Porter," "Darling, Stand by Me (Song for My Woman)," "If I Don't Love You This Way"

4/76 29 3 *Wings of Love* (Jeffrey Bowen and Berry Gordy)
"Sweet Gypsy Jane," "Sweetness in the Dark," "Up the Creek (without a Paddle)," "China Doll," "Mary Ann," "Dream World (Wings of Love)," "Paradise"

8/76 53 10 *The Temptations Do the Temptations* (Tall "T" Productions and Suzee Ikeda)
"Why Can't You and Me Get Together," "Who Are You (and What Are You Doing the Rest of Your Life)," "I'm On Fire (Body Song)," "Put Your Trust in Me, Baby," "There Is No Stopping (Till We Set the Whole World Rockin')," "Let Me Count the Ways (I Love You)," "Is There Anybody Else," "I'll Take You In"

ATLANTIC RECORDS

12/77 113 38 *Hear to Tempt You* (Ron Baker, Norman Harris, Earl Young)
"Think for Yourself," "In a Lifetime," "Can We Come and Share in Love," "She's All I've Got," "Snake in the Grass," "It's Time for Love," "Let's Live in Peace," "Read Between the Lines," "I Could Never Stop Loving You"

Date	Pop	R&B	Title (producer)
3/78	—	46	*Bare Back* (Brian Holland)

"Mystic Woman (Love Me Over)," "I Just Don't Know How to Let You Go," "That's When You Need Love," "Bare Back," "Ever Ready Love," "Wake Up to Me," "You're So Easy to Love," "I See My Child," "Touch Me Again"

GORDY RECORDS

Date	Pop	R&B	Title (producer)
4/80	45	13	*Power* (Berry Gordy and Angelo Bond)

"Power," "Struck by Lightning Twice," "Isn't the Night Fantastic," "How Can I Resist Your Love," "Shadow of Your Love," "Can't You See Sweet Thing," "Go for It," "I'm Coming Home"

| 8/80 | — | — | *Give Love at Christmas* (Gil Askey, Harold Johnson, Teddy Randazzo) |

"Give Love on Christmas Day," "The Christmas Song," "Love Comes with Christmas," "Little Drummer Boy," "This Christmas," "Everything for Christmas," "Christmas Everyday," "Silent Night"

| 8/81 | 119 | 36 | *The Temptations* (Thom Bell) |

"Aiming at Your Heart," "Evil Woman (Gonna Take Your Love)," "The Best of Both Worlds," "Ready, Willing, and Able," "Open Their Eyes," "Oh, What a Night," "The Life of a Cowboy," "Just Ain't Havin' Fun," "What Else," "Your Lovin' Is Magic"

| 9/81 | — | — | *All the Million-Sellers* |

"My Girl," "Ain't Too Proud to Beg," "I Wish It Would Rain," "Cloud Nine," "Run Away Child, Running Wild," "I Can't Get Next to You," "Psychedelic Shack," "Ball of Confusion (That's What the World Is Today)," "Just My Imagination (Running Away with Me)," "Papa Was a Rollin' Stone"

Date	Pop	R&B	Title (producer)
4/82	37	2	*Reunion* (Berry Gordy, others) "Standing on the Top" (with Rick James), "You Better Beware," "Lock It in the Pocket," "I've Never Been to Me," "Backstage," "More on the Inside," "Money's Hard to Get"
2/83	159	19	*Surface Thrills* (Dennis Lambert and Steve Barri) "Surface Thrills," "Love on My Mind Tonight," "One Man Woman," "Show Me Your Love," "The Seeker," "What a Way to Put It," "Bring Your Body Here (Exercise Chant)," "Made in America"
8/83	—	—	*The Temptations* (greatest hits compilation) "Get Ready," "Ain't Too Proud to Beg," "My Girl," "I Can't Get Next to You," "(I Know) I'm Losing You," "I Wish It Would Rain," "I Could Never Love Another (After Loving You)," "Ball of Confusion (That's What the World is Today)," "Cloud Nine," "Run Away Child, Running Wild," "Papa Was a Rollin' Stone"
10/83	152	51	*Back to Basics* (Berry Gordy and Norman Whitfield) "Miss Busy Body (Get Your Body Busy)," "Sail Away," "Outlaw," "Stop the World Right Here (I Wanna Get Off)," "The Battle Song (I'm the One)" (with the Four Tops), "Hollywood," "Isn't the Night Fantastic," "Make Me Believe in Love Again"
10/84	55	3	*Truly for You* (Albert Philip McKay and Ralph Randolph Johnson) "Running," "Treat Her Like a Lady," "How Can You Say That It's Over," "My Love Is True (Truly for You)," "Memories," "Just to Keep You in My Life," "Set Your Love Right," "I'll Keep My Light in My Window"
10/85	146	20	*Touch Me* (the Temptations, others) "Magic," "Givehersomeattention," "Deeper Than Love," "I'm Fascinated," "Touch Me," "Don't Break Your Promise to Me" (with Alfie Silas), "She Got Tired of Loving Me," "Do You Really Love Your Baby" (with Luther Vandross), "Oh Lover"

MOTOWN RECORDS

Date	Pop	R&B	Title (producer)
4/86	140	55	*The Temptations 25th Anniversary* [2 LPs]

"I Want a Love I Can See," "So Much Joy," "It Don't Have to Be This Way," "The Further You Look, the Less You See," "My Girl," "Since I Lost My Baby," "A Tear from a Woman's Eyes," "Wherever I Lay My Hat (That's My Home)," "Don't Look Back," "Get Ready," "Ain't Too Proud to Beg," "Truly Yours," "I Can't Get Next to You," "Cloud Nine," "Just My Imagination (Running Away with Me)," "Come to Me," "Soulmate," "Papa Was a Rollin' Stone," "Thanks to You," "Glass House," "Power," "Treat Her Like a Lady"

GORDY RECORDS

3/86	74	4	*To Be Continued* (Peter Bunetta and Rick Chudacoff)

"Lady Soul," "Message to the World," "To Be Continued," "Put Us Together Again," "Someone," "Girls (They Like It)," "More Love, Your Love," "A Fine Mess," "You're the One," "Love Me Right"

MOTOWN RECORDS

9/87	112	12	*Together Again* (Peter Bunetta and Rick Chudacoff)

"Look What You Started," "I Wonder Who She's Seeing Now," "10 × 10," "Do You Wanna Go with Me," "Little Things," "I Got Your Number," "Every Time I Close My Eyes," "Lucky," "Put Your Foot Down"

The Temptations with
Diana Ross and the Supremes

MOTOWN RECORDS

Date	Pop	R&B	Title (producer)
11/68	2	na[6]	*Diana Ross and the Supremes Join the Temptations*
12/68	1	na	*TCB*
9/69	28	na	*Together*
12/69	38	na	*On Broadway*

1. All chart positions on the singles and album discographies and the text of this book are based on *Billboard* magazine's weekly record sales charts and are compiled in a series of books published by Joel Whitburn's Record Research. These books are available by writing: Record Research, Post Office Box 200, Menomonee Falls, Wisconsin 53051.
2. *Billboard's* black-music charts have appeared under the titles "race records," "R&B," "soul," and, currently, "black." We've used R&B because it saves space and eliminates the confusion of changing the category title several times in the book.
3. The Temptations recording as the Pirates.
4. nc = "no chart." Between November 1963 and January 1965, *Billboard* did not publish an R&B chart, instead consolidating the pop and black-music charts into one pop chart. "My Girl" was one of the first number-one records to appear on the "revived" R&B chart in early 1965.
5. With the Supremes, on the Motown label.

Top 10 Otis'isms

1. "Feel like a penny waitin' for change"

2. "From amazing grace to a floatin' opportunity"

3. "The girl looks good enough to sop with a biscuit"

4. "Eyes red as two cherries in a glass of milk"

5. "Heavy is the head that wears the crown"

6. "Stretch a mile before it tears an inch"

7. "Some people don't believe fat meat is greasy"

8. "Sometimes that's the way the side walks"

9. "Kiss the monkey on the bald spot"

10. "It ain't the magic in the wand, it's the magician who uses it"